Intelligence Analysis
Fundamentals

Intelligence Analysis
Fundamentals

Patrick McGlynn
Godfrey Garner

CRC Press
Taylor & Francis Group
Boca Raton London New York

CRC Press is an imprint of the
Taylor & Francis Group, an **informa** business

The views expressed in this text are the authors' and do not imply endorsement by the Office of the Director of National Intelligence (ODNI) or any other U.S. Government agency.

CRC Press
Taylor & Francis Group
6000 Broken Sound Parkway NW, Suite 300
Boca Raton, FL 33487-2742

First issued in paperback 2021

© 2018 by Taylor & Francis Group, LLC
CRC Press is an imprint of Taylor & Francis Group, an Informa business

No claim to original U.S. Government works

ISBN-13: 978-0-367-77864-4 (pbk)
ISBN-13: 978-0-8153-6940-0 (hbk)

Library of Congress Cataloging-in-Publication Data

Names: McGlynn, Patrick, 1960- author. | Garner, Godfrey, author.
Title: Intelligence analysis fundamentals / Patrick McGlynn and Dr. Godfrey Garner.
Description: Boca Raton, FL : CRC Press, 2018. | Includes bibliographical references and index.
Identifiers: LCCN 2017059787| ISBN 9780815369400 (hardback : alk. paper) | ISBN 9781351249355 (ebook)
Subjects: LCSH: Intelligence service--Methodology.
Classification: LCC JF1525.I6 M34 2018 | DDC 327.12--dc23
LC record available at https://lccn.loc.gov/2017059787

**Visit the Taylor & Francis Web site at
http://www.taylorandfrancis.com**

**and the CRC Press Web site at
http://www.crcpress.com**

CONTENTS

PREFACE

In most cases, this book exercises the approach of using military intelligence examples as a starting point to explain concepts. There is a fundamental reason for this approach. Historically, military organizations have practiced the profession of "intelligence." Remembering a Sunday school lesson from my youth as an illustration, I recollect being told that as Moses approached the Promised Land with the army of Israel at his side, "the Lord directed Moses to spy on the land of Canaan."

> And the LORD spoke to Moses, saying, "Send men to spy out the land of Canaan, which I am giving to the children of Israel; from each tribe of their fathers you shall send a man, every one a leader among them."
>
> Numbers 13, New King James Version (NKJV)

Sending "spies" or scouts into an unknown land to collect intelligence on terrain, roads, watering points, and potential enemies could be called wise or just common sense. Whichever label you choose, it is difficult to argue the logic. With "criminal intelligence" and "business intelligence" being constructs of the 20th century for the most part (perhaps a few hundred years old, at best), the argument that the roots of military intelligence reach back thousands of years is self-evident. The fact that military intelligence has been around that long makes the body of knowledge collected over those thousands of years far larger, richer, and more extensive. In that context, this book takes every opportunity to compare, contrast, and cite similar examples where military intelligence methods and concepts can be applied to business and criminal intelligence problem sets.

Historically, the U.S. intelligence community has faced criticism for failing to adequately predict or warn of a given attack taken on the United States, thereby allowing the enemy to gain the element of surprise. World War II has multiple examples of these surprise attacks. Most notably they include Pearl Harbor, Kasserine Pass (North Africa), and the Battle of the Bulge. During the Korean campaigns, the U.S. military was surprised at the outbreak of the war and again when China entered on the side of the North Koreans. Vietnam gave us the Tet Offensive, followed by the collapse of the Iron Curtain and Soviet Union. Such incidents, in addition to the events of 9/11, have produced an outcry that have led to numerous studies to determine "what went wrong." Government hearings, think-tank studies, and independent researchers have offered their proposals and advice on how to fix the intelligence community (IC).

More often than not, the prescribed answers have been to throw more money and resources at the problem. However, subject matter experts believe the major reason for the failure of analysis more likely lies with faulty analytical thinking. This book seeks to provides analytical instruction, which addresses this faulty analytical thinking, while creating a process where the analyst can develop, practice, and internalize a systematic analytical process using real-world and hypothetical (though real-world–related) problem sets.

Most topics covered within the book are germane to all fields (i.e., military, national, political, criminal, and business) of intelligence analysis. However, certain chapters and sections, as well as most of the instructional examples, scenarios, exercises, and learning activities, provide focus on (or can be applied to) the Homeland Security mission and its associated problem sets. The Department of Homeland Security (DHS) mission statement is as follows:

> The vision of homeland security is to ensure a homeland that is safe, secure, and resilient against terrorism and other hazards.
>
> Three key concepts form the foundation of our national homeland security strategy designed to achieve this vision:
>
> - Security;
> - Resilience; and
> - Customs and Exchange.[1]

The training presentation methods and instructional approaches embodied within the lesson material in this book are all products of much thought, research, and discussion. Many tested and proven government and commercial analytical training methodologies are utilized to explain and demonstrate concepts and assist the student to internalize the instructional materials.

Where possible, lesson materials contain actual unclassified Homeland Security products, document formats, and situational scenarios. To simulate classified scenarios and examples for instructional purposes, hypothetical instruments use unclassified Department of Homeland Security

---

[1] United States Department of Homeland Security, 2015, http://www.dhs.gov/our-mission.

document formats or other unclassified federal/foreign government document formats in order to provide a higher level of authenticity to the learner.

Books using DHS-based learning activities/exercises are rare, but weaving homeland security-focused content with various instructional approaches makes this book unique among its peers.

ABOUT THE AUTHORS

Patrick McGlynn is a retired army intelligence officer. He has authored multiple authoritative strategic-level intelligence reports addressing terrorism, irregular warfare, weapons of mass destruction (WMD), and information operations (IO). His military career has included assignments with the U.S. Defense Intelligence Agency (DIA); and military and civilian contractor tours in Afghanistan, Iraq, and other Middle East locations, where he served in various senior theater-level staff intelligence positions. Since retiring from the military in 2007, McGlynn has authored technical papers on targeting, articles for various intelligence professional periodicals, and has developed analytical training courses for Counter-Improvised Explosive Devices (C-IED); Counter Insurgency Operation (COIN); and Analytical Tradecraft, Terrorism, Information Operations, Collection Management, and Network Analysis. McGlynn has a master's in adult education and industrial technology from Georgia Southern University.

Godfrey Garner is a professor at Mississippi College and adjunct professor at Tulane University, teaching Counterterrorism and Intelligence Analysis for the Homeland Security degree programs. Dr. Garner is director for Mississippi College Center for Counterterror Studies and is a locally recognized authority on terrorism, counterterrorism, and conflicts in the Middle East. His work has appeared in *Homeland Security Today*, *Journal of American Diplomacy*, and *Foreign Policy Journal*. He is the author of the novels *The Balance of Exodus*, *Danny Kane and the Hunt for Mullah Omar*, and *Clothed in White Raiment*. He served in Vietnam and Afghanistan and completed two military and eight civilian government-, intelligence-, and counterintelligence-related tours in Afghanistan.

1

Defining Intelligence Analysis

INTRODUCTION

This course of instruction begins with defining *intelligence analysis*. Chapter 1 guides the student through multiple definitions, using several widely accepted examples as foundational information. First, by pointing out the various divergent perspectives on intelligence analysis, then by segregating the commonalities. To aid in instruction and minimize confusion, the book provides a broad definition for intelligence analysis for use through the remainder of the course. The intelligence analysis definition discussion ends with the introduction of the intelligence analysis process. The chapter then introduces, along with its origins, the purpose of intelligence analysis. This book continues, discussing other intelligence analysis processes and how they are used in business, product marketing, counter terrorism, crime prevention, military applications, and so on. This book does not, however, advocate for a single process, only that there should be a formal process. The United States military process for intelligence analysis will be the initial intelligence analysis process explained during this course of instruction. Later chapters cover the advantages, process structure, and applications of other (non-military–related) processes in more detail. After briefly discussing the analysis process framework, the chapter's instructional materials identify and describe the analysis process starting point: Requirements. The instruction describes the three analysis requirement categories along with their subtypes, providing real-world examples of each supporting category subtype.

This chapter discusses some of the applications and more specific examples of crime analysis and military intelligence analysis integration in tackling the Homeland Security intelligence analysis problem set, including the hybrid threat.

WHAT IS INTELLIGENCE?

What is *intelligence?* A basic definition of intelligence: The ability to obtain and apply knowledge and skills. Sounds simple, so why is it perceived to be so difficult and why are there so many varying definitions? Taking it a step further, it becomes more apparent. Each individual (or organization) has differing definitions of the terms *abilities* and *apply*. Later in the text we will investigate deeper into what is meant by "abilities to obtain" and how to better "apply" them.

WHAT IS INTELLIGENCE ANALYSIS?

Presently, there exists no broadly agreed upon definition for what intelligence analysis is or what it means to accomplish. The lack of a consensus definition for intelligence analysis stems from the fact that there is no agreement on the meaning of the term *intelligence*.

Intelligence subject matter experts (SMEs) tend to view the term through the microscope of their own specialties. The Federal Bureau of Investigation's (FBI) perspective is oriented more toward the wishes of policymakers, whereas the military's definition aligns more with the desires of the commander. According to the Rand Corporation, a nonprofit research organization:

> Intelligence analysis is the process by which the information collected about an enemy is used to answer tactical questions about current operations or to predict future behavior.[1]

Adding to our discussion of intelligence analysis, let us look now at origins and how intelligence analysis is segregated based upon differing aspects and characteristics.

---

[1] Rand Corporation, Intelligence Analysis, 2015, http://www.rand.org/topics/intelligence-analysis.html.

Origins

Intelligence (the ability to obtain and apply knowledge and skills) has been around in its most basic form since prehistoric times. Humans have been collecting and applying knowledge and skills since they began to walk upright. The application of intelligence for military purposes soon followed. The following is an early historical example of military intelligence from ancient Egyptian times, specifically during the reign of Rameses II at the Battle of Kadesh (roughly 1274 BC).

Rameses II had collected information from two captured enemy spies on the size and disposition of Hittite enemy forces. Ramesses, having been misled by the spies, thought the Hittite forces were many days' march away, and decided to make camp near Kadesh with the limited military force accompanying him. In reality, the Hittite forces and their allies were well within striking distance. When the Hittites attacked, Rameses was surprised and outnumbered. Only the opportune arrival of the remainder of the Egyptian chariot forces and infantry on the battlefield turned the tide of battle and saved Rameses from what would have been certain defeat.

One could argue the Hittites had better intelligence than the Egyptians. Perhaps this perception is partially correct. However, if that were the actual case, the Hittites should have known about the Egyptian reinforcements closing in on their position and picked a better opportunity to attack. However, this example clearly does show how critical intelligence properly applied can tip the scales in one's favor.

Differences

To further compound the subject, intelligence analysis is often further classified or divided into:

- Terms of information or data sources (e.g., human, imagery, signals, open source)
- Who the intelligence product end users/consumers are (e.g., business intelligence, military intelligence, political intelligence)
- Number of sources used in production (e.g., single source, all source)
- Types (e.g., strategic, tactical, scientific/technical)
- Product usability aspects (e.g., actionable vs. nonactionable)

Commonalities

Even though the definition is unclear, the mental processes for producing intelligence products are essentially identical. The major identifiable distinctions among all of these intelligence production processes are who performs the analysis and who the product end users are.

Most intelligence community (IC) organizations' analysis process descriptions contain two parts: (1) an *analysis phase* (separating or breaking up any whole into its parts for examination), and (2) a *synthesis phase* (putting together of parts or elements to form a whole). Throughout the IC, aspects other than analysis and synthesis may (or may not) be present in the definition, but the essential elements of analysis and synthesis are always resident.

For purposes of simplicity, this book uses the term *intelligence analysis* as a process including all the activities from exploring the given question or problem through providing the final intelligence products (in whatever form they may take; e.g., assessments, imagery, signals reporting).

Setting aside the definition of intelligence analysis for the moment, in this chapter we will limit the discussion to analytical process starting points, which are no more than questions needing answers or unsolved problems. Whether working for the military, a law enforcement organization, news organization, commercial business, or as a Homeland Security analyst, at the most fundamental level, this is the work of the intelligence analyst.

STARTING WITH ANALYSIS REQUIREMENTS

Intelligence analysis must result in an outcome, that is, at the very least, both descriptive and explanatory of any given set of circumstances and, at best, provide forecasts of future events.[2]

Regardless of the field of intelligence analysis, at the beginning of the process there is always at least one unanswered question or unsolved problem. Those questions (also known as *requirements*) are the starting point for the analysis process. Intelligence analysis requirements generally fall into three categories: descriptive, explanatory, and anticipatory. See Figure 1.1.

---

[2] Don McDowell, Intelligence Study Center, *Strategic Intelligence Analysis; Guidelines on Methodology & Applications*, Chapter 2, Section 2.21, 1997.

Figure 1.1 Analysis requirement categories.

Descriptive Requirements

Starting with descriptive requirements, what do we mean when we say *descriptive*? Descriptive intelligence requirements are factual or relational in nature. Factual requirements are immutable and clear cut. In the journalism trade, the lead paragraph should contain certain "factual" items. Journalists call those factual items the "five Ws." Factual analysis requirements utilize four, of five, Ws. The five Ws are:

1. Who? (e.g., green force, red force, friendly, enemy)
2. What? (e.g., five soldiers, two tanks, three submarines)
3. Where? (e.g., crossing the border, leaving port)
4. When? (e.g., 06:30, Tuesday, 15 July)
5. Why? (Why will not be used because it is considered to be more explanatory than factual)

Relational requirements describe associations, comparisons, connections, or involvement; for discussion purposes, an example of the potential relationship between red and green force tanks is as follows.

Example

While analyzing potential adversaries, a comparison of green and red force tanks has determined they are fundamentally identical. The reason for similarity stems from the fact that both countries have a common heavy weapons supplier.

Explanatory Requirements

The next category of analysis requirements is *explanatory*. Explanatory requirements may be interpretative, casual, or evidential. The interpretive perspective looks to find meaning in the data (e.g., why are drug smugglers following a new route?). The casual viewpoint requires looking for

5

the cause(s) (e.g., what is forcing drug smugglers to abandon their established smuggling routes and take another?) Evidential-oriented requirements seek sensor data, imagery, or other reporting that prove or disprove the hypothesis. The following is an example of such a hypothesis and associated (in this case disproving evidence) imagery data (IMINT) and human intelligence (HUMINT) reporting.

Example

Requirement Hypothesis Statement: South American drug traffickers are using a particular coastal home to continuously process drugs for later shipment to the United States.

Intelligence Surveillance Reconnaissance (ISR) Collection Data:

- Commercial (day and night) imagery, collected every day for the last week, show no lights or human traffic or activity in or around the target coordinate; a "For Rent" sign is posted in front of building facing the street-side approach.
- Intermittent IMINT collection for the last month show no lights or human traffic activity in or around the target coordinates; "For Rent" sign also present in imagery.
- HUMINT collections show that, according to three separate and unrelated real estate agents, the home is a rental property and has had no recorded tenants in more than four months.
- Other HUMINT reporting based on second-hand reported conversations with two local neighbors (names not provided) corroborates previous real estate agent reporting.

Anticipatory Requirements

The final category of requirements is *anticipatory*. Two subcategories, predictive and speculative, further subdivide anticipatory analysis requirements to provide forecasts and gauge the probability of anticipated events. Predictive types of analysis requirements seek the likelihood of a given scenario or chain of events, whereas speculative requirements seek to know what will happen in some given timespan into the future based upon various assumptions. Shown below are examples of predictive and speculative intelligence analysis requirements.

Example of a Predictive Analysis Requirement

Are the chances of the Sinaloa Drug Cartel merging with another drug trafficking cartel(s) in the next five years greater than 50 percent?

Example of a Speculative Analysis Requirement

If host nations do not step up drug interdiction efforts (above present and historical levels), what will the Sinaloa Drug Cartel look like in five years? Provide analysis results in terms of staffing, territorial control, smuggling operations, drug market share, and government influence.

CRIME ANALYSIS

Crime analysis is a law enforcement function that involves systematic analysis for identifying and analyzing patterns and trends in crime and disorder. Information analysis on patterns can help law enforcement agencies deploy resources in a more effective manner and assist detectives in identifying and apprehending suspects. Crime analysis also plays a role in devising solutions to crime problems and formulating crime prevention strategies. Quantitative social science data analysis methods are part of the crime analysis process, though qualitative methods such as examining police report narratives also play a role.[3]

Crime analysis has advantages and shortcomings when applied to homeland security issues/threats. One advantage of criminal analysis groups is that they are generally very familiar with criminal enterprises and have high levels of institutional and street-level knowledge of many known criminal organizations. Additionally, they can usually leverage the profiles of known organizations to identify and exploit the unknown criminal organizations.

Crime analysis is generally more reactive in nature, waiting for crimes to be committed rather that proactively looking for criminal vulnerabilities and proactively prosecuting crimes and disrupting criminal organizations and activities. Criminal analysts must always be aware of the likelihood of successful prosecution. If their analysis is insufficient to obtain a criminal conviction, they must continue to search for evidentiary data to support their analysis. Further, crime analysis is often artificially constrained by territorial borders and by limited and sometimes very restricted data resources. See the example scenario.

---

[3] International Association of Crime Analysts (IACA), Definition of Crime Analysis, http://www.iaca.net.

Example Scenario

A local law enforcement organization (LEO), located near the U.S. southern border, arrests a drug smuggler for related crimes within their jurisdiction. The criminal cooperates with interrogators and gives a full confession. The smuggler's confession points to criminal accomplices and ties that reach far into South America and to multiple worldwide terror groups. The local LEO is ill-equipped, both analytically and authoritatively, to follow the smuggler's trail. The local LEO's authority to legally further pursue (often to even use other intelligence resources) generally halt at the limits of their local jurisdiction. Should the LEO gain cooperation of other county, state, and federal law enforcement, the trail most definitely stops at the international border.

MILITARY INTELLIGENCE ANALYSIS

The military intelligence approach to analysis is more aggressive than crime analysis in that it consists of assessment of an adversary's capabilities and vulnerabilities or analysis of potential threats and opportunities. Military analysts generally look for the least defended or most fragile resource that is necessary for important military capabilities. The military analyst then designates these "perceived vulnerabilities" as "critical vulnerabilities" and proposes them for attack, degradation, destruction, interdiction, or some combination.

The military intelligence analyst is the reciprocal of American crime analyst. Where U.S. law enforcement agencies have significant ability to investigate/analyze criminal activities within our borders, military analysts have limited legal authority in the United States and its territories (or U.S. citizens overseas, for that matter). Specifically, Department of Defense (DoD) Directive 5240.01, *DoD Intelligence Activities*, severely restricts U.S. military personnel (except where specified exemptions apply) from collecting information on U.S. persons.[4]

This restriction potentially hampers investigation and analysis of criminal- and terrorism-related activities against the United States committed by U.S. nationals, but detected by the military intelligence elements outside the United States and its territories.

---

[4] Department of Defense (DoD) Directive 5240.1, DoD Intelligence Activities, 27 August, 2014.

HOMELAND SECURITY PROBLEM SET

The Department of Homeland Security (DHS; see Figure 1.2) was founded in the wake of the 9/11 attacks, established in 2002. DHS combined 22 different federal departments and agencies into a unified, integrated cabinet agency to secure the homeland.

There are the five homeland security missions:

1. Prevent terrorism and enhance security
2. Secure and manage our borders
3. Enforce and administer our immigration laws
4. Safeguard and secure cyberspace
5. Ensure resilience to disasters[5]

Figure 1.2   DHS seal.

From the mission statement alone, the DHS threat problem set includes terrorism (foreign and domestic), cyber threats (foreign and domestic), and border security; to include smuggling and illegal immigration.

To address this problem set, the DHS uses law enforcement (Customs and Border Protection, Immigration and Customs Enforcement, and United States Secret Service), a unique military organization (the U.S. Coast Guard), and an intelligence organization (the Office of Intelligence and Analysis). Other organizations under the DHS contribute also address the problem set. However, for instructional purposes, this text limits the list to these four elements.

Note: While the U.S. Coast Guard does have military capabilities and comes under the command of the U.S. Navy in times of war, the Coast Guard has the authority under Title 14 USC 89 to make inquires, examinations, inspections, searches, seizures, and arrests upon the high seas and

---

[5] U.S. Department of Homeland Security, *Mission Statement and History*, 2015, http://www .dhs.gov.

waters over which the United States has jurisdiction, in order to enforce federal laws.[6]

THE HYBRID THREAT

When criminals, terrorists, and other bad actors synergize their personnel, efforts, and resources to do wrong, the threat to civilization becomes a "hybrid" of the many parts, and more likely than not, more efficient and dangerous.

Because the homeland security threat/problem set is "hybrid" in nature and scope (e.g., criminal, terrorism), a more conventional, a strictly military, or strictly law enforcement approach is inadequate to the threat.

Presently there is no consensus (military, academic, or open source) definition of *hybrid threats*. For instructional purposes, the book uses the U.S. Army definition of hybrid threat: "The diverse and dynamic combination of regular forces, irregular forces, and/or criminal elements all unified to achieve mutually benefitting effects."[7]

Based upon the U.S. Army definition of *hybrid threat* and comparing the Homeland Security Mission Statement, one can easily see that hybrid as well as strictly criminal or terrorism-based threats should be considered by DHS threat analysis groups. By combining criminal and military intelligence analysis perspectives, the homeland security analyst can leverage to the fullest extent the advantages while mitigating the shortfalls of either.

Homeland security analysts have extensive access to criminal and crime organization records via shared law enforcement databases in addition to multiple terrorist data resources. By using a combined military intelligence and crime analysis approach against the hybrid threat, DHS intelligence analysts can focus on capabilities and vulnerabilities in order to strike the threat organization(s) where it is most vulnerable, as opposed to where legal advisors assess they can best obtain a criminal conviction.

---

[6] U.S. Code, *Law Enforcement*, Title 14, Chapter 5, § 89.
[7] U.S. Department of the Army, *Hybrid Threat*, Training Circular 7-100, November 26, 2010, 1-1.

Practical Exercise

The instructor will provide a practical exercise sheet and facilitate the learning activity. Read the hybrid threat scenario and be prepared to participate in a facilitated discussion. While reading the scenario, look for answers to the following questions.

- Is the criminal activity described multijurisdictional?
- Are there terror threat aspects associated with the criminal activity?
- What are some of the crimes identified in the scenario?
- What is the host nation's law enforcement involvement in the criminal activities? Are they interdicting the flow of drugs and arms?
- Do these criminal activities fall under DHS? If yes, why? If no, then who and why?

CHAPTER SUMMARY

Following is a summary of the major informational points elaborated on in Chapter 1. It provides only a brief review of the chapter learning materials to aid in retention.

The summary section is just that—a summary. Students should not utilize it as a definitive guide for exam review, in that it does not address all pertinent chapter information.

Defining Intelligence

An agreed on definition for *intelligence analysis* remains elusive. The main reason for the lack of consensus is the fact that the term *intelligence* is ill-defined.

For the purpose of simplicity, this book uses the term *intelligence analysis* as a process including all the activities from exploring the given question or problem through providing the final intelligence products (in whatever form they may take; e.g., assessments, imagery, signals reporting).

Analysis Requirements

The intelligence analysis process always begins with at least one unanswered question or unsolved problem. Those questions (also known as *requirements*) generally fall into three categories: descriptive, explanatory, and anticipatory.

Crime Analysis

Crime analysis is a law enforcement function that involves systematic analysis for identifying and analyzing patterns and trends in crime and disorder.

Military Intelligence Analysis

Military intelligence analysis is more aggressive than crime analysis in that it consists of assessment of an adversary's capabilities and vulnerabilities in order to determine where it is best to attack.

Homeland Security Problem Set

The DHS threat problem set includes terrorism (foreign and domestic), cyber threats (foreign and domestic), and border security; to include smuggling and illegal immigration.

The Hybrid Threat

Due to the reciprocal nature of military intelligence and crime analysis approaches, the U.S. military's lack of domestic collection authority and most law enforcement organizations limited intelligence resources; using a strictly military intelligence analysis (or crime analysis) approach to the hybrid threat is inadequate.

However, by using a combined intelligence analysis approach (military intelligence and crime analysis) against the combined threat, DHS intelligence analysts can focus on hybrid threat capabilities and vulnerabilities in order to strike them where it is most vulnerable.

2

The Intelligence Cycle

INTRODUCTION

This chapter describes and briefly explores the process of taking known information or data about situations and entities (military, criminal, or other threat) and characterizing the known, and (with appropriate statements of probability or risk) predicting future trend actions in those situations/entities. The chapter material also introduces and discusses the *Intelligence Cycle*, commonly used by selected members of the intelligence community (IC) to collect, process, and disseminate intelligence.

Figure 2.1 and Figure 2.2 depict intelligence process cycles, in which the analysis process is part of but one phase of the total. Figure 2.2 represents the Federal Bureau of Investigation (FBI) and it represents the Federal Law Enforcement version of the Intelligence Cycle. The second graphic depicts the military's version and its source is

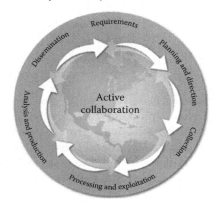

Figure 2.1   FBI intelligence cycle graphic.

Figure 2.2 U.S. military intelligence cycle graphic. (From Department of Defense, Joint Publication 2.0, *Joint Intelligence.*)

Joint Publication 2.0.[1] Notice that "Analysis and Production" is in the same location for both figures.

ANALYSIS IS A SINGLE PART OF THE CYCLE

Doctrinally, analysis is one of the last steps in the process, coming just before production and dissemination.

The Intelligence Cycle is the basis for most forms of intelligence (Figure 2.2), mainly because it logically and methodically moves one through each phase of the process.

With slight variations, the cycle, the component phases, and the sub-components are the traditional foundation for intelligence training used by law enforcement, the military, and the business community.

There are negligible differences in the cycles. The only visible differences in the two figures are that there is a separate Requirements phase in the FBI graphic (Requirements is synonymous with mission), and Active Collaboration is in the center of the FBI graphic (Active Collaboration and Evaluation and Feedback are synonymous processes).

THE INTELLIGENCE CYCLE

The intelligence cycle consists of six interrelated phases of intelligence operations typified by broad activities conducted by intelligence groups and organizations in an effort to provide clients, consumers, and decision makers with relevant and timely intelligence.

To limit confusion, the text uses the law enforcement version of the intelligence cycle for explanation and discussion.

---

[1] Department of Defense (DoD), Joint Publication 2.0, *Joint Intelligence,* http://www.dtic .mil/doctrine/new_pubs/jp2_0.pdf.

Cycle Phases

The intelligence cycle is composed of six phases: Requirements, Planning and Direction, Collection, Processing and Exploitation, Analysis and Production, and Dissemination. There is a continuous evaluation and feedback process associated with each phase known as "active collaboration." (See Figure 2.1.)

Requirements

As discussed in Chapter 1, regardless of the intelligence analysis field, at the beginning of the process there is always at least one unanswered question or unsolved problem. The unanswered question or unsolved problem is known as an *intelligence* (or *analytical*) *requirement*.

Problems, however, are often misunderstood, resulting in poorly defined requirements. It is essential that the intelligence consumer and the analyst thoroughly understand the requirements and that it is a shared understanding. Otherwise, intelligence resources and efforts are unduly extended and the analytical result will disappoint the intelligence end user. Following is an example of a vague and poorly understood intelligence requirement.

Example Scenario

A DHS intelligence consumer submits an intelligence requirement. The request reads: "Request an assessment of the amount of illegal border traffic crossing the Canadian border."

What is wrong with this request? The following bullets outline but a few of the vague and possibly misleading aspects of the requirement:

- The complete Canadian Border? ... Or just a portion? (Need greater specificity)
- For what period? (Time period not stated)
- When is the information required? (Intelligence has an expiration date!)
- Illegal traffic across the border in which direction? (South, into the United States, or perhaps north?)

The analyst might make reasonable assumptions to address any of the bullets and they may be correct ... or perhaps not.

Planning and Direction

In the Planning and Direction Phase, the analyst performs the planning and generates at a minimum the initial tasking for all later phases of the Intelligence Cycle. Analysis and production responsibilities assigned during this phase establish the anticipated flow of information and the development of the appropriate intelligence dissemination architecture.

Analysts will make many assumptions throughout the intelligence process. One of those assumptions appears at the start of the Planning and Direction Phase. Analysts must assume there exists a "clear and common" understanding of the requirements provided. If this is not the case, they should make every effort to rectify the situation. Failure to obtain a clear and common understanding of the requirements (between analyst and client) imperils further planning steps and all results from further analysis and collection efforts.

DHS "all source" intelligence production is a collaborative and federated information sharing process, often between many geographically dispersed and diverse organizations (federal, state, and local law enforcement; and occasionally foreign governments). This approach involves dividing the analysis and production effort among intelligence facilities and law enforcement organizations (often worldwide) to meet DHS intelligence needs.

Intelligence Requirement (IR) Refinement

The analyst then performs some level of basic research in the intelligence problem. A period of requirements refinement should also take place to identify the "must-know" information. In military circles, this must-know information is known as *commander's critical information requirements* (CCIR).

The CCIR is identified by the commander as being critical in facilitating timely information management in the decision-making process that affects successful mission accomplishment. The CCIR should be the result of an exchange between the intelligence officer/analyst and the client. In the military's case, the client is the commander. Others will use finished intelligence products; they are the "consumers" or "end-users," but the "client" is the prime "stakeholder" in the requirements negotiation process and has the last word. The following is an example of an unrefined intelligence requirement.

Example of an Information Requirement (IR)

Will terrorists attack? If so, where, when, and how will they appear?

These all may be valid client concerns, but the requirements are so multiple, broad, and vague that they are virtually impossible to satisfy. In the example scenario, the analyst's task is to:

- Reduce the number of requirements (preferably to one).
- Further develop the specifics (e.g., where, a two-mile strip of border; terrorists, which terror group/cell).
- Determine client/commander's end purpose (or decision), which drives the intelligence need. (Knowing the end purpose helps mold collection planning.)

Example of an IR: 1st Refinement

(Based upon client discussions and some level of research and intelligence collaboration effort; military term: *war-gaming*.)

Will the Islamic State of Iraq and the Levant (ISIL) attack the United States in the next two months?

(This first refinement has narrowed the threat scope and the time span, thereby making the collection effort more practical, but still very difficult.)

Understanding the Operational Environment

Knowing how the operational environment affects friendly and adversary operations also weighs on the planning process.

Example of an IR: 2nd Refinement

Is ISIL more likely to attack the United States in the next two months using affiliates from outside U.S. borders or by using assets already in the United States?

(The second refinement is likely the result of a growing analytical draft hypothesis to determine the most likely threat course of action. Since it is impossible to look at everyone, everywhere, all the time, the analyst(s) must develop a more workable hypothesis based on an appropriate threat model.)

Military intelligence professionals refer to the process of creating a "workable hypothesis/threat modeling" as the *Intelligence Preparation of the Operational Environment* (formerly Intelligence Preparation of the Battlefield/ Battle Space). Since DHS (friendly forces) are not alone, the threat (or enemy) also has "operational environment" constraints. The analyst must consider both threat and friendly factors in the planning phase. Figure 2.3 depicts the effects of the "operational environment on the intelligence planning process."[2]

For example, a terror group may try to encourage sympathizers within the United States to attack. However, the terror group must consider other factors: what controls do they have on the who, what, where, or when their sympathizers will attack. Unless reasonable command and control (C2) ties exist between the sympathizer and the terror C2 element, target types and timing are difficult and unless the sympathizer(s) have ample

---

[2] Department of Defense (DoD), Joint Publication 2.0, *Joint Intelligence*, http://www.dtic .mil/doctrine/new_pubs/jp2_0.pdf.

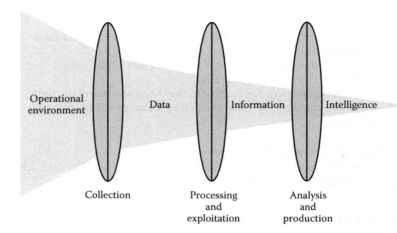

Figure 2.3 Relationship of the environment on the intelligence process.

personal resources (weapons, explosives, transport, access, staffing, etc.), the logistics issues for the terror group become more complicated.

Understanding the operational environment yields potential threat C2 vulnerabilities (weaknesses), providing intelligence collection opportunities. The analyst has now modified the hypotheses to reflect a "most likely" threat scenario where the terror group would use sympathizers, potentially already in the United States, and plans and tasks collection requirements around this hypothesis. (See Example of an IR: 3rd Refinement.)

Example of an IR: 3rd Refinement

Are ISIL C2 elements (see collection plan for specifics) using messenger services or commercial communications (directly) or the Internet (indirectly) to contact potential sympathizers already in U.S. borders as part of an attack planning process, which may occur in the next two months?

(The third refinement is the result of a more mature hypothesis. It contains a more finite and defined target set to direct collection assets; the collection manager also understands that the collection plan will focus on using signals intelligence [SIGINT] platforms [possibly HUMINT if feasible] and those SIGINT collection assets would need to exploit signal/message content.)

18

Practical Exercise

The instructor will provide a practical exercise sheet with an example information/intelligence requirement (IR) and facilitate a learning activity. Using the IR and associated scenario provided refine the requirement into meaningful and observable requirements.

Collection

Planning for, and tasking of "collection assets" (e.g., aerial surveillance, wire taps) takes place during the Collection Phase. Analysts need an understanding of what is being asked and why the information is needed to properly generate collection requests. The "what" and "why" help to better define the collection plan. Collection asset requests are generated by a collection manager, then routed to higher authority for approval and scheduling.

(**Note:** Planning of what information needs collecting is identified in the previous Planning and Direction Phase.)

The collection plan specifies the types of information and data required. It does not specify the collection platform. The collection plan should also state when the information is required (e.g., the "not later than," or NTL, date is 4 JUN). Without the NTL date, the required information may be collected, but it may also arrive when it is no longer of value. As well, length of the collection period and frequency must also be determined based upon the "why aspect" of the requirement. See the example below.

Example Scenario

A determination of illegal crossing activity, along a specified two-mile portion of the U.S. southern border, is the subject of the collection effort. The information will drive border patrol staffing, scheduling, and interdiction efforts. The developed collection plan outlines a continuous 24-hour video collection effort, for one month, starting one week from today's date. A quick terrain study shows that only foot traffic is possible along that particular stretch of the border. Therefore, the collection manager adds remote ground vibration sensors to the video surveillance package.

Processing and Exploitation

The Processing and Exploitation Phase converts raw collected data into usable forms more readily understood by clients, decision makers, intelligence analysts, and other intelligence consumers. Today processing and exploitation is becoming more and more automated, especially IMINT, SIGINT, and MASINT; however, much processing is still manual. Additionally, the Processing and Exploitation Phase combines and collates the data to fill in the information gaps.

Not all raw data forms are understandable to the consumer. Most imagery forms, for example, must first be processed and interpreted. Something as basic as an aerial photograph may require mensuration (the measuring of geometric magnitudes, lengths, areas, and volumes) to determine proper scale/size of depicted objects for purposes of identification and targeting.

Similarly, not all data confirms or denies the hypothesis. Some data is erroneous or misleading and therefore multiple collections help to provide a more thorough understanding and complete picture. HUMINT collects generally require credibility and reliability evaluations.

Other processing and exploitation may be required, such as signals decryption, documents or recorded voice translations, explosive forensics, or technical exploitation of a piece of equipment (e.g., a laptop computer).[3] Even something as basic as translating an unencrypted document into the English language for further exploitation and analysis is a rather involved process—see Figure 2.4.

Analysis and Production
Collection capabilities assigned or attached to the DHS and other government/law enforcement related groups gather information and raw data for analysis. The Analysis and Production Phase creates the final intelligence products using the refined, compiled and processed information and data provided by subordinate units and external organizations. All available processed information is integrated, evaluated, analyzed, and interpreted to create products that will satisfy the information/intelligence requirements (IRs). Intelligence products can take many presentation forms. They may be oral presentations, hard copy publications, or electronic media. All-source intelligence products are the result of multidiscipline fusion efforts.

A recent beneficial refinement to IC all-source intelligence processing is the requirement to comply with *Intelligence Community Directive*

---

[3] Department of Defense (DoD), Joint Publication 2.0, *Joint Intelligence*, http://www.dtic .mil/doctrine/new_pubs/jp2_0.pdf.

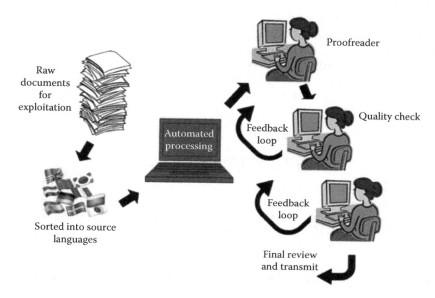

Figure 2.4 Simplified diagram of unencrypted document exploitation.

#203, Analytic Standards.[4] Prior to the creation of Office of the Director of National Intelligence (ODNI) analytic standards, all-source processing, analysis, content and quality control of intelligence products could vary from one member of the IC to the next.

This section only introduces the Analysis and Production Phase as part of the Intelligence Cycle. Later chapters contain more discussion and explanation of the Analysis and Production Phase and includes multiple and varied methods of analysis and how they are utilized.

Dissemination

The purpose of the Dissemination and Integration Phase is to appropriately distribute and deliver finished intelligence to the intelligence consumer or end user to be consumed in the completion of their organizational missions. Various mechanisms facilitate dissemination. Product classification, availability of viable distribution pathways, and the needs

---

[4] Office of the Director of National Intelligence (ODNI), Intelligence Community Directive #203, *Analytic Standards*, 2015, http://www.dni.gov/files/documents/ICD/ICD%20203%20 Analytic%20Standards.pdf.

of the end-user determines the mechanisms for delivery of the finished intelligence products. As long as the dissemination route is properly accredited and certified, delivery can utilize computer networks, couriers, registered mail, and other delivery systems.

The multiplicity of dissemination paths underpins the need for communications and computer systems interoperability among the IC and law enforcement.

CHAPTER SUMMARY

This chapter briefly described and explored the process of taking known information or data about situations and entities (military, criminal, or other threat), characterizing the known, and (with appropriate statements of probability or risk) predicting future trend actions in those situations/ entities. The intelligence cycle is that process and has multiple phases— analysis and production being but one of the phases. U.S. military and federal law enforcement versions of the intelligence cycle are essentially the same.

The Intelligence Cycle

The intelligence cycle consists of six interrelated phases of intelligence operations typified by broad activities conducted by intelligence groups and organizations in an effort to provide clients, consumers, and decision makers with relevant and timely intelligence.

Requirements, Planning and Direction, Collection, Processing and Exploitation, Analysis and Production, and Dissemination are the phases of the intelligence cycle.

Requirements
Requirement(s) that start the Intelligence Cycle are always based upon at least one unanswered question or unsolved problem.

Failure to obtain a "clear and common" understanding of the requirements (between analyst and client) imperils further planning steps and all results from further analysis and collection efforts.

Planning and Direction

The Planning and Direction Phase will perform the planning and generate, at a minimum, the initial tasking for all later phases of the Intelligence Cycle. Analysis and production responsibilities assigned during the Planning and Direction Phase establish the anticipated flow of information and the development of the appropriate intelligence dissemination architecture.

Collection

Planning for and tasking of collection assets (e.g., aerial surveillance, wire taps) takes place in the Collection Phase. Analysts need an understanding of "what is being asked" and "why the information is needed" to properly generate collection requests. The "what" and "why" help to better define the collection plan. Collection asset requests are generated by a collection manager, then routed to higher for approval and scheduling.

Processing and Exploitation

The Processing and Exploitation Phase converts raw collected data into usable forms more readily understood by clients, decision makers, intelligence analysts, and other intelligence consumers.

Analysis and Production

The Analysis and Production Phase creates the final intelligence products using the refined, compiled, and processed information and data provided by subordinate units and external organizations.

Dissemination

The purpose of the Dissemination and Integration Phase is to appropriately distribute and deliver finished intelligence to the intelligence consumer or end user to be consumed in the completion of their organizational missions.

3

Thinking about Thinking

INTRODUCTION

The stock and trade of analysts is their ability to think, both objectively and methodically, about problems using a structured process, which avoids personal or cultural biases. Chapter 3 introduces the various types of thinking included in the cognitive domain routinely used by analysts. Topics include critical thinking, reflective thinking, and higher-order thinking, as well as the cognitive factors that affect thinking quality. The chapter also describes the benefits and pitfalls of each thought process.

PROBLEM SOLVING

Problem solving is another one of those ill-defined terms that many use routinely. However, it is a necessary skill for the intelligence analyst. It often is just as important to know how one got to the answer as it is to know the answer. Without knowing the steps to solve the problem, how can one replicate the results, or, if there is an error in the logic, how can the error be found?

Problem solving starts with problem definition and that is where intelligence analysis begins. We start with dividing problems into two categories: poorly defined and well defined. A *poorly defined problem* does not have an easily recognized outcome, remedy, or expected solution. A *well-defined problem* is the reciprocal. For example, some people would call getting a bill a "well-defined problem." The remedies are obvious, straightforward, and sometime intuitive. Pay the bill or do not pay the bill. Each remedy has clearly identified and predictable consequences.

The poorly defined problem (or undefined problem) is the reciprocal of the well-defined problem. A complexity exists and usually several steps, moves/countermoves, direct or indirect variables are at play. Therefore, since the solution is less obvious (or even incalculable), a plan, structure, or methodical process becomes quite useful for getting started toward obtaining an answer.

According to Richards J. Heuer Jr., a thought leader in analytical thought processes, the human mind has a limited capacity of working memory, which causes many problems in doing intelligence analysis. There are two basic tools for dealing with complexity in analysis: decomposition and externalization.

Decomposition means breaking a problem down into its component parts. The basis of problem-solving analysis is to divide and conquer: Decompose a complex problem into simpler problems, get one's thinking straight in these simpler problems, and then reconnect these analytical solutions within a rational construct.

Externalization means getting the decomposed problem onto paper (and outside of one's mind) in some simplified form that shows the major variables or elements and how they pertain to each other. Writing out math problems are basic examples of externalizing an analytical problem.[1]

The concepts of decomposition and externalization will be explored further in Chapter 7.

CRITICAL THINKING

As with most analytical terminology, critical thinking has many varying definitions. The book uses the following definition when referring to critical thinking:

> Thinking about one's thinking in a manner designed to organize and clarify, raise the efficiency of, and recognize errors and biases in one's own thinking. Critical thinking is not "hard" thinking nor is it directed at solving problems (other than improving one's own thinking). Critical

---

[1] Richards J. Heuer, Jr., *Psychology of Intelligence Analysis*, 2nd Edition, Pherson Associates LLC, 2007.

thinking is inward directed with the intent of maximizing the rationality of the thinker. One does not use critical thinking to solve problems ... one uses critical thinking to improve one's process of thinking.

Kirby Carmichael
Letter to Olivetti, Laguna Salada Union School District, May 1997

Using the above definition, one can rationalize some of the characteristics of critical thought which include:

- Ability to interpret raw information, to appraise evidence, and to evaluate arguments and thought processes
- Recognition of the existence of logical relationships, or lack thereof
- Willingness to test one's ideas, conclusions, and hypotheses
- Ability to restructure one's beliefs/bias patterns and determine their level of influence on cognitive processes

In light of these characteristics, it becomes apparent that critical thinking skills are integral to performing intelligence analysis in which the analyst would minimize and possibly negate the influences of their own biases and possibly recognize logical errors.

REFLECTIVE THINKING

Intelligence analysts should have a firm understanding of multiple problem-solving methods in order to use as tools in order to break down, scrutinize, and continuously develop their analysis processes. Reflective thinking is a recognized and tested problem-solving procedure.

Reflective thinking is a basic thought model developed in the last century by John Dewey. Reflective thought differs from random thought in its "chaining" feature, which entails a consecutive ordering of ideas so that each idea establishes its successor while referring to its forerunner.

Dewey Sequence Problem Solving

One of the most effective methods of problem solving is the Dewey Sequence (Figure 3.1). This method uses the reflective thinking process, which is a structured organized series of questions. The process is described by the questions listed below.

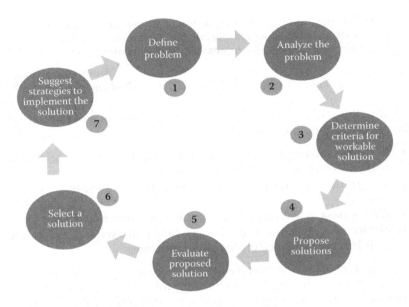

Figure 3.1   The Dewey Sequence Problem-Solving Process.

Step 1: Define the Problem

1. What is the specific problem?
2. What terms, concepts, or ideas need defining or further explanation?

Step 2: Analyze the Problem

1. What is the history of the problem?
2. What are the causes of the problem?
3. What are the symptoms of the problem?
4. What methods currently exist for dealing with the problem?
5. What are the limitations of these methods?

Step 3: Determine Criteria for a Workable Solution

What are the guidelines for a workable solution?

Step 4: Propose Solutions

After the analyst(s) has analyzed the problem and suggested criteria for a solution (e.g., brainstorming).

Step 5: Evaluate Proposed Solution

After compiling a list of possible solutions, evaluate the solutions using the questions below.

1. Are there any disadvantages to the solution? Do the disadvantages outweigh the advantages?
2. Does the solution conform to the formulated criteria (see Step 3)?

Step 6: Select a Solution

1. Weigh the merits and deficiencies.
2. If adopted, what would be the long-term and short-term effects of this solution?

Step 7: Suggest Strategies to Implement the Solution

1. How can the analyst(s) gain support and approval for the proposed solution? What is the internal/external review process?
2. What specific steps are necessary to implement the solution?
3. How can the solution be evaluated/validated?

Practical Exercise

Break into groups of more than two but less than five. The instructor will provide a practical exercise sheet and facilitate the learning activity. Use the Dewey Sequence Problem-Solving Process to develop and evaluate a solution to the problem provided.

HIGHER-ORDER THINKING

Higher-order thinking skills (HOTS) is part of a taxonomy developed in 1956 by educational psychologist Dr. Benjamin Bloom. HOTS cognitive skill categories are composed of creating, analyzing, and evaluating. This course encourages the exercise of higher-order thinking in all aspects of analysis.

Analysis

Analysis, as defined by Robert Marzano, consists of matching, classifying, error analysis, generalizing, and specifying. By engaging in these processes, intelligence analysts can use what they are learning about a threat or problem to create new insights and invent ways of using the information in new situations. When analysts use analysis skills to determine the validity and worth of a particular piece of information, they are engaging in critical thought.[2]

It would seem intuitive that intelligence analysts would need to be analytical. However, the intelligence analyst takes analysis to a new level of complexity. They not only need to be able to analyze bits of data, imagery, and other information provided to solve the problem or satisfy an IR, but they have to be critical of those information sources, their potential personal cultural biases, and at the same time be able to identify and analyze the process they used for the original analysis. Simply put, analysts analyze the source information, they analyze themselves, and they analyze the analytical process.

Evaluation

To evaluate information, analysts need to be able to distinguish essential data from information that is simply interesting. They must be able to identify core themes; form and support opinions; and identify inconsistencies, bias, or lack of coherence or accuracy in a text. They must also be able to use background information, prior knowledge, and other textual sources to assess the validity of the text. For example, when reading a raw HUMINT intelligence report from a new source, analysts with strong evaluation skills might compare the reports of two other vetted sources. Questions analysts use to evaluate the original source and reporting might include:

- Where reporting topics overlap, do they agree with new source reporting? Are there inconsistencies? (*Comparing/Contrasting/ Critiquing*)
- What are the "bona fides" of the new source? What are the source's motivations for providing the information? (*Assessing/Appraising*)
- Does he or she have reasonable placement and access to the information they are providing? If yes, how did they obtain placement and access? If no, how did they obtain the information? (*Defending/ Justifying/Supporting*)

---

[2] R. J. Marzano, *Designing a New Taxonomy of Educational Objectives*, Corwin Press, 2000.

Creating

It may not be immediately apparent to the nonprofessional as to why "creativity" is critical to analytic processes. However, creativity is often what distinguishes the good analyst from the extraordinary. Creativity allows the analyst to diverge from the mainstream group thought perspective. They are the one who "thinks outside the box." Creativity and imagination skills come quite in handy when analysts perform exercises like *Red Cell Analysis*. Red Cell Analysis is where the analyst attempts to put him or herself in the mind of adversaries and contemplate their next move.

The DHS has had an established Analytic Red Cell Program dating back to 2004. The Red Cell compares results with terrorism analysis from Homeland Security's intelligence professionals who examine real-life threat information. Written reports on Red Cell sessions are then forwarded to terrorism analysts inside the department, as well as to local and state police and security experts in private industry. Most Red Cell reports note they are "alternative assessments intended to provoke thought and stimulate discussion."[3]

COGNITIVE FACTORS THAT AFFECT THINKING QUALITY

According to Richards J. Heuer Jr. and other supporting research, the principal challenges affecting critical thought are often human limitations. Humans are limited in their ability to address complexity issues and situations, by their inability in handling uncertainty, by their personal biases, and often by a lack of subject matter expertise.[4]

Complexity

The complexity of information/data in the analysis stream can often be very intricate, far beyond the human mind's ability to comprehend and create a significant analytical challenge. Today, computer algorithms and data processing reduce some of that complexity. Automated processing is an excellent mechanism for handling thousands of simple and repetitive

---

[3] John Mintz, Homeland Security Employs Imagination Outsiders Help Devise Possible Terrorism Plots, *Washington Post*, June 18, 2004.

[4] Richards J. Heuer, Jr., *Psychology of Intelligence Analysis*, 2nd Edition, Pherson Associates LLC, 2007.

calculations. However, relationships' variability are more difficult to conceptualize into models or algorithms.

In attempting to adequately deal with the more complex information sets, analysts often try to simplify the problem. Those simplifying strategies may lead to biased results, such as using analogous examples or valuing more vivid, immediate cases rather than on more abstract, bland statistical data which often is of much greater value.[5]

Uncertainty

Unlike criminal investigations, where compiled evidence meets a judicial level of satisfaction that leads to an arrest, suspect interrogation, and possibly confession, intelligence analysis rarely achieves similar levels of certainty. Intelligence analysis normally operates under varying degrees of uncertainty. Most real-world analytical problem sets, due to the associated variables, cannot easily fit into statistical equations and therefore it becomes difficult for the intelligence analyst to provide hard mathematical percentages defining the confidence level of the analysis or level of risk involved. The following examples better describe this conundrum.

Examples

Imagine you are trying to predict the likelihood of men walking on the moon and the year is 1900. Where do you begin? (At this time, airplanes do not yet exist, and the concept of space flight resides within the pages of H. G. Wells's science fiction novels.)

Same problem, but the year is 1950. Can you see the difficulty? (Now airplanes are commonplace; even jets and ballistic missiles exist. However, Sputnik will not launch for another seven years.)

Note: Intelligence analysts often get similar information requests (e.g., How can we stop the flow of illegal drugs into the United States? What will be the next great technological advance of our adversaries?).

Since it is often impossible to remove uncertainty in analysis, the analyst will describe or qualify the level of uncertainty in the final analysis product so that the intelligence consumer can better assess the value or

---

[5] Douglas H. Harris and V. Alan Spiker, *Ergonomics: A Systems Approach, Critical Thinking Skills for Intelligence Analysis*, Chapter 10, Anacapa Sciences, Inc., 2012, www.intechopen.com.

Table 3.1 ODNI Directive 203, Analytic Standard, Likelihood or Probability Terminology

Almost No Chance	Very Unlikely	Unlikely	Roughly Even Chance	Likely	Very Likely	Almost Certain
Remote	Highly improbable	Improbable (Improbably)	Roughly even odds	Probable (Probably)	Highly probable	Nearly certain
1–5%	5–20%	20–45%	45–55%	55–80%	80–95%	95–99%

Source: Office of the Director of National Intelligence (ODNI), Intelligence Community Directive #203, Analytic Standards, 2015, http://www.dni.gov /files/documents/ICD/ICD%20203%20Analytic%20Standards.pdf.

usefulness the information provides when integrated into the decision-making process.

To aid in normalizing the assessment of analytical uncertainty, the Office of the Director of National Intelligence (ODNI) provides a standard. See Table 3.1.

Bias

Bias can also skew the analysis, but for the intelligence analyst (or the scientific researcher), the prevention of selection bias is a significant challenge.[6] *Selection bias* (or biased sampling) is when the analyst selectively cherry picks the information that supports their hypothesis or what the client already believes and disregards contradicting data.

It is difficult to eliminate analytical bias because it can occur unconsciously, but analysts (and researchers) can minimize it by peer reviews, quality assurance procedures, using multiple sources, including and explaining contradicting results in final product, and having an outside and independent group solve the same problem.

Subject Matter Expertise

Lastly, often there exists an expectation that analysts possess a high level of expertise on many topics in many areas of analysis and fields of investigation. They can mitigate their lack of knowledge by using structured analytical processes and critical thinking skills to facilitate analysis while

---

[6] Richards J. Heuer, Jr., *Psychology of Intelligence Analysis*, 2nd Edition, Pherson Associates LLC, 2007.

33

building subject matter expertise. Additionally, analysts can reduce confusion by segregating or sorting less useful data or irrelevant information to reduce the amount of information to assimilate, comprehend, and evaluate. Where information gaps exist, using assumptions to satisfy the gaps until hard data is available allows more time for analysts to increase their level of knowledge.

CHAPTER SUMMARY

In Chapter 3 analytical thought processes were introduced. The uses of problem solving in the analysis process and the concept of critical thinking were discussed. Other topics included reflective thinking and higher-order thinking, as well as the cognitive factors that affect thinking quality. The chapter also described the benefits and pitfalls of each thought process.

Problem Solving

Problem solving starts with problem definition and that is where intelligence analysis begins. First, we divide problems into two categories: Poorly defined and well defined. A poorly defined problem does not have an easily recognized outcome, remedy, or expected solution. In a well-defined problem, the remedies are obvious, straightforward, and sometime intuitive; and each remedy has clearly identified and predictable consequences.

Critical Thinking

The text uses the following definition when referring to critical thinking:

> Thinking about one's thinking in a manner designed to organize and clarify, raise the efficiency of, and recognize errors and biases in one's own thinking. Critical thinking is not "hard" thinking nor is it directed at solving problems (other than improving one's own thinking). Critical thinking is inward directed with the intent of maximizing the rationality of the thinker. One does not use critical thinking to solve problems ... one uses critical thinking to improve one's process of thinking.

Kirby Carmichael
Letter to Olivetti, Laguna Salada Union School District, May 1997

Some of the characteristics of critical thought include:

- Ability to interpret raw information, to appraise evidence, and to evaluate arguments and thought processes
- Recognition of the existence of logical relationships, or lack thereof
- Willingness to test one's ideas, conclusions, and hypotheses
- Ability to restructure one's beliefs/bias patterns and determine their level of influence on cognitive processes

Reflective Thinking

Reflective thinking is a recognized and tested problem-solving procedure that uses a basic thought model developed in the last century by John Dewey. Reflective thought differs from random thought in its "chaining" feature, which entails a consecutive ordering of ideas so that each idea establishes its successor while referring to its forerunner.

Higher-Order Thinking

Higher-order thinking skills (HOTS) is part of a taxonomy developed in 1956 by educational psychologist Dr. Benjamin Bloom. HOTS cognitive skill categories are composed of creating, analyzing, and evaluating. This course encourages the exercise of higher-order thinking in all aspects of analysis.

Cognitive Factors That Affect Thinking Quality

Research identifies that the principal challenges affecting critical thought are often human limitations. Humans are limited in their ability to address complexity issues and situations, by their inability in handling uncertainty, by personal biases, and, often, by a lack of subject matter expertise.[7]

---

[7] Richards J. Heuer, Jr., *Psychology of Intelligence Analysis,* 2nd edition, Pherson Associates LLC, 2007.

4

Perception and Deception

INTRODUCTION

For the uninitiated, the intelligence analyst's duties are encompassed by collecting information on an adversary, analyzing the data, then creating and distributing the report. This limited view of the analyst's responsibilities is, however, sorely lacking.

In Chapter 4, the reader gains an improved understanding of the intelligence process and the fact that there is considerably more to the profession and skill of analyzing intelligence. Analysts must initially uncover the information they seek, which becomes problematical when the enemy is adept at concealment. The situation becomes even more difficult when an opponent distracts friendly collection sensors while concealing or distorting beyond recognition the appearance of the desired information. Further complicating matters is the fact that the analyst's psychological profile may be aiding the opposition in their concealment efforts.

This chapter explains how the human mind perceives the environment and how that environment can mislead the observer. Accurate and effective intelligence analysis depends on the analyst's disciplined and critical perceptions of the data provided. This chapter discusses how military organizations and criminals use deception practices to fool analysts and investigators. Personal or self-deception—when the mind tricks itself by its own senses—is also detailed. The book provides various deception examples, as well as analytical tools and methods used to minimize their effects.

PERCEPTION

What is human perception? The *Oxford Advanced Learners Dictionary* defines *perception* as "the ability to see, hear, or become aware of something through the senses"; or "the awareness of something through the senses."[1]

Psychologists view *perception* as "the human sensory experience of their environment." It involves both the recognition of sensory stimuli and actions in response to these stimuli. Human beings gain information about their environment through perceptual stimuli in order to survive; for example, the stove is hot.

Perception includes the five senses of touch, sight, hearing, smell, and taste. It also includes the cognitive processes required to process sensory information, such as recognizing the favorite song, face of a friend, or the smell of grandma's cookies.

Practical Exercise

The following is a sensory perception exercise. See Figure 4.1. Visualize that you are standing in a hallway next to three light switches, which are all off. There is another room down the hall, where there are three incandescent light bulbs. You are informed that one of the switches in the hallway operates one light bulb (as illustrated in Figure 4.1). From your position in the hall, you cannot see the light bulbs.

If only allowed to enter the room with the light bulbs one time, and only one time, how would you determine which switch operates which light bulb?

Hint: Most successful participants are those who routinely depend on multiple sensory stimuli to perceive their environment.

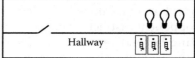

Figure 4.1 Sensory perception exercise.

Misperception

Accurate human perception can increase chances of survival just as misperception can decrease our chances. Factors that influence the level at which we perceive our environment include (1) the perspective of the

---

[1] *Oxford Advanced Learner's Dictionary*, Oxford University Press, 2015.

observer, (2) the *object* being perceived, and (3) the observed object's *background or surroundings*. As these factors vary, the level of human perception (or misperception) also varies.

Observer

Each individual brings his or her own personal experiences and perspectives to bear when observing a given situation. For example, when a crime is committed and there are five eyewitnesses, why are there often five opposing accounts? What causes this observational disparity?

The reasons for this quandary are varied. In all likelihood, each eyewitness has a different location from which to observe the crime. Environmental reasons for discrepancies may include separate physical locations, which may cause differing views of the same scene as result of dissimilar visual perspective, lighting, and shadow effects. Aside from the different observers' positions, the observers themselves are unique. Some may be old and have poor sight or hearing. Others may not have been paying attention during the commission of the crime, or possibly they were unconsciously subject to the influence of other eyewitness accounts or their own personal experiences and biases.

Object Being Perceived

The object itself may attract or distract the perception of the observer. Most are familiar with the following examples of objects that attract our attention (e.g., blue flashing lights of a police car, emergency sirens, and car alarms). Distracters may include things we do not like, such as a couple arguing in public or a crying child not getting their way on a crowded plane.

Background and Surroundings

Background and surroundings may also affect perceptions. Camouflage, deodorants, and loud white noise are good examples of backgrounds reducing one's perception, and conversely, contrasting colors, dead silence, and heavy perfumes or scents can increase one's perception of an object.

The combination of observer experience and situational arrangement associated with these factors (observer, object, and background) determine whether the observer effectively and efficiently cognitively perceives (or misperceives) the object.

DECEPTION

Unlike misperception, where the observer inadvertently misperceives the object due to experience or circumstance, deception is a deliberate effort to alter the perception of the observer. For example, focus on Figure 4.2. As your eyes observe from left to right, are the figures of the three men gradually getting larger, smaller, or remaining the same size?

Figure 4.2 Optical illusion.

(*Note*: Use only your eyes. We will measure the figures later.)

You, the observer, perhaps already suspect trickery and falsely assume your initial assessment that "the figures are getting larger" is erroneous. Therefore, the optical pattern of converging lines and personal bias (your assumption that the image was purposely misleading) combine to fool your mind into believing the figures are actually getting larger (from left to right). However, they are approximately the same size.

However, to detect deception, a skill that is vital to the gatherer of intelligence, one must first have some understanding of what deception is and how it works. A broad definition of deception includes terms such as deceit, bluff, disorientation, trick, and other acts to create and spread untrue beliefs. Additionally, not all deceptions are complete lies. The most effective deceptions use some truth, or just leave out critical facts (half-truths or significant omissions). Deception comes in the form of propaganda, distraction, misdirection, camouflage, and concealment.

Deceptions can be elaborate or quite simple and obvious, therefore, one might think they should be relatively easy to detect.[2] In practice, though, this may not be the case.

Adversarial deception can easily mislead intelligence analysts, primarily because unless prompted otherwise, they do not look for it and therefore assume it is not present. According to Richards J. Heuer Jr., analysts often reject the possibility of deception because they see no evidence of it. Heuer

---

[2] Barton Whaley, *Textbook of Political-Military Counterdeception*, National Defense College, 2007.

Table 4.1 Terror/Criminal Deceptive Practices

Terror Group	Criminal Organization
Hezbollah sending operatives to South America to learn Spanish and blend with the local population	Use of semi-submersibles to move drugs from South/Central America north for distribution and sale
Use of border tunnels (Gaza/Israeli Border) for smuggling and other illicit activities	Use of border tunnels (U.S. southern border) to for smuggling and other illicit activities
ISIS/ISIL laundering millions of oil dollars from illicit Syrian oil trading	Cartels laundering millions of drug dollars from the illicit drug trade
Terrorists, posing as a TV news team, assassinate Ahmad Shah Massoud, leader of the Afghan Northern Alliance, September 9, 2001	Human trafficking under the guise of Eastern European "mail order brides"

persuasively argues that if an adversary plans and executes the deception properly, the analyst should not expect to see evidence of the deceit.[3]

Most analysts can more easily understand deception by a nation-state, such as China, Russia, or Iran. However, visualizing criminal or terrorist organizations using deception is often more difficult. Many illicit deceptive practices fall under various government classifications or are, by nature, "law enforcement sensitive" and therefore cannot be discussed here. However, the following table contains a sampling of the more notable real-world examples describing criminal organizations and terror groups using deception against the United States and other nations of the world.

Each of the deceptive practices listed in Table 4.1 are attempts by an adversary to conceal or deceive in order to avoid discovery or true intent. This is known as 'classic deception'.

Personal (Self) Deception

Sackeim and Gur define and empirically demonstrate self-deception which incorporates many of the basic elements postulated by other psychologists and philosophers, including Plato, Freud, Fingarette, and

---

[3] Richards J. Heuer, Jr., *Psychology of Intelligence Analysis*, 2nd edition, Pherson Associates LLC, 2007.

41

Sartre.[4-6] Sackeim and Gur argue that certain criteria were necessary and sufficient in order to attribute self-deception to any given event. One must

1. Simultaneously
2. Hold two contradictory beliefs
3. One of which the individual is not aware of
4. Because of a motivated act

Using these criteria, self-deception contrasts with other types of deception and is thought to occur when individuals confront aspects of themselves that they find difficult to accept.

Personal, or self, deception is a process of denying or rationalizing away the significance, factual basis, or substance of conflicting evidence or logical argument. Self-deception involves convincing oneself to believe something as "factual" in such a manner that one does not realize they are discounting logical and factual arguments and deceiving themselves. To emphasize the point, refer to an infamous and classic example of self-deception, Custer's Last Stand.

General George Custer, at the time of the Battle of Little Bighorn, was not the brilliant tactician history books might imply. He was, however, decisive and unafraid to take risks. Custer strongly exhibited these character traits when he disregarded multiple reports of an overwhelmingly large enemy force awaiting his troops in the Little Bighorn River valley.[7] Custer was said to have been grossly overconfident of the 7th Cavalry's ability to handle the hostiles. His self-assurance developed from years of actual Civil War combat, but by comparison, he had few and brief battlefield engagements fighting the Sioux Nation. In Custer's limited experience of fighting the Plains Indians, the common thread seemed to be that when his troops attacked the Sioux war parties, the Sioux generally did not stand and fight. Therefore, the general erroneously assumed that at Little Bighorn, the Sioux warriors would retreat in the face of the 7th Calvary's determined assault. Unfortunately for Custer (and the 7th Calvary), he was self-deceived.

---

[4] R. C. Gur and H. A. Sackeim, Self-deception, self-confrontation, and consciousness, in G. Schwartz and D. Shapiro (Eds.), *Consciousness and Self-Regulation: Advances in Research and Theory*, vol. 2, pp. 139–197, New York: Plenum Press, 1978.

[5] H. A. Sackeim, Self-deception: A synthesis, in J. S. Lockard and D. L. Paulhus (Eds.), *Self-Deception: An Adaptive Mechanism?*, pp. 146–165, Englewood Cliffs, NJ: Prentice Hall, 1988.

[6] R. C. Gur and H. A. Sackeim, Self-deception: A concept in search of a phenomenon, *Journal of Personality and Social Psychology*, 37, 1979.

[7] Charles Windolph, Frazier Hunt, Robert Hunt, Neil Mangum, *I Fought with Custer: The Story of Sergeant Windolph, Last Survivor of the Battle of the Little Bighorn*, University of Nebraska Press, 1987.

Custer's experience fighting the Sioux war parties stemmed from a limited data set and his own faulty analysis of the data at hand. In Custer's few engagements (less than five) with Sioux war parties, the Sioux were heavily outnumbered when attacked and showed reasonable tactical competence by recognizing the severe force ratio imbalance weighed against them. They routinely fled the battlefield to fight another day.[8]

In addition to ignoring hostile strength reports with estimates of 1,500 to 2,500 warriors from his Crow scouts and the sound advice of his subordinate, Major Reno, and his superior, General Terry, Custer made the tactical decision to attack an overwhelmingly large force.[9] Worse, Custer made several other severe tactical mistakes, namely spurning the offer of reinforcements (he only had 210 soldiers with him at his last stand), leaving two Gatling guns in the rear, and dividing his forces into smaller and physically separate elements (Reno having roughly 350 troops), now no longer capable of providing any timely support.[10]

Custer's actions at the Little Bighorn fit perfectly the concept of self-deception. He convinced himself to believe something as "factual": Precisely that he and the 7th Calvary alone could defeat a significantly larger force, to the extent that he did not realize he was discounting logical and factual arguments.

Self-deception is a significant concern for analysts. To avoid self-deception, analysts must use multiple procedures to mitigate the negative and possibly catastrophic effects. Such methods include peer reviews, structured analytical techniques (SATs), parallel collaboration, alternatives analysis, and others which will be discussed later in the text.

A similar and more modern military example would be Operation Market Garden. Market Garden was a failed Allied military operation fought in the Netherlands and Germany during World II. Prior to the launch of the operation, several confirmed reports of German troop movements, including details of German armored formations near drop zones were presented to British Field Marshall Bernard Montgomery. Montgomery refused to alter the plans for the landing of 1st Airborne Division at Arnhem.[11] Other intelligence reports of German armored units just outside Arnhem were presented to Lieutenant-General Fredrick

---

8   Evan S. Connell, *Son of the Morning Star*, New York: Harper Perennial, 1997.
9   James Donovan, *A Terrible Glory: Custer and the Little Bighorn*, Little, Brown, and Co, 2008.
10 James Donovan, *A Terrible Glory: Custer and the Little Bighorn—The Last Great Battle of the American West*, Back Bay Books, 2009.
11 Peter Harclerode, *Wings Of War: Airborne Warfare 1918–1945*, Weidenfeld & Nicolson, 2005.

Browning, 1st Airborne Corps Commander, but were similarly dismissed.[12] Since Officers Montgomery and Browning were both provided with solid intelligence analysis, buttressed by multiple reliable and confirming reports, yet still discounted the information and proceeded with the operation, arguably, one could say they suffered from self-deceit.

How to Deceive

Barton Whaley goes into extensive specifics of deception in his *Textbook of Political-Military Counterdeception*. He elaborates on the theory and processes used in creating deception and countering deception. Because they provide full and rich discussion and examples on the topic, this text uses Whaley's theories and practices over other sources, which explain the deception trades (e.g., magic, politics, propaganda, war).

Barton Whaley's 10-Step Deception Process

Dr. Barton Whaley, a scholar in the science of deception, received his doctorate in strategic deception analysis at MIT in 1969. Whaley was a military intelligencer, historian, and amateur student of magic. He served in a U.S. Army psychological warfare intelligence unit headquartered in Tokyo during the Korean War. In later years, he served as a research professor at the U.S. Naval Postgraduate School.

The following step-by-step process of the deception planning and execution process was developed by Dr. Whaley.

1. In planning a deception, planners must know the ultimate goal(s). For the magician, the goal is to entertain with a pleasing surprise or puzzle. For the military commander, it may be to launch a surprise attack, minimize opposition forces at the point of an expected attack, or simply provide a distraction to cover another operation such as reconnaissance or rescue. These goals pose the kinds of problems planners initially face; they are the "givens" they must work with.

2. Planners must decide how they want the target to react in such a given situation. The magician requires only that his or her audience concentrate their attention and interest on the presented effect (or distraction) and not on the trick. For the military

---

[12] Martin Middlebrook, *Arnhem 1944: The Airborne Battle*, Penguin, 1995.

deception planner, however, the problem is subtler. This essential element of effective deception planning is in determining what you want the enemy to do. For the military planner, often it is not enough to make the enemy refocus their attention. In other words, if a commander wants to reduce enemy forces in a particular area of the battlefront in advance of a major attack he or she is planning, he or she must do more than get the enemy to send scouts or reconnaissance elements to different location. He or she must make the enemy physically move significant forces somewhere else—preferably depleting the enemy's combat strength in the area he or she desires to launch the attack.

3. Only after the magicians/planners determines the deception's purpose(s) (e.g., distract the audience, relocate or tie down enemy forces), then they must decide what they want the target to think about the facts or event—precisely what it is they should "perceive."

4. After determining what the target should perceive, planners decide specifically what facts or impending events to conceal and what to present in their stead. In doing this, they should remember the caveat that hiding and showing ideally take place simultaneously, as any deviation from simultaneity gives the target more time to discover the switch. (In military practice, hiding usually takes place prior to showing; only sometimes simultaneously; and fortunately, because it is most risky, rarely afterwards.)

5. Planners now analyze the pattern of the real thing they want to hide to identify its distinguishing characteristics, specifically, which of these characteristics they must delete or emphasize to give another pattern that suitably masks, repackages, or dazzles.

6. The process repeats itself for the presentation of the false thing, which provides another pattern that plausibly mimics, distracts, or decoys.

7. At this point, planners have designed a desired effect together with its hidden method. They must now explore the means available for presenting this effect to the target. A magician's limitation may include availability of appropriate types of deception apparatus; his or her ability to purchase or construct appropriate new apparatus; or his or her theatrical ability. Military commanders or practitioners of intelligence limitations may include their available deception assets, and too often, inadequate time available to acquire additional resources. They must make do or go

45

back to Step 4 of the deception process plan and entertain possible alternative designs.

8. Having the effect and the means, the planning phase has ended and the operational phase begins. In magic, the planner is usually also the performer. In the military and intelligence fields, the deception planner usually hands over to operational units to present (sell) the effect.

9. Channels through which the false information, characteristics, and patterns flow or present themselves must be channels which are open (directly or indirectly) to the target's sensors. That is to say that a magician should not use a "false count" of clicking coins before a deaf spectator or an intelligence officer should not plant disinformation in a newspaper unless he has reason to believe the enemy monitors that paper.

10. Last, for the deception to succeed, the target must accept (buy) the effect, perceiving the illusion as fact. Deception will fail at this point only if the target takes no notice of the presented effect, notices it but judges it irrelevant, misconstrues its intended meaning, or detects its method. Conversely, the target will:
    - Take notice, if the effect is designed to attract his or her attention
    - Find it relevant, if the effect can hold his or her interest
    - Form the intended hypothesis about its meaning, if the projected pattern of characteristics is congruent with patterns already part of his or her experience and memory
    - Fail to detect the deception, if none of the ever-present characteristics that are incongruent are accessible to his or her sensors

Effective deception planning must anticipate all four of these contingencies and seek feedback, monitoring the target's responses, to assure that these four contingencies are being met.[13]

---

[13] Barton Whaley, *Textbook of Political-Military Counterdeception*, National Defense College, 2007.

HOW TO DETECT DECEPTION

There are dozens of specific theories, principles, and methods for detecting deception. However, all have been adopted into one or more other disciplines, particularly by consistently successful analysts who more or less deal regularly with deception. Of these many theories, principles, and methods, only three are covered here and are particularly appropriate for use by intelligence analysts.

According to Dr. Whaley, 143 different fields and disciplines were surveyed to identify the key to detecting deception. The key presented itself as *congruity/incongruity analysis,* or in short, *incongruity analysis.*[14]

Finding Patterns of Congruity and Incongruity (Scientific Method)

We start with a process many learned in grade school, the scientific method. Actually, the scientific method is made up of several interlocking methods, a set of principles and procedures that scientists are expected to follow when doing research.

Having defined the set of facts appropriate to his or her specialty, the scientist then observes those facts; proceeds to make a guess (develop hypothesis) about their nature or relationship; then predicts that, if this guess were true, we should expect to see a predictable outcome; and ends with an experiment to test that prediction (and its underlying) hypothesis. If the hypothesis is not disproven, scientists tentatively accept it, subject to repeated test experiments (replication). This method places great value on skepticism. This skepticism extends to all steps in the process of scientific investigation, accuracy of observation and data collection, hypothesis formation, experimental design, analytical methods, and conclusions.

All discoveries or detections in science and technology are made by perceiving either a new congruity or an unexpected incongruity. These fresh perceptions can arise either during an experiment using some systematic (scientific) method or from chance observation of a natural event.[15]

---

[14] Barton Whaley, *Textbook of Political-Military Counterdeception,* National Defense College, 2007.

[15] Barton Whaley, *Textbook of Political-Military Counterdeception,* National Defense College, 2007.

Congruity

If two things fit together perfectly, they are congruous. If they do not fit, they are incongruous. Every coincidence is a perceived congruity. Normal science is the master of congruity. It busies itself by applying currently fashionable theories and received knowledge to immediate problems. Such plodding and systematic experimental procedure gives us the precise tables of measurements and data that fill the handbooks of medicine, chemistry, engineering, physics, astronomy, and other sciences. Without it there would be no scientists, only mechanics and philosophers.

Normal science is intolerant of surprises. If a test or experiment results in an unexpected finding, the scientist will dismiss it as either "experimenter error" (failure to follow the procedures called for) or "instrument error" (defective or maladjusted apparatus). The scientist then reviews the procedures used or checks the apparatus and adjusts the measuring instruments and proceeds to repeat the experiment. Usually this will give the expected test result and eliminate the anomaly. If, in those rare cases where the anomaly persists, the scientist will tend to question their competence and, in most cases, this will be the full and correct explanation. There is, however, the very rare occasion where the unexpected observation is not a phantom conjured up by either bungled technique or faulty equipment.[16] The scientist now realizes that he or she has been working from a flawed hypothesis or theory. This is the moment of truth when the scientist is on the verge of a genuinely revolutionary discovery.

Incongruity

Any unexpected observation in science is said to be an anomaly. It is simply the most usual term used by most physical scientists for an incongruity. It is what some military deception planners and most magicians and computer scientists call a discrepancy, or what some forensic scientists mean when they declare findings to be inconsistent, or what some social psychologists call dissonance.

Incongruities arise in science in only two circumstances: during mental play or by accident. The first, which is the more usual, occurs whenever a scientist toys in their mind with various possible connections between two phenomena and comes up with an unlikely pair that does seem to fit together.

---

[16] Barton Whaley, *Textbook of Political-Military Counterdeception*, National Defense College, 2007.

This, as Dr. James D. Watson's highly personal account, *The Double Helix* (1968), recalls, frequently happened during his three-year winding intellectual journey toward the revolutionary codiscovery (with Bernard Crick) in 1953 of the double-helix structure of the DNA molecule.[17]

The other, less usual, source of an incongruous event is accident, although an accident of a very special kind, namely one that is first noticed, then perceived to have relevance to science, then stated as a formal hypothesis that can be verified (tested), and finally proved by what is called a *crucial experiment*.

The scientist's opposite path to creativity is by recognizing an incongruity, a puzzling chance occurrence. One example must suffice. Italian physicist Dr. Enrico Fermi was one year into researching the newly discovered neutron at the University of Rome in October 1934 when he and his team observed a puzzling anomaly in the silver samples they were irradiating with neutrons. They observed that the silver became much more radioactive when the experiments were done on a wooden table instead of a marble bench. A few days later Fermi tried an experiment by placing a radiation filter between the neutron stream and the target metal. He had decided on lead as the obvious filter, however, at the last moment, he noticed a handy slab of paraffin and on a whim, used it instead. To everyone's surprise it increased the rates of nuclear activity by a hundred-fold.

Baffled by what all these unexpected events could possibly mean, he went home for lunch and a nap. He was alone. At 3:00 that afternoon, still alone, he returned to his lab with the answer. The paraffin molecules had slowed the bombarding neutrons to the point where these slow neutrons could produce more effective collisions with the target than normal fast neutrons. Fermi had instantly invented a new branch of experimental physics (neutron-induced radioactivity). Four years later, it won him a Nobel Prize.[18]

This extraordinarily valuable ability to perceive an incongruity and, by devising a new theory that will make it congruous, is precisely what creates all "revolutions" in science.[19]

---

[17] James D. Watson, *The Double Helix: A Personal Account of the Discovery of the Structure of DNA*, New York: Atheneum, 1968.

[18] Dan Cooper, *Enrico Fermi: And the Revolutions in Modern Physics*, New York: Oxford University Press, 1999.

[19] Barton Whaley, *Textbook of Political-Military Counterdeception*, National Defense College, 2007.

Balancing Congruities and Incongruities

Whenever a scientist or mathematician expresses a conclusion in the form of an equation, it proves that he or she has perceived and proved a congruity (identity or analogy) between the terms on both sides of the equation. These equalities range from the simple math equation ($2 + 2 = 4$), to the complex approximation of pi ($\pi = 3.1416$), to the Nobel Prize–winning Einstein equation ($E = mc^2$).

However, to perceive and prove an incongruity, one must assess the authenticity of the observed. To do this, one must ask the following three basic questions:

What is there that should be?
What is missing? (i.e., what is not there that should be?)
What is there, if anything, that should not be?[20]

Incongruity Analysis

Because nature never deceives, there can be no incongruities in nature. Consequently, whenever we find an incongruity (discrepancy, anomaly), we are entitled to draw three inferences:

1. We have misread our instruments or sensors and need to double-check. Then, if the incongruity still persists, we are on the verge of an exciting discovery, namely that
2. Our relevant hypothesis is incorrect and, in this case, there are two possible causes:
    - There is some real characteristic in nature that requires us to adjust our hypothesis to incorporate this newly perceived characteristic.
    - There is some false characteristic introduced by a human deceiver.
3. In that case incongruity analysis will, in theory, reveal one or both of the two incongruities created by every deception; namely, the real thing the deceiver is trying to hide (dissimulate) and the false thing being shown (simulated) in its place.

Because the process of detecting deception is fundamentally simple in both theory and practice, a sure sign of an ineffective deception analyst is one who subscribes to and applies complex theories, at least at the

---

[20] Barton Whaley, *Textbook of Political-Military Counterdeception*, National Defense College, 2007.

beginning. Conversely, an effective deception analyst is one who systematically applies incongruity analysis.

The Plus or Minus Rule

Each real thing has a large but finite number of identifiable characteristics. In other words, every real object must have its complete set of defining characteristics not one more, nor one less. All imitations will share at least one, and often many, of these characteristics, however, every imitation must lack at least one characteristic that marks the real thing and it will usually have additional ones not in the original. Even identical twins have a different history starting in the womb and even the most perfect clone lacks two characteristics of the original: it is not the first and it has had a different history.

Then if either a plus (added) or a minus (missing) characteristic is detected, the imitation stands revealed. Note that a most important corollary of this Plus or Minus Rule is that the analyst need not discover all or even many of the discrepancies or incongruities. A single false characteristic, whether plus (added) or minus (missing), is sufficient to prove fakery. This is why complicated deceptions tend to be weak. For example, the cadaver of *The Man Who Never Was* (Operation Mincemeat was a successful British disinformation plan during the Second World War) died from the wrong cause (poison-induced pneumonia rather than drowning), his body was far too decomposed for the pretended time since death, and the personal effects bore not his but another man's fingerprints.[21] Here were at least three absolutely or presumptively incongruous characteristics, any one of which, if detected by the enemy, would have completely blown or at least raised grave suspicions about that major British military deception operation.

Military examples of the Plus or Minus Rule are common. They are most common in ambush situations where often the only life-saving warning is a vague awareness of something wrong; a sense that either something is there that shouldn't be (a seemingly abandoned knapsack perhaps) or that something is missing (an empty village square during rush hour).

The Plus or Minus Rule greatly helps the analyst identify the key pieces of evidence to focus on. Therefore, we may conclude that the greater number of uniquely distinguishing characteristics we know about

---

[21] Denis Smyth, *Deathly Deception: The Real Story of Operation Mincemeat*, New York: Oxford Press, 2010.

something, the greater our chances of recognizing its counterfeit, if either (1) any incongruous characteristic is present, or (2) any congruous characteristic is missing.

The Congruity/Incongruity Rule and the Analyst's Advantage

Every real thing is always, necessarily, completely congruent with all its distinguishing characteristics. Conversely, every false thing will display at least two incongruities. Because every deception involves simultaneously showing at least one false thing and hiding a corresponding real thing, the Congruity–Incongruity Rule tells us that the detective has two independent chances to detect any deception. Thus, a deception will be confirmed if we detect either its simulated or its dissimulated half. Moreover, even this half-disclosure focuses the detective's guesses about what the remaining part could be, thereby greatly simplifying the effort to detect it as well. This one simple fact gives the detective a crucial advantage against every deceiver.

American art expert and museum curator Thomas Pearsall Field Hoving applied his version of the Congruity–Incongruity Rule to his own specialty:

> Embedded in every art forgery, no matter how ambitious or paltry, is a stupid mistake left by the faker—a physical property that didn't exist in ancient times, or a kind of aging that cannot be natural, or an amusing error in style—a blunder that anybody with concentration and common sense might be able to spot.[22]

Thomas Pearsall Field Hoving, Former Curator
Metropolitan Museum of Art

Two other recent examples where the direct detection approach failed yet the indirect one succeeded were the mole hunting cases of Aldrich Ames (former Central Intelligence Agency officer turned KGB mole, convicted of espionage in 1994)[23] and Robert Hanssen (former Federal Bureau of Investigation agent who spied for Soviet and Russian intelligence services against the United States for 22 years from 1979 to 2001).[24] Ames's

---

[22] Thomas Hoving, *False Impressions: The Hunt for Big-Time Art Fakes*, New York: Simon & Schuster, 1997.

[23] Tim Weiner, David Johnston, and Neil A. Lewis, *Betrayal: The Story of Aldrich Ames, An American Spy*, Random House Publishers, 1995.

[24] David Wise, *Spy: The Inside Story of How the FBI's Robert Hanssen Betrayed America*, Random House Publishers, 2003.

extravagant lifestyle was significantly incongruent with his $60,000 a year salary and Hanssen's identity as a mole was purchased via a confidential informant.

CHAPTER SUMMARY

Chapter 4 explained the concepts of perception and deception, focusing on how the human mind perceives the environment and how that environment can mislead the observer. It was emphasized that accurate and effective intelligence analysis depends on the analyst's disciplined and critical perceptions of the data provided for analysis. How adversary military organizations and criminals use deception practices to fool analysts and investigators was highlighted. Personal, or self-deception, when the mind tricks itself by its own senses, was also covered.

Perception

In lay terms, psychologists view *perception* as the human sensory experience of their environment. It involves both the recognition of sensory stimuli and actions in response to these stimuli. Human beings gain information about their environment through perceptual stimuli in order to survive; for example, the stove is hot.

Perception includes the five senses of touch, sight, hearing, smell, and taste. It also includes the cognitive processes required to process sensory information, such as recognizing the favorite song, face of a friend, or the smell of grandma's cookies.

Misperception
Accurate human perception can increase chances of survival just as misperception can decrease our chances. Factors that influence the level at which we perceive our environment include (1) the perspective of the *observer*, (2) the *object* being perceived, and (3) the observed object's *background or surroundings*. As these factors vary, the level of human perception (or misperception) also varies.

Deception
Unlike misperception, where the observer inadvertently misperceives the object due to experience or circumstance, deception is a deliberate effort to alter the perception of the observer.

53

Personal (or Self) Deception
Personal, or self, deception is a process of denying or rationalizing away the significance, factual basis, or substance of conflicting evidence or logical argument. Self-deception involves convincing oneself to believe something as "factual" in such a manner that one does not realize they are discounting logical and factual arguments and deceiving themselves.

How to Deceive
The section highlights the theories and processes for creating and detecting deception as described in D. Barton Whaley's book, *Textbook of Political-Military Counterdeception.*

Barton Whaley's 10-Step Deception Process
Dr. Barton Whaley's 10-Step Deception Process is a step-by-step process for deception planning and execution process.

How to Detect Deception
According to Dr. Whaley, the key to detecting deception is "congruity/incongruity analysis"—in short, incongruity analysis.

Finding Patterns of Congruity and Incongruity (Scientific Method)
Because the process of detecting deception is fundamentally simple in both theory and practice, a sure sign of an ineffective deception analyst is one who subscribes to and applies complex theories, at least at the beginning. Conversely, an effective deception analyst is one who systematically applies incongruity analysis.

The Plus or Minus Rule
The Plus or Minus Rule greatly helps the analyst identify the key pieces of evidence to focus on. Therefore, we may conclude that the greater number of uniquely distinguishing characteristics we know about something, the greater our chances of recognizing its counterfeit, if either (1) any incongruous characteristic is present, or (2) any congruous characteristic is missing.

The Congruity/Incongruity Rule and the Analyst's Advantage
Because every deception involves simultaneously showing at least one false thing and hiding a corresponding real thing, the Congruity–Incongruity Rule tells us that the detective has two independent chances to detect any deception. Thus, a deception will be confirmed if we detect either its simulated or its dissimulated half.

5

Knowing Your Audience

INTRODUCTION

The maxim "don't kill the messenger" originates in ancient Greek literature. Plutarch, a Greek historian and biographer, in a quotation from *Plutarch's Lives* (The Parallel Lives), writes:

> The first messenger, that gave notice of Lucullus' coming was so far from pleasing Tigranes that, he had his head cut off for his pains; and no man dared to bring further information. Without any intelligence at all, Tigranes sat while war was already blazing around him, giving ear only to those who flattered him.

> Plutarch

Like Tigranes, human beings dislike bad news and unfortunately often associate the negative information with the bearer of bad news. As an analyst, good fortune will allow you to produce many valuable intelligence products over a long and distinguished career. However, your analysis may or may not delight all of your intelligence consumers. This chapter does not address why people associate bad news with the bearer. However, it does give the intelligence analyst tools and information on how to prepare intelligence products which users are more likely to read and appreciate.

So to avoid cases where users want to "shoot the messenger" or ignore the analyst and waste his or her efforts, Chapter 5 helps the analyst develop an analytical product that not only answers the right question, but encourages the user to "want" the information provided.

IDENTIFY AND WRITE FOR YOUR AUDIENCE

Whether it's a winning lottery number or the latest Hollywood rumors about their favorite soap opera star, analysts, like novelists, must capture the intelligence consumers' attention early if they want to get their message across. Generally, humans only want information they can "use" or that "interests them," but preferably "both."

The best way an analyst can seize and hold someone's attention is to know his or her audience and what they want to know. As discussed in Chapter 2, analysts identify this information early on in the Planning and Directions Phase of the Intelligence Cycle.

TIPS ON HOOKING YOUR AUDIENCE INCLUDE

- **Remember, your first chance to get your reader's attention may be your last.**
- **Know what interests your audience.**
- **Give them what they want early.**
- **Do not make them look for it.**
- **Use simple and direct language.**
- **Pair the "hook" text with a visual (e.g., a graphic), if appropriate.**

Therefore, since you have already identified "what" information the end user needs or wants, do not make them search for it because it is buried three pages deep in the report.

Identifying your audience will do more than ensure you write clearly by including the most-wanted information, it will also aid the analyst in focusing on the audience's "needs." See the following example scenario.

Example Scenario

You are a DHS analyst and you just received an intelligence/information requirement (IR) from the Drug Enforcement Agency (DEA).

"Identify the major cocaine drug smuggling routes crossing the Texas land border into the United States." You are tasked to rewrite the IR in order to forward it for collection.

Who is your audience? Is it the DEA? ... DHS? ... CBP management? ... CBP patrol agents? ... Cocaine smugglers?

Answer: The request would logically go to the Customs and Border Protection (CBP) agents located on the Texas Border. Unless DHS has a well-placed confidential informant (CI) inside one or more of the smuggling gangs, DEA (they created the IR), DHS (is asking to forward the IR), and CBP management (has no access or placement to obtain the information) would not be logical collection assets for this IR.

What does the audience already know about the subject? How does one locate a major cocaine smuggling route? Are they labeled "major cocaine smuggling route"? ... Not very likely. However, CBP agents would plausibly know what significantly large drug shipments look like. For example, a couple of grams of cocaine found in the backpack of a non–U.S. national found outside El Paso, in this case, probably does not fit the IR criteria. Plot the information collected from this IR on a map, and the analyst will eventually start to see patterns form. With enough data collected, those patterns will begin to show routes and amounts of throughput.

What does the audience (the CBP agents) need to know? The analyst must translate clear criteria to the CBP agents, which satisfies the "intent" of the DEA IR.

Answer: Request information on all cocaine seizures greater than 1 kilogram reported in the vicinity (50 miles) of the Texas–Mexico land border. Specifics include weight, date, and time of seizure, names of perpetrator(s) involved, gang/cartel/organizational affiliation, direction traveling when captured, reported origin, destination, and route information, if available.

What questions might the audience have? At this point, to save possible reiterations of drafting, revising, and resending the IR, the analyst might call or email a CBP office near the Texas border and bounce the IR off a CBP agent. If it does not make sense to the agent, the analyst should listen to their concerns, make adjustments, and forward the IR for release.

CHOOSING YOUR SUPPORTING EVIDENCE

In an effort to prevent misunderstanding, the book is not endorsing the "selection of supporting evidence" for presentation based upon what agrees or does not agree with one's hypothesis. However, if for example, your audience generally does not accept (or prefer) certain types of evidence (i.e., statistics or expert opinion), it will not matter how much statistical data or expert opinion–related evidence you have, the consumer may ignore it or disregard it based on the "packaging" rather than the "content." If intelligence products are ignored or disregarded, in either case, you have failed. In intelligence analysis, one does not always get to choose the types of supporting information or data that is available. However, if there are differing forms available to support the analysis, the analyst should make an effort to choose those forms which are most likely the consumer will read.

Generally, one can support an intelligence argument by using three different methods. An analyst can use them separately or in combination according to their purpose and audience. These methods are statistics, examples, and expert opinion. From an intelligence consumer's perspective, each form has its advantages and detractors.

Statistics

Some intelligence consumers want statistical evidence in their reports. Statistics present information in seemingly unbiased numerical format. According to Webster, *statistics* is a branch of mathematics dealing with the collection, analysis, interpretation, and presentation of masses of numerical data.[1] Therefore, one must understand statistical information can be presented in various legitimate ways and yet suggest dramatically different conclusions.

Statistics Example

Scenario: Some may be familiar with the popular statistic that 52 percent of car accidents occur within 5 miles and 69 percent of all car accidents occur with 10 miles of the home (refer to Figure 5.1).[2] That factual statistic could make some concerned that, for some unknown reason, it might be more dangerous to drive the roads within a 10-mile radius of one's home. However, looking a little deeper, a casual skeptic might recognize that

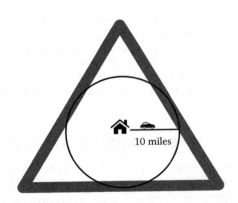

Figure 5.1 Statistics example.

---

[1] Merriam-Webster, *Dictionary*, 2015.
[2] National Highway Traffic Safety Association (NHTSA), *Traffic Safety Facts Annual Report*, 2008.

no matter what destination or direction you set off to (e.g., the store, work, golf course), 100 percent of the time you leave your home as point of origin and return to the same location. Therefore, statistically you will be within 10 miles of your home a much higher percentage of the time and will more likely get into an accident within that 10-mile radius than any area outside that radius.

Notice the same factual statistic can yield two drastically different inferences.

If your audience is comfortable with statistical information sets and understands their pitfalls, using statistics to support your analysis may be most appropriate. However, not all datasets or numerical samples (small or skewed datasets in particular) readily support statistical analysis. Because of this shortfall of statistical calculation, the statistical analytical results may be seriously flawed and therefore using statistical evidence is not always appropriate, even when the consumer desires that it be included in the overall analysis.

FACTUAL EXAMPLES

Specific factual examples (not analogies) that support (as well as those that do not support) the analyst's claim(s) should be included. Examples can provide specifics and supporting details often giving the analysis a visual description, which can grab and hold the intelligence consumer's attention. Examples can be in the form of HUMINT reporting, photographic evidence, video or audio recordings, or raw scientific or forensic data. Each example dataset requires some additional contextual information (e.g., date and time of data; and/or language translation, names of individuals in the photos, videos, and voice recordings). Although some interpretation is required, it is generally minimal.

Analysts should organize samples logically or sequentially, whichever is easiest to understand by the reader and that best supports the analysis. The contradictory data should also be included along with some explanation or rationale so that user understands why the information is not considered valid.

Some intelligence consumers are like the characters from the old TV show *Dragnet* from the 1950s and, later, the 1970s. The most famous line from the TV series was detective Joe Friday (played by Jack Webb) saying, "the facts, just the facts." Just like Detective Friday, intelligence consumers are not interested in opinions or mathematical algorithms (regardless of their accuracy); they only want "the facts."

Expert Opinions

Factual evidence is the basis for expert opinions, however, expert opinions differ from fact in that they are interpretations of fact from the perspective of an expert.

For example, a physicist may consider mountains of data when determining whether a foreign chemical processing facility is producing weapons-grade Uranium (U^{235}) or, peanut butter. The same dataset reviewed by different expert observers may yield differing interpretations of the same information. Political decisions on whether to do nothing, exercise sanctions or bomb the facility are balanced based upon which argument is most convincing.

Intelligence analysts often must use subject matter experts (SMEs) to interpret data because they themselves do not have the best background information or subject matter knowledge to properly weigh the facts presented. However, some consumers are not interested in highly technical and lengthy scientific reports. They just want a clean quick assessment. Nevertheless, by providing that "clean quick assessment" to the consumer, the analyst is not relieved of the burden of due diligence and of performing thorough and complete analysis. Even if the analyst does not provide the raw scientific data as part of the deliverable, they should have it available and reference it in the final report.

ORGANIZING INFORMATION FOR THE USER

One should recognize that most intelligence consumers are similar to you in that they do not want to waste their time reading many pages of marginally related information just to find what they were looking for 15 pages into the document or, even worse, not at all.

To ensure the intelligence consumer can easily locate desired reporting content, an analyst should have a logical plan to present findings and make (support) their case in a brief and logical fashion (for further discussion on this subject, refer to the chapter on briefings). The format can be based upon a template (if driven by organization requirement) or of your own design. Whichever way you choose to present your findings, it should be consistent, verifiable, straightforward, and logically supportable.

Findings Intelligence Assessments

Analytical findings, also known as your assessments, is/are based upon the evidence or information (e.g., facts, opinions, and statistics) collected and your analysis of that information. One must show linkage between your findings and the supporting evidence. To demonstrate this linkage, an analyst normally states his or her claim/finding as the topic sentence of the paragraph, followed by supporting evidence or information from which the claim or finding derives its support, as well as the justification or logical reasoning linking the evidence to their finding.

Findings (Focused to the Audience) Example

FICTITIOUS SCENARIO

You are a DHS analyst and have been informed that an alien invasion of Texas is coming across news channels (Figure 5.2). You must prepare a quick assessment for federal, state, and local law enforcement, as well as for the National Guard units in affected areas to assist them with containing the situation.

The IR reads: Determine size, strength, route(s), speed of movement, and intentions/destination(s) of space invasion force. Below are the first field reports and your first finding.

- Media and Internet reports pour in

- Local TV news stations announce "Invasion from Space," citing NASA public advisory announcements and video reports (using cell phone video sources and station video clips).
- Video clips show spacecraft landing footage at five separate locations in Texas.

- Local police reports corroborate those five landing sites. No TV reports have yet to locate a landing site not already reported by police.
- *Analyst comment*: It is likely that news agencies found landing sites based upon police scanner reports or locals sending in their cell phone clips.
- Hundreds of cell phone video clips flood the Internet.
  - *Analyst comment*: Presently, only 25 video clips match up to military, air traffic, or police reports with any level of confidence.
  - Seven other sightings are still under investigation.
- Multiple conspiracy theories circulate on social networks citing that China, Russia, the CIA, angels, and creatures from outer space are attacking.
- NASA reports verify that the alien craft trajectories originated from or near Mars: First suspected to be a series of asteroids which had a near-miss of the planet Mars; later confirmed to be under intelligent control after a series of course and speed changes. Radio contact was attempted with no response.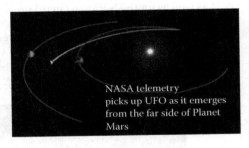

NASA telemetry picks up UFO as it emerges from the far side of Planet Mars

Ultimate origin cannot be confirmed at this time.
- U.S. military satellite imagery depicts multiple large (300 yards long × 50 yards wide) spacecraft at multiple landing sites (>25 known sites, multiple suspected) across Texas. Cloud cover and commercial and private aircraft in the vicinity confuse observations.
- Military and federal air traffic controllers track on radar and attempt radio contact also, with no response.
- Highway traffic cameras along Interstates 10 and 20 show > 100 unidentified vehicles moving east at approximately 50 mph. Forward limit of progress, roughly along Texas–Louisiana border. (See Figure 5.2.)
- Local police reports:
  - Visible ray causing officers at roadblocks to become physically nauseated and temporarily incapacitated; no further information (NFI).
  - Landing craft (visually reported to be more than 200 yards long) are deploying multiple (>100 total)

smaller craft/vehicles (each approximately 30 feet long), which hover above the ground (10 to 20 feet).

- Multiple deployed craft/ vehicles approach road-blocks; officers give verbal orders to stop in English and Spanish as well as hand signals and warning shots. Aliens respond with incapacitating ray; unidentified backwash from hovering craft brush patrol cars and personnel aside as they bypass roadblocks and move eastward towards interstate. Multiple reports submitted with similar results. No known deaths reported at this time.

Figure 5.2 Southern U.S. map.

- Unidentified aquatic/amphibious craft being transported by other self-propelled vehicles.

Now taking the information on hand, we break it down into the following categories: "Supporting Evidence," "Inferences," "Assumptions," and "Gaps."

- Supporting Evidence (What do we know?):
  - Military satellite imagery depicting large (300 yards long × 50 yards wide) spacecraft at multiple landing sites (>25 known sites, multiple suspected) across Texas.
  - NASA telemetry showing point of origin as the planet Mars.
  - Local law enforcement organizations eyewitness reports:
    - Unable to contain in landing zones
    - Using unidentified incapacitating ray against any resistance
    - Large numbers (>100) of unidentified air- and land-craft levitating and moving east at 50 mph along Interstates 10 and 20
    - Other unidentified craft in columns appear to be aquatic or amphibious
    - Unidentified aquatic/amphibious craft being transported by other self-propelled vehicles

- Inferences (What do we suspect?):
  - Possibly hostile; use of incapacitating ray to remove resistance, no reported attempts to communicate or respond to human attempts
  - Over 100; local LEO report large numbers (>100) of unidentified air- and landcraft (if manned 1 per craft, number would be >100)
  - Movement based upon eyewitness reports: moving east at 50 mph along Interstates 10 and 20 (possibly I-30)
  - Intermediate destination likely Mississippi River:
    - Based upon unidentified craft in columns appearing to be aquatic or amphibious.
    - Only large body of water in path for hundreds of miles and the path of march is the Mississippi River.
    - If were heading to Atlantic, they would have likely landed closer to the coast.
    - They landed near I-10 and I-20, so they will likely use them for travel east.
- Assumptions (What must we assume):
  - Invaders are extraterrestrial, possibly from Mars; but could have originally come from another planet in the Solar System or outside the Solar System and used the backside of Mars as an assembly area for attack preparations.
- Gaps (missing information?):
  - Intentions and ultimate destination are unknown:
    - Hostile possibly, purpose may be occupation? … Raid? … Going for a swim in the Mississippi? … Presently undeterminable.
    - Not indiscriminately killing or destroying property, but they are also are not communicating.
    - Apparently highly advanced technologically—why are they not communicating?
  - Point of origin is unknown: NASA telemetry only can observe the side of Mars facing Earth.
  - Final destination(s) is (are) unknown.
  - Propulsion systems of all craft are unknown.
  - Are they living creatures? What is their physiology? No reported sightings of actual "beings," only spacecraft and ground-effect vehicles. Therefore, could be unmanned (robotic) spacecraft/vehicles.

Foundational Evidence

Foundational or supporting evidence refers to the information the analysts are using upon which to base their findings. Notice, under Example Finding #1, the sources (see source footnotes) that are used to support the particular finding are specified, for example, military satellite imagery, NASA telemetry, and local law enforcement organization (LEO) reports. Factual evidence generally speaks for itself. However, inferences need some level of explanation; assumptions should be recognized as "assumptions," and intelligence gaps need to be identified as collection requirements.

Facts

A fact is piece of information considered to be "true." In the analytical field, that is generally a piece of information that has multiple independent and known reliable sourcing. For example, a report that identifies a suspect by name and is supported by video and DNA evidence. There is still a chance that the video footage or DNA evidence are fake or somehow manipulated. However, the chances of this being the case are extremely low, but not zero.

Inferences

Inferences by their very nature are not facts. However, inferences should be supported by facts and described in the findings using presumptive or suggestive terminology, for example, likely, highly likely, unlikely, and so on. The destination of "Mississippi River" is cited as a "likely" destination. The rationale for the probable destination is based upon the route of movement (east) and the unidentified aquatic or amphibious craft being moved by self-propelled vehicles. The analyst's rationale for making the inference is usually included in the finding/assessment to assist the intelligence consumer in understanding the analyst's perspective.

Assumptions

Would it be reasonable to assume that the invaders are "extraterrestrial"? Possibly, as they appeared to come from somewhere other than Earth. You have many indicators, but no incontrovertible proof positive. The next logical question would be, how could you obtain that irrefutable proof? Unless the analyst captures and examines a spacecraft or ground-effect vehicle, or perhaps if an alien steps out and shakes somebody's hand, the analyst is at an impasse. Rather than wasting precious collection assets to obtain hard or impossible to find data for the experts to argue over, the analyst will make a few logical assumptions and move on.

It may very well be an elaborate hoax, but to pull this hoax off, all sensor data and video footage from a host of independent (and some quite reliable) sources would have to be falsified and everyone providing the information would need to be involved in the hoax.

Assumptions should be few in number and clearly identified as assumptions in the analysis document.

Gaps

Would it be reasonable to assume that the invaders came from Mars? Possibly, since they appeared to come from there on the way to Earth. NASA's telemetry supports the Mars-to-Earth portion of the travel route. However, the point of origin is beyond the reasonable scope of the evidence available and therefore is considered an intelligence "gap."

Intelligence "gaps" are unknowns. They may be questions left unanswered form the original IR or new questions generated during the analysis process. In either case, analysts should submit collection requirements to address any intelligence gaps.

Justification (Logical Reasoning)

Once collected, information sorts into the appropriate categories. Weighing all available data, one must make some logical and justified assessments (findings) based upon that information. However, the analyst must keep the audience in mind.

Who is the audience? A combination of lightly armed state national guardsmen and law enforcement professionals.

What is our audience's most likely mission? Is it "defeat the invaders"? If this is the case, do they have the capacity? Does a state of "war" exist? Are the invaders attacking anyone? There are no reported casualties (save the temporarily incapacitated police). Perhaps our audience's mission is to "protect the public."

First, one must recall, what the IR specified.

> **IR: "Determine size, strength, route(s), and speed of movement and intentions/destination(s) of space invasion force."**

Did the IR specify something to the effect of "identify possible physical weaknesses for tactical exploitation"?

The U.S. military (and in this case, NATO forces) is far better-suited to attack the invaders, if required. Would it not be more advantageous for everyone, if police and National Guard were to focus on evacuating civilian populations to prevent potential collateral casualties? Should it ultimately be determined to be a "hostile" invasion and if the military does have to attack/defend, military forces will need clear fields of fire. What if the invaders are not hostile? What if the extraterrestrials did not even know the planet was inhabited? … What if we attack and start a war that could have been avoided?

> *Finding #1*: More than 100 extraterrestrial spacecraft approximately 300 yards long × 50 yards wide (origins unknown) have landed in Texas at 25-plus confirmed locations.[1] Multiple smaller (approximately 30 feet long) ground-effect vehicles have emerged (specific numbers unknown, estimated to <50 per spacecraft based upon parent volume) from the parent craft and are moving east along Interstates 10, 20, and possibly 30 at approximately 50 mph.[2]
>
> *Finding #2*: Likely headed towards the Mississippi River (could cross Mississippi) at two, probably three, locations (I-10/I-20/I-30? bridges), intentions—whether friendly or hostile—unknown (no fatalities yet reported), and ultimate destination(s) presently unknown.[3]
>
> *Finding #3*: Unidentified ground-effect craft are extremely mobile. However, vehicular movement patterns appear to indicate preference or probably require relatively flat surfaces to obtain/maintain present speed (approximately 50 mph); resulting in the observed preferential movement along interstates.[4] NFI (no further information).

Assumption 1: Invaders are extraterrestrial in origin.

Assumption 2: Extremely advanced technologically; superior weapons and propulsion capabilities.

Source Footnotes
---

[1] NASA ground station radar and satellite telemetry tracks, National OPIR imagery collection.

[2] Multiple state and local police reports and interstate traffic cameras footage collected and collated by Southwest Texas Fusion Center.

[3] Analyst assessment based upon available field reports and pattern/movement analysis.

[4] Analyst assessment based upon multiple eyewitness police reports, video footage, and traffic camera footage.

Looking at each bulleted item above, ask yourself if the IR was answered, yes, no, or partially? Regardless of the answer, was there adequate support for the finding? Is the IR response more helpful when it focuses on the needs of the intelligence consumer (i.e., the intended audience)?

CHAPTER SUMMARY

As mentioned in the introduction, this chapter did not address "why" people associate bad news with the bearer. However, it did give the intelligence analyst tools and information on how to prepare intelligence products which users are more likely to read and appreciate. By having a full understanding of one's audience (the intelligence consumer) and their mission, the analyst fine-tunes information requirements (IRs) to more accurately collect information as well as more precisely address the information needs of their customers.

Identify and Write for Your Audience

Identifying your audience will do more than ensure you write clearly by including the most wanted information, it also aids the analyst to focus on the audience's "needs."

Choosing Your Supporting Evidence

Generally, one can support an intelligence argument by using three different methods. An analyst can use them separately or in combination, according to their purpose and audience. The types are statistics, factual examples, and expert opinion. From an intelligence consumer's perspective, each form has its advantages and detractors. Knowing what type(s) the intelligence consumer is more receptive to increases the likelihood that an intelligence product will be properly received and the information contained, understood, and accepted.

Statistics
If your audience is comfortable with statistical information sets and understands their pitfalls, using statistics to support your analysis may be most appropriate. However, not all datasets or numerical samples (small or skewed datasets in particular) readily support statistical analysis. Because of this shortfall of statistical calculation, the statistical analytical results

may be seriously flawed and therefore, using statistical evidence is not always appropriate, even when the consumer desires that it be included in the overall analysis.

Factual Examples
Examples can provide specifics and supporting details often giving the analysis a visual description, which can grab and hold the intelligence consumer's attention. Examples can be in the form of HUMINT reporting, photographic evidence, video or audio recordings, or raw scientific or forensic data. Each example dataset requires some additional contextual information (e.g., date and time of data, names of individuals in the photos, videos, and voice recordings). Although some interpretation is required, it is generally minimal.

Expert Opinion
Factual evidence is the basis for expert opinions; however, expert opinions differ from fact in that they are interpretations of fact. Intelligence analysts often must use subject matter experts (SMEs) to interpret data because they do not have the background information to properly weigh the facts presented. However, some consumers are not interested in highly technical and lengthy scientific reports. They just want a clean quick assessment. Nevertheless, by providing that "clean quick assessment" to the consumer, the analyst is not relieved of the burden of due diligence and performing thorough and complete analysis. Even if the analyst does not provide the raw scientific data as part of the deliverable, they should have it available and reference it in the final report.

Organizing Information for the User

To ensure the intelligence consumer can easily locate desired reporting content, an analyst should have a logical plan to present his or her findings and make (support) his or her case in a brief and logical fashion. The format can be based upon a template (if driven by organization requirement) or of your own design. Whichever way you choose to present your findings, it should be consistent, verifiable, straightforward, and logically supportable.

Foundational Evidence

Foundational or supporting evidence is the information the analyst is using to base his or her claim/finding. Factual evidence generally speaks for itself. However, inferences need some level of explanation, assumptions should be recognized as assumptions, and intelligence gaps need to be identified as collection requirements.

Finding(s) (Intelligence Assessments)

Analytical finding(s) (also known as assessments) is based upon the evidence or information (e.g., facts, opinions, and statistics) collected and your analysis of that information. One must show linkage between your findings and the supporting evidence.

Facts

A fact is piece of information considered to be "true." In the analytical field, that is generally a piece of information that has multiple independent and known reliable sourcing. There is still a chance that the evidence is fake or somehow manipulated. However, the chances of this being the case are extremely low, but not zero.

Inferences

Inferences should be supported by facts and described in the findings using presumptive or suggestive terminology, for example, likely, highly likely, unlikely, and so on. The analyst's rationale for making the inference is usually included in the finding/assessment to assist the intelligence consumer in understanding the analyst's perspective.

Assumptions

Analysts may use assumptions when there are many indicators, but no incontrovertible proof. If something is "self-evident" or "extremely difficult to determine," rather than wasting precious collection assets to obtain impossible to find data, the analyst just makes a few logical assumptions and moves on.

Assumptions should be few in number and clearly identified as assumptions in the analysis document.

Gaps

Intelligence "gaps" are unknowns. They may be questions left unanswered form the original IR or new questions generated during the analysis process. In either case, analysts should submit collection requirements to address any intelligence gaps.

Justification: Logical Reasoning

Keeping the audience in mind, the analyst weighs all available data and makes some logical and justified assessments (findings) based upon that information. Once the analyst has drafted his or her findings, he or she reviews each of them to ensure they are each logical and justified.

6

Analytical Communication

INTRODUCTION

Analytical communication takes many forms. It includes everything from formulating an analytical product pitch, to peer-to-peer collaboration, to outreach to experts outside the intelligence community, to formatting the final product so that it conveys the proper message in an easily understood format. This chapter explores these concepts and provides guidance, formats, an explanation of writing for release, and checklists to support the analyst in achieving effective communication between collaborators/peers and end users.

Professional intelligence organizations, whether governmental or commercially operated, adopt writing standards or style guide(s) that govern the grammar, content, and format for writing intelligence documents, products, and memorandums. These guides address conventional writing, formats, style, grammar, and punctuation topics that are the basis for standardizing written materials. This section introduces and advocates the development and use of writing standards or style guides for professional communications and intelligence production.

BASIC WORKINGS OF ANALYTICAL COMMUNICATION

Professional communication in general requires thoughtful preparation. Analytical communication is no exception. If anything, because of the critical nature of analytical communication, it requires a more rigorous and rigid structure to ensure product standardization that reduces the chances misunderstanding and miscommunication.

Communication Preparation

One must take the time to carefully plan and prepare analytical communication in order to satisfy production requirements and avoid needless confusion. No matter what type of written communication instrument you are dealing with, there are four basic preparation steps: Analyze the purpose, know your audience, determine the medium, and assemble the information.[1]

1. Analyze the purpose.
   a. What is the purpose of the communication?
   b. Is your goal to direct, inform, influence, or motivate?
2. Know your audience.
   a. Who is going to read this? Depending on the type of communication and coordination, analysts may deal with one or more individuals in the following categories: Primary receiver, secondary receiver, and coordinators/facilitators.
      i. Primary: The primary is the intended audience.
      ii. Secondary: The secondary receivers are an indirect audience. They indirectly receive the contents of your communication via the primary.
      iii. Coordinators/facilitators: Those who staff and review communications and follow procedures for tasking, tracking, processing, and disseminating communications.
3. Determine the communication medium to use (e.g., letter, memorandum, formal intelligence product).
4. Assemble the supporting information (e.g., new data, research reports, background information).

Communication Execution

After completing your preparation steps, visualize your message and make every effort to ensure it is clear and can be easily understood.

1. Get to the point quickly and state your purpose up front. When writing intelligence assessments, this arrangement of putting the main

---

[1] Office of the Director of National Intelligence (ODNI), *Writing Guide*, 2011.

idea or point first is known as the "bottom line up front" format, or BLUF. We will discuss the BLUF format of writing intelligence products later in the chapter. Then make certain to include any information needed to understand the context of the communication.

2. Organize the thoughts and paragraphs logically; use transitions to make sure your audience knows where the thought trail leads.
3. Ensure sentences are clear and direct.
4. End the message by summarizing the purpose and desired result.[2]

OTHER TIPS

- **Write with nouns and verbs. Though adjectives and adverbs are important, nouns and verbs are the key to concise, powerful writing.**
- **Avoid using power-draining qualifiers such as rather, very, little, or pretty.**
- **Use active voice, which is usually stronger and direct. This should be the rule.**
- **Use strong, active words by avoiding empty actors such as "it is," "there are," and all their variations because they interfere with clarity.**
- **Use clear verbs instead of hidden verbs, such as "implement, perform, and determine" versus "implementation, performance, and determination."**

Besides the tips listed in the box at the right, you are referred to the Office of the Director of National Intelligence (ODNI) Writing Guide, which is referenced in the footnotes and provided in .pdf form in the online supplemental lesson materials available from your instructor and included with the instructor edition textbook.

PRODUCT WRITING STYLE

This book is not designed to assist the student in developing effective, appropriate analytical writing skills however, it may enhance or perhaps

---

[2] Office of the Director of National Intelligence (ODNI), *Writing Guide*, 2011.

refine existing good writing skills into a style, which adds clarity, succinctness, and precision to intelligence products.

Clarity

Analytical writing thrives on clarity. The report writer's rule, *Never use three words when one while suffice*, is paramount to good analytical writing. The only exception to this rule is when reducing the word count confuses the message. Some guidelines to assist in clarifying intelligence products include:

- Avoid lengthy introductory clauses. For example: The enemy guerilla forces, which had suffered seven major engagement losses this year prior to yesterday's defeat, were beaten again today. (*Note*: The gist of the statement is the "enemy guerilla forces were defeated today"; the rest of the clause adds wordiness without a great deal of new information.)
- Avoid nominalization. For example: Destabilize, not destabilization.
- Avoid "passive voice" and embrace "active voice." Using active voice is not always possible, but it should always be the goal.

Succinctness

The essence of succinctness is the art of coming to the point as quickly as possible. To illustrate the point:

> In reference to analytical writing, that is authoritative and professional in nature, there is a common misconception that analytical products must be written in a verbose manner in order to come across as an expert in the field.

Now look at the same sentence restructured:

> A brief but accurate analysis product is superior to one that is wordy and imprecise.

What was the difference in the two sentences? See the following table for the answer.

First Sentence	Second Sentence
Passive	Active
38 words	15 words
Nonessential clause	No clause
Reading Level: 19.8 grade	Reading Level: 11.5 grade

Notice the two sentences express essentially the same idea, but the second sentence does it in less than half the words and is far easier to read.

Precision

Precision in analytical writing is analogous to hitting the bull's eye in marksmanship. Analytical writers become more precise in their writing when they use more nouns and verbs and less adjectives and adverbs; when they use simpler terms, such as "use" versus "utilize"; and when they avoid jargon. The following is an example of increasing degrees of precision in noun and verb usage.

Examples: "Vague" to "Precise" Analytical Writing Style

> An Eastern European supplier provides armaments to terrorists. (Vague)
> Former Communist-bloc supplier provides arms to terrorists. (Less vague)
> Romanian arms dealer provides small arms to terrorists. (Precise)
> Romanian arms dealer sells Kalashnikov rifles to Taliban. (More precise)
> Nicolai Anatov[3] sells AK47s to Pakistani Taliban. (Precise and actionable)

Notice the examples progressively become more precise using more specific noun and verb usage. "An Eastern European supplier" becomes a proper name and the action verb morphs from "provides" to the more accurate transaction "sells." The result is a sentence that is roughly the same length, but is less vague and provides more information that is actionable. By "actionable" we mean that with a proper name analysts can now search databases, identify possible aliases, possibly make positive identification, and further the intelligence collection process.

---

[3] Nicolai Anatov is a fictitious name. Any resemblance to real persons, living or dead, is purely coincidental.

BRIEFINGS

Communications can be oral or written, and of the many types of intelligence support activities, preparing and conducting intelligence briefings is one of the more common. Because developing, preparing for, and conducting intelligence briefing is a critical, but lengthy subject, the book has dedicated a full chapter to the subject. See Chapter 16 for more information.

USING PRODUCT TEMPLATES

Written products are far more common than oral types. Just as briefings have formatting guidance tools for performance, so do written intelligence products. A type of formatting guidance tool, which has come into vogue with the advent of electronic word processing, is the automated template.

Why use intelligence product templates? There are a multitude of reasons beyond uniformity or standardization. Cognizant of the need for uniformity and standardization, meeting a minimum product standard and ensuring an analyst organizes information such that the intelligence consumer can easily locate specific pieces of information is essential. Other reasons include efficiency, mitigating writer's block, facilitating review routing process, and so on.

Writer's block does not just affect novelists; analysts also suffer from it. Product template files provide the analyst a place to start. Not only do they give a starting point, they can also force your product team to be a team. By looking at a blank template, the analyst sees a "to-do" list of the content he or she needs to complete. The product template outlines and "cues" the analyst to what types of information he or she must collect, analyze, source, route for review, and deliver to the client or end user. The template can also assist in proper classification of the information contained.

Electronic product templates also allow for data access automation. Once the individual fields of a properly linked and network-associated product or report template are in place, the information can become accessible and searchable by any linked database, thereby allowing collaboration and data sharing unheard of just 20 years ago.

A properly executed product template file, or series of product template files, as mentioned previously instills standardization and increases efficiency. Standards are created and enforced because the template file uses built-in product styles, identifies needed content and sourcing requirements, and more. Since these intelligence product attributes are preinstalled, it also saves time and creates efficiency.

Sample Product Template

You will be provided an unclassified template similar to ones used by the Department of Homeland Security (DHS) for Open Source Information Reporting. It includes "boiler plate" information as well as explanatory information for required and recommended content. The document fields electronically link to databases to allow instant updates to searchable relational knowledge bases.

The instructor will provide a DHS Open Source Intelligence Report (OSIR) template for use in the following Practical Exercise.

Note: Government reports are replete with acronyms and DHS is no exception. Below is a list of acronyms that appear in the hyperlinked document and their meanings:

- CYB: Cyber
- DHS: Department of Homeland Security
- IA: Office of Intelligence and Analysis
- HSEC: Homeland Security
- OSCAR-MS
- OSIR: Open Source Information Report
- U: Unclassified

Note: OSCAR-MS is a web-based service sponsored by the Office of the Assistant Deputy Director of National Intelligence for Open Source (ADDNI/OS) to provide the National Open Source Enterprise (NOSE) with an application for managing open-source collection requirements.[4]

---

[4] U.S. Army, Army Doctrine and Training Publications, *Intelligence*, (ADRP 2-0), August 31, 2012.

Practical Exercise

In this analytical communications practical exercise, you will take information provided by your instructor and enter it into the OSIR template accessible by hyperlink. After entering the information in the proper locations, save and print the report and bring it back to class for review and comment.

MASTERING THE BLUF FORMAT

This section attempts to answer two questions often voiced by new analysts in the IC: Why do intelligence analysts care about learning how to write in the BLUF format? What makes it so effective?

The BLUF format tailors products to meet the needs of intelligence consumers or end users. These consumers may be high-ranking members of government or the military. Generally, they are busy men and women who rely on clear, concise, and accurate intelligence reporting to make daily decisions that affect U.S. national security and other critical issues. Arranging intelligence reporting in the BLUF format helps more efficiently situate the information in the more understandable layout that they require.

The instructor will provide a copy of the Department of Justice (DoJ) instructions for the BLUF writing format for your review.

In the BLUF format, the first sentence of each paragraph sums up all of the information in the paragraph. The BLUF should address all of the information in a paragraph. If the paragraph contains any information that does not fall under the BLUF, that information should be moved to a more appropriate paragraph or the BLUF should be revised to include the additional information. Following the BLUF format arranges the component sentences in the paragraph from most to least important. Arranging sentences from most to least important ensures readers immediately are aware of the intelligence product's most important points, allowing readers to locate information more easily.

As stated previously in the Communication Execution section, it is most effective to get to the point immediately, which is why BLUF is the best way for intelligence analysts to communicate with their clients and consumers. Summarizing paragraphs in the first sentence allows decision-makers the ability to skim intelligence products without sacrificing clarity.

Other documents that are not in the BLUF format, such as academic white papers, texts, and research reports, may contain paragraphs with several important ideas scattered throughout the document. When the main idea, and other more vital data are scattered through the text, the reader may skim these publications inadvertently, failing to comprehend critical information. More importantly, the BLUF format aids readers in locating information.

The BLUF formatted intelligence product normally contains the following sections:

- Executive Summary
- Introduction
- Analysis
- Background
- Conclusion

Title

The title is not a section. However, it is important because it "sells" the product.

The title, introduction, and executive summary will usually be the last part of your product, because each of these components acts to summarize the product contents.

> **Tip:**
> **The product title may be your hook for potential indirect intelligence consumers, so it must be accurate, concise, representative, and catch the reader's attention.**

The title succinctly represents the contents of the product, marketing the contents and promising to provide the reader with the information the title suggests. Creating an accurate title is extremely important because the title is often your first and only opportunity to catch the reader's attention.

Executive Summary and Introduction

A properly formatted BLUF intelligence product usually starts with an executive summary–style section followed by the introduction. The introduction and executive summary (like the title) are written last, because each of these components must summarize everything contained in the product. The executive summary may be called "Executive Summary," "Key Findings," or "Key Judgments." The name is not important, what is important is that it is usually written last and summarizes the entire document. Therefore, once the product is written, the analyst only has to cut and paste the first sentence of each paragraph into the executive summary, then review and revise for grammatical correctness. Sometimes when an executive summary is used, the introduction is omitted.

Generally, executive summaries can be provided as stand-alone documents of one to two pages that convey the analytical impact of the full intelligence product (minus the details). An introduction should briefly and generally sum up the main points of the paper, like a less-detailed executive summary.

Background

The background section follows the introduction and provides whatever background information the reader needs in order to understand the analysis contained. The background is situated in the document to allow the next section to focus entirely on the analysis without being mired in unnecessary explanatory details and technical speak. The background section allows the analysis section to focus primarily on the results of the analysis rather than the research conducted to create it.

Analysis

The body of the BLUF-formatted intelligence product contains the analysis and sources used to create the product and will generally be the longest part of the document. Call out sourcing in the document using footnotes or endnotes. Footnotes are preferred because they can be used to provide extra information to aid the flow of paragraphs, provide needed definitions and background information, and reduce paragraph clutter.

Document your analysis in a brief, accurate, and clear fashion. Writing clear and concise products forces analysts to carefully order their thoughts and think critically, thus avoiding accidental or intentional misrepresentation of the facts and improving the final analytical product.

There is no room for bias, personal opinion, or "gut feelings" in intelligence analysis. All analysis and subsequent inference or assessment must be supported by and based upon the facts. Any intelligence gaps identified during the process, if included in the final product, should be cited as "gaps." Likewise, any assumptions used in the analysis must be adequately identified so that the reader fully understands the basis of your analysis and properly weighs it into the decision process.

Organizational format or doctrine usually decides the title of the analysis section. Whichever the case, organizational format, doctrine, or personal preference, the title should be appropriate to the contents (e.g., body, contents, supporting arguments).

Conclusion

The BLUF-formatted document ends with the conclusion (referred to as "Summary" or "Outlook" paragraph), which should efficiently sum up the content of the document. As such, the conclusion should not introduce new material. The conclusion can expand upon previous material already addressed in the body of the document.

WRITING FOR RELEASE

Intelligence products have diminished value if we cannot share the information with our friends and allies. Therefore, there are mechanisms available to facilitate that sharing process. Formally releasing classified information is far different from covertly disclosing information to adversaries or the unauthorized leaking of classified document to the press.

Often in the normal course of duties, intelligence analysts collect or create classified information, which may be of great value to our friends in law enforcement and allies in the common effort to stem international crime and terrorism. Besides common cause, America shares intelligence with foreign partners for other reasons, such as quid pro quo, influence, and to encourage new partnerships.

Declassifying already overclassified information can be inefficient and needlessly time-consuming. Therefore, analysts are encouraged to "write for release." Writing for release means that you provide an intelligence product that meets a specific classification caveat threshold, which allows release to a specific partner.

To be successful, and to avoid multiple declassification/reclassification iterations and reviews, the process usually starts with a product proposal meeting where all stakeholders and reviewers attend. At this meeting, it will be determined if it is even feasible to release the information to a given partner. If so, the analyst creates a U.S. version and submits it through the release review chain and to the Foreign Disclosure Officer

(FDO), if the product is to go outside U.S. custody. This is but a brief over-view of the release process. Many other procedural requirements exist, depending on the specifics of the information, level of classification, and the specific organizational protocols of the origination intelligence organization.

PRODUCT VISUALS

Analyst often ask, "Should I include visuals (e.g., graphics, photos, maps) in my intelligence products?" The answer is yes, provided the organization allows it. A picture is worth a thousand words. Today, visual communication is omnipresent. Visuals, more effectively than text alone, impress and engage on both a cognitive and emotional level.

- Cognitively: Graphics expedite and increase our level of communication. They increase comprehension, recollection, and retention. Visual clues help us decode text and attract attention to information or direct attention increasing the likelihood that the audience will remember.[5]
- Emotionally: Pictures enhance or affect emotions and attitudes.[6] Graphics engage our imagination and heighten our creative thinking by stimulating other areas of our brain (which in turn leads to a more profound and accurate understanding of the presented material).[7]

The computer/Internet age has made its mark on the intelligence community.

Not only are various graphics routinely included in IC web products, but also interactive media, including maps, Google Earth, and hyperlinks are included to add impact. Reference sources are routinely imbedded into web-based intelligence products. Pictures interact with text to produce

---

[5] W.H. Levie and R. Lentz, Effects of text illustrations: A review of research, *Educational Communications and Technology Journal*, 1982.

[6] W.H. Levie and R. Lentz, Effects of text illustrations: A review of research, *Educational Communications and Technology Journal*, 1982.

[7] D. Bobrow and D. Norman, Some Principles of Memory Schemata, Representation and Understanding: Studies in Cognitive Science, New York: Academic Press, 1975; D. Rumelhart, Schemata: The Building Blocks of Cognition, Theoretical Issues in Reading Comprehension, Hillsdale, New Jersey: Lawrence Erlbaum Associate, 1980.

levels of comprehension and memory that can exceed what is produced by text alone. Studies demonstrate that visuals imbedded in web-based intelligence products make the product more likely to be read and if read, more likely to have a greater impact.[8] If you still doubt the impact of visuals in intelligence products, look at the picture and the text and then ask yourself a question: *Which has more impact, the text or the photo?*

Please pet the pretty puppy

TEXT BOXES

Text boxes are useful for helping to organize your product and provide additional information. Along with other visuals to improve the presentation of a product (or webpage), text boxes visually flow with text to assist in readability.

Today, analysts commonly use text boxes in the body of intelligence products to draw attention to important concepts, findings, assumptions; to highlight anecdotal material; and to present alternative analysis or dissent, administrative (or scope) notes, background information, or other appropriate uses. When using text boxes to highlight anecdotal material, the analyst is pointing out the subjectivity or unreliability of the information. Shaded or tinted text boxes can highlight important information of special significance or to catch the reader's attention and alert them that the material is necessary to understand one or more portions of the product.

Text box fonts, sizing, number of sentences, color or shading, and titling are all functions of the style guidance and formatting of the parent organization/agency creating the product.

Some members of the IC use various color shades, or tones, to signify the purpose of the text box and refer to them as "tone boxes."

---

[8] J.R. Levin, A Transfer of Appropriate Processing Perspective of Pictures in Prose, Knowledge Acquisition from Text and Prose, Amsterdam: Elsevier Science, 1989.

ANALYTICAL COMMUNICATIONS CHECKLIST

The following checklist provides a take-away for future use and as a tool to reinforce the analytical communications instruction covered in this chapter. No matter if the analytical communication is written, verbal, or web-based, the checklist of typical self-test questions will aid the analyst in performing a quality control check.

1. Before making the first draft, did I make an outline of all pertinent information, contacts, and organizations needed to collect the required information?
2. Did I use appropriate nouns and verbs and minimize the use of adjectives and adverbs?
   - Did I use strong, active words by avoiding empty actors such as "it is," "there are," and all their variations because they interfere with clarity?
   - Did I use clear verbs instead of hidden verbs, such as "implement, perform, and determine" versus "implementation, performance, and determination"?
3. Did I avoid using power-draining qualifiers such as "rather," "very," little," or "pretty"?
4. Did I use active voice, versus passive voice, whenever possible?
5. Am I writing as accurately and succinctly as possible?
   - Can I make my point with less text?
   - Is my language vague or precise?
   - Have my words conveyed my meaning?
   - Can someone be confused by what I said/wrote?
6. Did I use the Bottom Line Up Front (BLUF) format?
7. Is each paragraph properly classified?
8. Did I focus on my audience and is my content "written for release"?
9. If I had a template, did I follow it?
10. Does my text provide substantial factual information, better presented in a graphic or visual?
11. Do my text boxes effectively emphasize information that may otherwise be lost in the text?
12. Do I have so many text boxes that they detract from the text?
13. Do the fonts, sizing, number of sentences, color of shading, and titling match style guidance and formatting?

CHAPTER SUMMARY

This chapter discussed the many forms of analytical communication. Additionally, the text demonstrated, discussed, and explained writing standards or style guides that govern the grammar, content, and format for writing intelligence documents, products, and memorandums. In addition, the "Do's" and "Don'ts" of analytical communication, writing, and product production were presented along with a checklist for future use. The content summary of each chapter section follows.

Basic Workings of Analytical Communication

Professional communication in general requires thoughtful preparation, and analytical communication is no exception. If anything, due to the critical nature of analytical communication, it requires a more rigorous and rigid structure to ensure product standardization and reduce chances of misunderstanding and miscommunication.

Communication Preparation

One must take the time to carefully plan and prepare analytical communication in order to satisfy production requirements and avoid needless confusion. No matter what type of written communication instrument you are dealing with, there are four basic preparation steps: (1) Analyze the purpose, (2) know your audience, (3) determine the medium, and (4) assemble the information.[9]

Communication Execution

After completing your preparation steps, visualize your message and make every effort to ensure it is clear and can be easily understood.

Product Writing Style

Adding clarity, succinctness, and precision enhances and refines your writing skills to produce a professional style that reflects the quality of your intelligence products.

---

[9] Office of the Director of National Intelligence (ODNI), *Writing Guide*, 2011.

Briefings

Communications can be oral or written. Of the many types of intelligence support activities, preparing and conducting intelligence briefings is one of the more common. See Chapter 16 for details on developing, preparing for, and conducting intelligence briefings.

Using Product Templates

A type of formatting guidance tool that has come into vogue with the advent of electronic word processing is the automated template. Intelligence product templates provide efficiency, mitigate writer's block, facilitate review routing process, and so on. Electronic templates allow for data access automation.

Mastering the BLUF Format

The BLUF format tailors products to meet the needs of intelligence consumers or end users; some may be high-ranking members of government or military. Arranging intelligence reporting in the BLUF format helps more efficiently situate the information in the more understandable layout that they require.

In the BLUF format, the first sentence of each paragraph sums up all of the information in the paragraph. The BLUF should address all of the information in a paragraph. Following the BLUF format arranges the component sentences in the paragraph from most to least important and ensures readers immediately are aware of the intelligence product's most important points, allowing readers to locate information more easily.

As stated previously in the Communication Execution section, it is most effective to get the point immediately, which is why BLUF is the best way for intelligence analysts to communicate with their clients and consumers. Summarizing paragraphs in the first sentence gives decision-makers the ability to skim intelligence products without sacrificing clarity.

The BLUF formatted intelligence product includes a product title and normally contains the following sections: Executive summary, introduction, analysis, background, and the conclusion.

Writing for Release

America shares intelligence with foreign partners for other reasons, such as quid pro quo, influence, and to encourage new partnerships. Intelligence products have diminished value if we cannot share the information with our friends and allies. Therefore, there are mechanisms available to facilitate that sharing process. Formally releasing classified information is far different from covertly disclosing information to adversaries or the unauthorized leaking of classified document to the press.

Product Visuals

Product visuals that appear in intelligence products include visuals (e.g., graphics, photos, maps). Today, visual communication is omnipresent. Visuals accomplish what text alone cannot, because visuals quickly affect us both cognitively and emotionally.

Text Boxes

Text boxes are useful for helping to organize your product and to provide additional information. They effectively emphasize information that may otherwise be lost in the text.

Today analysts commonly use text boxes in the body of intelligence products to draw attention to important concepts, findings, and assumptions; to highlight anecdotal material; to present alternative analysis or dissent, administrative (or scope) notes, background information, or other appropriate uses.

Analytical Communications Checklist

The text-provided checklist provides a take-away for future use and as a tool to reinforce the analytical communications instruction covered in this chapter. It provides a list of typical self-test questions to aid the analyst in performing a quality control check of analytical communications written, verbal, or web- based.

7

Defining the Problem

INTRODUCTION

Defining the problem is often where analysts go astray. Intelligence consumers have questions based on their intelligence requirements. Sometimes questions come to the analyst in a clear, concise fashion and easily shape into intelligence requirements. Other times additional clarification is required. Just as analysts need to try to understand the thinking of the adversary, analysts need to know the thinking of their intelligence consumer. This chapter aids the analyst in orienting themselves to focus on the needs of the intelligence consumer when "defining the problem."

As introduced in Chapter 2, customer "needs" require interpretation or analysis by the intelligence service before becoming the intelligence requirements that drive the production process. This dialogue between intelligence producer and customer may begin with a simple set of questions, and if appropriate, progress to a more sophisticated analysis of the intelligence problem. "Defining the problem" is the designation given to this exercise of combining dialogue and analysis to produce requirements. The first situation we will discuss is a situation where there are virtually no boundaries and the second is where there are some reasonable limitations on expected outcomes.

MULTIPLE CONTINGENCY SITUATIONS

When the problem has no boundaries and few defining characteristics, defining the problem can be difficult. The analyst begins the process by asking, or being asked, the right questions. An extreme example would be a situation where multiple possible contingencies exist (e.g., when and where will the enemy attack?).

When dealing with hypothetical situations, it is difficult to introduce empirical or statistical data into the situation in order to drive the solution process. The most logical course of action is to find a more manageable number by eliminating contingencies. This, however, is not always achievable. Therefore, the analytical task now becomes to identify, characterize, and prepare for all potential outcomes. The analytical process is brainstorming (also called war-gaming) various scenarios and role-playing the adversary's perspective. After going through the various plausible scenarios, the players dutifully record and evaluate the potential outcomes, assessing which ones may be the most dangerous and the most likely. When no hard data is available to drive the analysis, the probability of error is high. Repetitive iterations of the brainstorming process (especially if using different brainstorming methods and different participants) can help reduce variability to establish a measure of confidence/reliability. Once they have defined the intelligence problem to a level of satisfaction and have come to an agreement, the intelligence analyst and the customer together can next generate intelligence requirements to drive the production process.

Brainstorming Contingencies

Brainstorming is intended to encourage the analyst to use their creativity to help identify contingencies and define problems. The idea of "brainstorming" implies an unfettered flow of thoughts and ideas that goes directly from brain to paper. Eliminating, sorting, and prioritizing these ideas comes later.

Brainstorming is most effective when done as group, but it works for individual analysts too. By letting the mind run free without critiquing any ideas can provide new perspectives which can cover most, if not all, potential contingencies. Be careful not to let one analyst dominate the session—this is prone to happen when several type-A personalities gather together.

Although there are several, we will introduce four types of analytical brainstorming techniques: Dumping, testing, mapping, and role-playing. These four brainstorming methods can be combined or used individually.

Dumping

Dumping is the simplest method, requiring analysts to "dump" all of their ideas onto paper (Figure 7.1). Dumping requires analysts to write down ideas without critique as fast as they enter their minds. In this process, analysts do not try to reduce the thought flow or censure sources. At this point in the process, the saying "there are no bad ideas" is taken quite

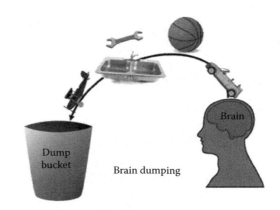

Figure 7.1   "Brain dumping" session figure.

literally. Do the freethinking exercises for 15 minutes and then cut off the idea contribution process. To ensure brainstormed ideas are properly identified and captured, put them into list form to keep them organized and review the list with the group. The facilitator should make corrections as required.

Be aware that even though 15 minutes is allowed for the exercise, the majority of dumping-style sessions yield the most valuable and usable material in the first five minutes.

Testing

While most brainstorming methods are creative processes, testing assumptions can eliminate ideas/ alternatives (as illustrated in Figure 7.2). Start with a given idea for the group and then systematically critique/test the idea during a "testing" brainstorming session. When challenging ideas by breaking them down into components and testing them, ideas and their

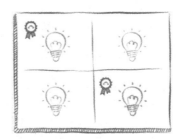

Figure 7.2   Idea testing session figure.

bases are validated, changed, or eliminated as unfeasible. Keep in mind that testing sessions are more than just eliminating ideas; they also involve identifying possible alternatives. These are frequently alternatives and contingencies not identified or considered in earlier brainstorming sessions.

The testing session takes an idea and first breaks it down into multiple parts. Once there is agreement that all the conceptual parts are present and in order (if there is an order), the group describes how one would feasibly accomplish each portion of the selected idea. See the following example.

Example: Terrorist Smuggling into the Country and Detonating a Dirty Bomb

- Target selection
- Collecting the nuclear and explosive materials and other components
- Moving the material and components into the country
- Assembly, emplacement, and detonation
- Escape

Mapping

Mapping assists the group in visualizing the problem (Figure 7.3) by arranging ideas into a conceptual "map" of sorts. Using sizes, shapes, colors, and positions on a blackboard, ideas and concepts are associated with degrees of meaning, priority, viability, and other types of information.

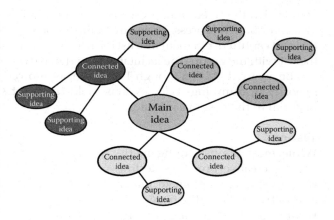

Figure 7.3 Mapping (brainstorming technique).

The mapping session is initiated by writing a central idea in the middle of the board (e.g., when and where will the enemy attack?). Then solicit and add ideas around it, grouping similar ideas together. After the solicitation phase, ask the group to draw connections and to annotate as required to show relationships, importance, precedence, and interrelations between concepts and how they connect to the central theme.

Role-Playing

Role-playing allows for a very different and possibly insightful perspective. Role-playing makes analysts look at a problem from the perspective of adversaries. It can be enlightening and often critical to identifying all potential contingencies.

It may be difficult for an analyst and may require some research and preparation, but during the role-playing session, analysts need to view ideas from the adversary's perspective.

ROLE-PLAYING ADVANTAGES

- Aids in converting abstract ideas into something more concrete
- Facilitates different perspectives
- Novelty of the exercise can reinforce knowledge and improve retention
- Provides immediate feedback
- Can develop sympathetic understanding of an issue
- Creates opportunities to speculate

For example, if you were working DHS problem sets, you might need to visualize from the perspective of a cartel member, a terrorist, or some other evildoer. Casting one's self in the role of different types of adversaries to view the problem can provide needed insights.

PROBLEMS WITH SOME DEFINITIONS

Intelligence requirements effectively translate end customer information needs into workable intelligence collection plans. However, this is often not the case. Even when the customer is confident that they know what the intelligence problem is and what the derivative information requirements should be, there is always a need to vet the requirement(s), at a minimum. The vetting (or refinement process) process described in Chapter 2 is critical to ensuring that the analysis process gets started correctly and that limited collection assets are not wasted.

The level of free-communication between the analytical group and customer at this stage often determines the quality of the subsequent intelligence product produced and whether it meets customer needs.

However, divergent perspectives between the intelligence customer and analytical group often make the negotiation process difficult.

To aid in the negotiations the analyst can use models as tools to help educate the customer and mold their expectations. One of those models is a Taxonomy of Problem Types.

TAXONOMY OF PROBLEM TYPES

Taxonomies provide a mechanism or model for classifying concepts, including the principles that underlie such classification. One such model for defining intelligence scenarios employs the Taxonomy of Problem Types.[1] Table 7.1 illustrates the factors that intelligence customers and analysts may take into account in expressing the nature of the intelligence problem and selecting a strategy for resolving it.

The following examples show how an analyst might use the Taxonomy of Intelligence Problem Types to understand some specifics and implications associated with various intelligence problems.

Example 1

A "definable" intelligence problem—What will the weather conditions be for tomorrow's mission? (See **bolded** table entries.)

Answer: Cloudy, 25 percent chance of rain, Temperature 72°, Winds out of the SW at 4 mph.

THE PROBLEM TAXONOMY TABLE...

- **Does not provide answers**
- **Only aids the analyst in understanding the parameters associated with the problem**
- **Facilitates analytical planning**
- **Is a useful explanatory tool to educate the customer and shape expectations**

Example 2

A "severely random" intelligence problem—Who will be the leading international terrorist 10 years from today?

Answer: Most likely will be someone alive today (and 10 years from now), potentially an Islamic extremist (but 10 years from now, Islamic extremism may not be a major international terror threat).

---

[1] Morgan D. Jones, *The Thinker's Toolkit*, New York: Random House, pp. 44–46, 1995.

Table 7.1 Taxonomy of Problem Types

Characteristics	Basic	Definable	Problem Types		
			Moderately Random	Severely Random	Undefined
Role of problem type	(Easiest) Simple research	5 Ws (Who, What, When, etc...)	Identify and rank outcomes	Identify and rank limitless outcomes	Predict future events/situations
Role of facts	Highest	High	Moderate	Low	Lowest
Role of judgments	Lowest	Low	Moderate	High	Highest
Analytical tasks	Find information	Collect sensor data, Find or develop calculation(s)	Generate all outcomes	Define all potential outcomes	Define future variables/factors
Analytical methods	Research sources	Match data to calculation(s)	Decision theory; utility analysis	Role-playing, brainstorming, war-gaming, etc.	Analysis via predictive modeling/scenarios
Analytical instruments	Matching	Mathematical calculation(s)	Influence diagram, utility, probability	Subject evaluation of outcomes	Use of SMEs

(Continued)

97

Table 7.1 (Continued) Taxonomy of Problem Types

			Problem Types		
Characteristics	Basic	Definable	Moderately Random	Severely Random	Undefined
Analytical outputs	Fact	Specific value, dataset, or number	Weighted alternatives or outcomes	*Plausible outcomes*	Elaboration of expected future(s)
Probability of error	Lowest*	Low*	Moderate*	*High**	Highest*
Follow-up tasks	None	None	Periodically monitor for change	*Continuously monitor*	Exhaustive research

Note: The Taxonomy of Intelligence Problem Types depicted above reflects minor edits and revisions from the original 1995 version.

*Dependent on data quality and reliability.

98

Since terrorists rarely go from obscurity to international notoriety overnight, the "leading international terrorist" 10 years from now is likely to be involved in radical/extremist or terror activities today. (See *italicized* table entries.)

Common understanding between the analyst (intelligence producer) and intelligence customer (client or end user) is essential. In the end, the analyst and the client must reconcile their differing viewpoints in order to agree on intelligence requirements and begin the collection process. Continuous free and open communication among the players fosters agreement on intelligence priorities and results in more usable and meaningful intelligence production. However, the communication process does not end with product delivery. Customer feedback on production quality leads to improving definition of future intelligence problems and requirements.

PRACTICAL EXERCISE

The facilitator will provide a handout for this small-group brainstorming exercise. You will be broken into groups of four to six and given a scenario. Using the scenario provided, take 10 minutes to brainstorm the idea and conceptually map it out. Then exchange your freshly mapped ideas with another group and conduct another 10-minute brainstorming session to test the idea. After completing the second brainstorming session, be prepared to discuss your observations with the instructor.

CHAPTER SUMMARY

This chapter identified the pitfalls of starting the analysis process with ill-defined intelligence requirements. It went on to explain how sometimes customer information questions shape easily into intelligence requirements, and at other times, additional clarification is required. To aid the process of understanding and "defining the problem," the chapter pointed out how analysts can orient themselves to focus on the needs of the intelligence consumer.

Customer "needs" often require interpretation or analysis by the intelligence service before becoming the intelligence requirements that drive the production process. This dialogue between intelligence producer and customer begins with a simple set of questions, and, if appropriate, progresses to a more sophisticated analysis of the intelligence problem. "Defining the problem" is the designation given to this exercise of combining dialogue and analysis to produce requirements. The content summary of each chapter section follows.

Multiple Contingency Situations

When the problem has no boundaries and few defining characteristics, defining the problem can be difficult. The analyst begins the process by asking, or being asked, the right questions.

When dealing with hypothetical situations, the most logical course of action would be to find a more manageable number by eliminating contingencies. However, that is not always achievable. Therefore, the analytical task now becomes to identify, characterize, and prepare for all potential outcomes. The analytical process is brainstorming (also called war-gaming) various scenarios and role-playing the adversary's perspective.

Brainstorming Contingencies

Brainstorming is intended to encourage the analyst to use his or her creativity to help identify contingencies and define problems. Brainstorming is most effective when done as a group, but it works for the individual analyst. Letting the mind run free without critiquing any ideas can provide new perspectives which can cover most, if not all, potential contingencies.

Although there are several, we will introduce four types of analytical brainstorming techniques: Dumping, testing, mapping, and role-playing. These four brainstorming methods can be combined or used individually.

Problems with Some Definitions

Intelligence requirements translate end customer information needs into a workable intelligence collection plan. Even when the customer is confident that they know what the intelligence problem is and what the derivative information requirements should be, there is a need to vet the requirement(s), at a minimum.

The level of free communication between the analytical group and customer at this stage often determines the quality of the subsequent intelligence product produced and whether it meets customer needs.

Taxonomy of Problem Types

To aid in negotiations, the analyst can use models as tools to help educate the customer and mold their expectations. Taxonomies provide a mechanism or model for classifying concepts, including the principles that underlie such classification. One such model for defining intelligence scenarios employs the Taxonomy of Problem Types.[2] The taxonomy illustrates the factors that intelligence customers and analysts may take into account in expressing the nature of the intelligence problem and selecting a strategy for resolving it.

---

[2] Morgan D. Jones, *The Thinker's Toolkit*, New York: Random House, pp. 44–46, 1995.

8

Generating the Hypothesis

INTRODUCTION

Once the problem is defined, the analyst is able to generate a reasonable hypothesis based on the question. However, rarely is there only one hypothesis. This chapter aids the analyst in the process of hypothesis formulation and introduces mechanisms used to weigh and ultimately select the best one.

If the analysis does not begin with the correct hypothesis, it is unlikely to get the correct answer. Before getting started with the generation of the hypothesis, it is worth noting that there exists a difference between generating a hypothesis and evaluating a hypothesis.

Assuming no existing intelligence requirement exists (e.g., scheduled requirements), the analyst will need to develop a new requirement. Analysts work to satisfy the specific customer need (unanswered question) through research, thought, and some level of negotiation to determine just what information is required. The intelligence analyst goes through a process similar to that of a research scientist to create the hypothesis. The chapter instruction begins with a simplified process to generate a hypothesis.

SIMPLE PROCESS TO GENERATE A HYPOTHESIS

A *hypothesis* is an explanation that proposes an answer to a specific question based upon a level of knowledge about a topic. This phase in the analysis process should identify all hypotheses worthy of detailed examination. Sometimes known as

When generating a hypothesis:

- Involve more analysts and seek more perspectives, which will result in more hypotheses generated
- Ensure it is measurable/testable
- Keep an open mind
- First try to disprove rather than prove it

an "educated guess," a hypothesis rests upon some existing level of knowledge of a given subject. However, rather than a guess, we are going to propose an answer to a specific question based upon a level of knowledge about a topic. It can be generated using the following six-step process.

Note: An analyst does not have to use the specific method presented in the text. It belongs to the authors and evolved from the scientific method of hypothesis generation and many years of military and law enforcement of experience.

Form question. Begin with an information requirement. For lesson purposes, we will take a real-world problem that exists on the U.S. southern border: Finding cross-border tunnels.

Note: The origin of the question does not matter, at present we are more interested in the hypothesis generation process.

Research question. Perform research on the subject. This step is not required if you already have subject matter expertise on border tunnels.

Analyze research. Perform a quick analysis to determine just how one goes about "finding border tunnels." This may require talking to experts, reviewing scientific research, reading reports where border tunnels were previously located, and so on.

Get specific. Generate a single question, for example, "Where are the tunnels along the U.S. southern border?" This may still be too involved, based upon collection assets, or the customer's ability to deal with the answer, therefore, it is necessary to work with the customer and your collection manager to refine it further. For example, "Where are illegal border tunnels >1 meter in diameter in the San Diego area?"

Ensure what you are looking for can be found/tested. In other words, a "source" or "sensor" exists that can collect the desired information. Now create a hypothesis based upon the refined original information/intelligence requirement until it is something you can definitively test. For example, your research shows that previously illegal tunnels discovered by law enforcement in the San Diego border area that were *approximately 1 meter in diameter (or larger), required electrical power to operate.*

Basic physics states that a current carry conductor (electric wires) creates an electromagnetic field (EMF). Therefore, any underground power cables produce an EMF that *can be measured*!

State your hypothesis. Once research on the question is complete and variables identified, write down your initial idea about how the variables might be related as a simple declarative

> **AUTHOR'S NOTES**
>
> • It was possible to use other scenarios for detecting the tunnels, such as radar, tomography, Sonde line locators, seismic measuring, electronic marker systems, and so on. EMF detection was selected because it is relatively simple and commonplace.
> • It is easier to construct the hypothesis by stating it as an "if/then" statement.

statement, for example: "If an illegal border tunnel in the San Diego area approximately 1 meter in diameter is operational, then it will produce a detectable EMF."

Analysts generate and evaluate hypotheses using three principal strategies: Situational logic, the application of theory, and comparison.[1] We will explore each of these.

SITUATIONAL LOGIC

This is the most common operating mode for intelligence analysts. Generation of the hypotheses starts with considering the "situation"

---

[1] Don McDowell, *Strategic Intelligence: A Handbook for Practitioners, Managers, and Users,* Scarecrow Press, 2008.

unique instead of an instance of a broader class of comparable situations. Situational logic is the framework for choice, and therefore action, defined by the actor's position within a given social structure in terms of his or her access to and control over resources. Analysts draw logical consequences and previous circumstances based on known facts and understanding of particular instances. A scenario develops that pulls together a plausible narrative. The analyst may work backward to explain the origins or causes of the current situation or forward to estimate the future outcome.

Situational logic commonly focuses on tracing cause–effect relationships when dealing with means–ends relationships. The analyst identifies the stated goals and explains why the involved player(s) are pursuing those goals. Situational logic thus involves more than intersecting roles and expectations (e.g., John Smith is a thief; something was sto-

> **SITUATIONAL LOGIC WEAKNESSES**
>
> - **Personal bias—Projecting your own personal interpretations onto the analysis**
> - **Failing to exploit theoretical knowledge obtained from the study of similar cases**
> - **Causal effects derived by situation logic may be just symptoms of more fundamental events, which can be explained by theory**

len; therefore, John Smith must have stolen it). By considering roles and expectations, one can easily see the inadequacy of the logic. Therefore, analysts should also weigh into the situational logic formula access to information, opportunity, resources, and the power that exploitation of these factors provides. The following example presents a hypothetical scenario using situational logic.

Example: Situational Logic

A series of intelligence reports are received as follows:

1 April, last year, analyst John Doe joins your intelligence organization.

5 April, John Doe is granted access to classified materials.

10 April, there is a security breach and several classified files go public on the Internet. It is the same classified material to which John Doe has access. However, several thousand others have access to those same files.

Analyst Comments:

Website that publishes the classified material proven to espouse Anarchist philosophies.

John Doe was a member of a group with Anarchist leanings in college, but that was several years ago. There are no reported connections between Doe and Anarchist groups since college. Doe's reason for joining the group was that he was dating a girl in the group and just wanted to hang out with her.

To date: Doe has not taken a CI or lifestyle polygraph.

Situational Logic Scenario/Hypothesis

If John Doe is the leak, either wittingly or unwittingly, then he will likely fail a polygraph or have an ongoing direct or indirect contact with an Anarchist Group.

Note: He may have genuine sympathies toward Anarchist philosophies or just be passing information to a third party under false pretense. However, his motivations are tangential issues.

To Test Scenario/Hypothesis

Administer a CI/lifestyle polygraph to eliminate Doe as a suspect. If he fails, do not alert the subject; conduct covert surveillance of John Doe, and determine if the polygraph is in error or whether he is still in contact with the girl from the college Anarchist Group, or others with links to similar groups.

AUTHOR'S NOTES:

- **The example hypothesis may not be a correct, but the tests will quickly validate (or disprove) it.**
- **Also notice that even if Doe fails the polygraph, further supporting (or possibly disproving) evidence is still pursued (e.g., covert surveillance).**
- **It is easier to construct the hypothesis by stating it as an "if/then" statement.**
- **Never forget that even if Doe is proven to be a "leaker," it doesn't mean he wasn't part of a deception or that he is alone!**

107

The strength of situational logic lies in its broad applicability and ability to bring large volumes of relevant detail to bear on a problem. Any situation, however unique, may be analyzed using situational logic.

APPLYING THEORY

Theory is a generalization based on the study of a large number of examples. It specifies that when a given set of conditions arise, certain other conditions will follow with some degree of probability. An example would be to label a country as a "failed state." This defines a set of conditions that imply conclusions concerning a state perceived as having failed at some of the basic conditions and responsibilities of a sovereign government, because analysts have an implicit if not explicit understanding of how these factors normally relate. Common characteristics of a failing state include a central government so weak or ineffective that it has little practical control over much of its territory and there is a non-provision of public services.

> **APPLYING THEORY WEAKNESSES**
>
> - **Can blind analysts to specifics of the current situation, which differentiate it from generalized theory**
> - **Often psychologically difficult to overcome an interpretation based on theory even in light of hard evidence to the contrary**

Applying a theory allows the analyst to see beyond short-term developments and recognize superficial or significant trends that currently leave little evidence.

HISTORICAL COMPARISON

Another approach for developing a hypothesis is comparison. An analyst seeks understanding of current events by comparing them with historical examples, or with similar events in other areas. Analogy is a form of comparison. When comparing historical examples to current circumstances, analysts use their understanding of the historical precedent to fill intelligence gaps in a given situation.

HISTORICAL COMPARISON WEAKNESSES

- **Conveniently assumes that the current situation and a past situation are equivalent based on known similarities, which can cause incorrect conclusions**
- **Vivid historical precedents often force themselves to the forefront of consideration**

Historical comparison depends upon the formation of analogies with specific situations in the past, thereby establishing a broad equivalence between the current situation and one or a few past situations. The analyst assumes the unknowns in current situations are equivalent and take on values of recognized values from prior situations. The limitation being that the values sought must be present and identifiable in the prior situation.

Historical comparison differs from situational logic in that the present situation is assessed against a conceptual model that is created by looking at similar situations in other times or places. It differs from theoretical analysis in that this conceptual model is based on one, or a limited number of cases, rather than on many similar cases.[2]

One of the strengths of historical comparison is that it allows analysts to develop a hypothesis when they cannot find enough situational data or a suitable theory.

---

[2] Don McDowell, *Strategic Intelligence: A Handbook for Practitioners, Managers, and Users,* Scarecrow Press, 2008.

CHOOSING BETWEEN STRATEGIES

There is no "best" strategy. After generating as many relevant hypotheses as possible while making maximum use of all potentially relevant information and using all three strategies (as appropriate) at the early hypothesis generation phase, methodically exclude the implausible and impossible until you have a workable handful of possible and probable hypotheses.

Table 8.1 compares and contrasts the applicability, advantages, and limitations of using situational logic, theory, and comparison as strategies for generating analytical hypotheses.

DEALING WITH MULTIPLE HYPOTHESES

To be thorough, analysts must identify all plausible hypotheses for consideration. Within time and resource constraints and employing diverse perspectives, create a catalog of as many credible hypotheses as reasonably achievable. Early rejection of unproven, but not disproved, hypotheses biases the analysis, because one does not then look for the evidence that might support them. Reserving judgment and excluding nonconvergent ideas and a liberal definition of plausibility as long as feasible will increase the probability of recognizing as many reasonable hypotheses as possible. Performing this exhaustive generation exercise minimizes the possibility of starting the analytical phase without the correct hypothesis identified.

There is no correct number of hypotheses to be considered. The number depends upon the nature of the analytical problem and how advanced you are in the analysis of it. As a general rule, the greater your level of uncertainty, or the greater the impact of your conclusion, the more alternatives you may wish to consider. More than seven hypotheses may be unmanageable. If this many alternatives exist, it may be advisable to group several of them together for your initial cut at the analysis.[3] After compiling a list of all plausible hypotheses, or if time has become a constraint, the reduction process begins. Reducing the number of hypothesis to something more practical is necessary because no intelligence organization can feasibly work with dozens of hypotheses. Even if it were possible it would likely be an inefficient use of analytical resources.

---

[3] Richards J. Heuer Jr., *Psychology of Intelligence Analysis*, Pherson Associates LLC, 2007.

Table 8.1 Strategies for Hypothesis Generation—Summary

	Situational Logic	Applying Theory	Historical Comparison
Application	✓ Use when data sources are available, but valid comparisons or theory is not	✓ Uses multiple examples to make generalizations to fill gaps	✓ Uses explicit conceptual model based on one or a few similar situations, from other times, or places
Advantages	✓ Can be used for practically any situation ✓ Able to integrate large amounts of data	✓ Enables an analyst to sort through a mass of less significant detail	✓ Convenient shortcut, chosen when data is limited or theoretical cases are not available
Limitations	✓ Susceptible to personal bias ✓ Fails to exploit theoretical knowledge obtained from the study of similar cases ✓ Derived causal effects may just be symptoms of more fundamental events	✓ Can blind analysts to specifics of the current situation ✓ Difficult for analysts to overcome an interpretation based on theory even in light of contrary hard evidence	✓ Assumes current situation and a past situation are equivalent based on known similarities ✓ Vivid historical precedents often dominate other evidence

Strategies for Choosing among Competing Hypotheses

A systematic analytical process requires selection among alternative hypotheses, and it is here that analytical practice often deviates significantly from the standard of the scientific method. The best case would be to generate a broad range of hypotheses,

ELIMINATING HYPOTHESES

- Is it really measurable/testable?
- Is it wrong/disproved?
- Collect evidence to prove/disprove.
- Use ACH to reduce biases.
- Preferentially try to disprove rather that prove.

systematically evaluate each hypothesis, and then choose the hypothesis that presents the best fit to the data. Scientific method specifies that one seeks to disprove hypotheses rather than confirm them.

When screening out the seemingly improbable hypotheses, it is necessary to distinguish hypotheses that appear to be disproved (i.e., improbable) from those that are simply unproven. An unproven hypothesis has no evidence that it is correct. A disproved hypothesis has evidence stating that it is wrong.

Unproven hypotheses should be continually considered until they can be disproved. One example of a hypothesis that often falls into this unproven but not disproved category is the hypothesis that an opponent is trying to deceive us. You may reject the possibility of denial and deception because you see no evidence of it, but rejection is not justified under these circumstances. If deception is planned well and properly implemented, one should not expect to find evidence of it readily at hand. The possibility should not be rejected until it is disproved, or, at least, until after a systematic search for evidence has been made, and none has been found.[4]

Less Preferred Strategies

Stanford University Professor Alexander George identified a number of lesser strategies for making decisions in the face of incomplete information and multiple, competing goals. Although George cited these as applicable strategies for political decision-makers, most also

---

[4] Richards J. Heuer Jr., *Psychology of Intelligence Analysis*, Pherson Associates LLC, 2007.

apply to how intelligence analysts might decide among alternative analytical hypotheses.

The relevant (but less preferred) strategies George identified are

Satisficing: Selecting the first identified alternative that appears "good enough" rather than examining all alternatives to determine which is "best."

Incrementalism: Focusing on a narrow range of alternatives representing marginal change without considering the need for dramatic change from an existing position.

Consensus: Opting for the alternative that will elicit the greatest agreement and support. Simply telling the boss what he or she wants to hear is one version of this.

Reasoning by analogy: Choosing the alternative that appears most likely to avoid some previous error or to duplicate a previous success.

Relying on a set of principles or maxims to choose between a "good" and a "bad" alternative.[5]

Intuitive Analysis

Intuitive analysis concentrates on proving or confirming a hypothesis and commonly grants more weight to evidence supporting a hypothesis than to evidence that weakens or disproves it. Generally an analyst should desire the opposite. Analysts should avoid using intuitive analysis since it often erroneously focuses too much on confirmation of a single hypothesis.

The simultaneous evaluation of multiple, competing hypotheses allows a more methodical and objective analysis than would normally be possible. The simultaneous evaluation of multiple, competing hypotheses entails far greater cognitive strain than examining a single, most-likely hypothesis. Retaining multiple hypotheses in working memory and noting how each item of evidence fits into each hypothesis adds up to a formidable cognitive task. That is why this approach is seldom employed in intuitive analysis of complex issues.[6]

Developing hypotheses and collecting evidence generates pattern development and understanding. Using the formal analysis of competing

[5] Alexander George, *Presidential Decisionmaking in Foreign Policy: The Effective Use of Information and Advice*, Westview Press, 1980.

[6] Richards J. Heuer Jr., Psychology of Intelligence Analysis, Pherson Associates LLC, 2007.

hypotheses (ACH) process developed by Richards Heuer while he was an analyst at the Central Intelligence Agency (CIA), one can systematically reduce the number of competing hypothesis. ACH draws on the scientific method, cognitive psychology, and decision analysis. ACH became widely available when the CIA published Heuer's *Psychology of Intelligence Analysis.*[7]

This chapter only contains a brief introduction to the ACH process. Chapter 10 contains a more complete discussion of ACH.

> **INTUITIVE ANALYSIS WEAKNESSES**
>
> - **Selective Perception: Only information that is relevant to the initial hypothesis is processed; if incorrect, information suggesting a different hypothesis is lost.**
> - **Failure to generate appropriate hypotheses: Most people are unable to identify and choose from the full range of potential hypotheses.**
> - **Failure to consider diagnostic ability of evidence: Without a full range of alternative hypotheses, evidence applicable to current hypotheses, as well as others, may be used to mistakenly verify current hypotheses.**

CHAPTER SUMMARY

This chapter provided guidance on how analysts generate multiple analytical hypotheses, as well introduces mechanisms used to weigh and ultimately select the best one.

The precept that if the analysis does not begin with the correct hypothesis, he or she is unlikely to get the correct answer, is established and repeatedly stressed.

Assuming that no existing intelligence requirement exists (e.g., scheduled requirements), the analyst will need to develop a new requirement. Analysts work to satisfy the specific customer need (unanswered question) through research, thought, and some level of negotiation to determine just what information is required. The intelligence analyst goes through a process similar to that of a research scientist to create the hypothesis.

---

[7] Richards J. Heuer Jr., Psychology of Intelligence Analysis, Pherson Associates LLC, 2007.

Simple Process to Generate a Hypothesis

A hypothesis is an explanation that proposes an answer to a specific question based upon a level of knowledge about a topic. It can be generated using the six-step process below:

1. Form question.
2. Research question.
3. Analyze research.
4. Get specific.
5. Ensure what you are looking for can be found/tested.
6. State your hypothesis.

Situational Logic, Applying Theory, Historical Comparison

See Table 8.1, Strategies for Hypothesis Generation—Summary.

Choosing between Strategies

There is no "best" strategy. After generating as many relevant hypotheses as possible while making maximum use of all potentially relevant information and use of all three strategies (as appropriate) at the early hypothesis generation phase, methodically exclude the implausible and impossible until you have a workable handful of possible and probable hypotheses.

Dealing with Multiple Hypotheses

The nature of a thorough analysis process creates multiple plausible hypotheses for consideration. However, there is no "correct" number of hypotheses to be considered. The number depends upon the nature of the analytical problem and how advanced you are in the analysis of it. As a general rule, the greater your level of uncertainty, or the greater the impact of your conclusion, the more alternatives you may wish to consider. More than seven hypotheses may be unmanageable; if there are this many alternatives, it may be advisable to group several of them together for your initial cut at the analysis.[8]

---

[8] Richards J. Heuer Jr., *Psychology of Intelligence Analysis*, Pherson Associates LLC, 2007.

Reducing the number of hypotheses to something more practical is necessary because no intelligence organization can feasibly work with dozens of hypotheses. Strategies for choosing among competing hypotheses include methodical and systematic approaches, as well as lesser-preferred methods. Heuer's ACH is the most preferred method. Intuitive analysis is the least preferred and should be avoided.

9

The Collection Process

INTRODUCTION

The collection process refers to the step in the formal intelligence cycle process. In many cases, the information needed by the analyst is either already available or is already being sought by collection assets. If not, the analyst may request collection on the subject/problem set, or if this is not possible, identify the information gap in their final intelligence product. Success, or failure, of the analysis process rests often on the quality and quantity of collection results.

A major aspect of the collection process is basic research, matching intelligence gaps or needs to available sources of information, with the results to be molded into usable intelligence. For decades Soviet intelligence organizations used publicly available information as a major collection source. The FBI estimated that up to 90 percent of the information obtained by the Soviets came from open sources.[1] There are no indications that Russian intelligence services have shifted from this pattern of using open source collections for intelligence production.

In order to provide realistic, but unclassified examples and exercises, the text will use some common open source data sources (public records, press reporting, historical records, various databases, etc.) data sources which are also commonly used by the intelligence community (IC).

---

[1] Jeffrey T. Richelson, *Sword and Shield: Soviet Intelligence and Security Apparatus*, Cambridge, MA: Ballinger Publishing, 1986.

COLLECTION MANAGEMENT

Collection management is the process of managing and organizing the collection of intelligence from various sources. The collection management element of a U.S. government/military intelligence organization may attempt basic validation (metadata type validations; that is, date, time, location, etc.) of collected data, but generally does not analyze its significance.

Analysts initially look to see if the answer to the intelligence requirement (IR) has already been generated. If it has, the analyst only needs to validate that it is still accurate and current.

COLLECTION TIPS

- **Has the IR already been answered?**
- **If "yes," validate that it is still accurate and current, then disseminate.**
- **Is someone else looking for the same info?**

If it is validated, then the information is distributed to the end user. If the answer is not current or is no longer valid, then the analyst uses research to answer the IR using existing intelligence and readily available data sources.

The collection management process is shown in Figure 9.1.

Traditional Methods

In the not-too-distant past, analysts would go to their own files or collections of data, also known as an "analyst's shoebox," to start their research. These data collections were literally map references, 3 × 5 notecards, and photos; whatever information the analyst had previously collected on a topic stuffed in one or more shoeboxes. With the advent of networked relational data resources, the analyst's shoebox has been relegated to history. Even though the tools have improved, the conceptual process is the same—it is still basic applied research.

Modern Methods

The U.S. IC has significantly benefited from algorithm networked search engines (such as Internet search engines Yahoo™ and Google™). Intelligence analysis software platforms such as Palantir™ Gotham (used

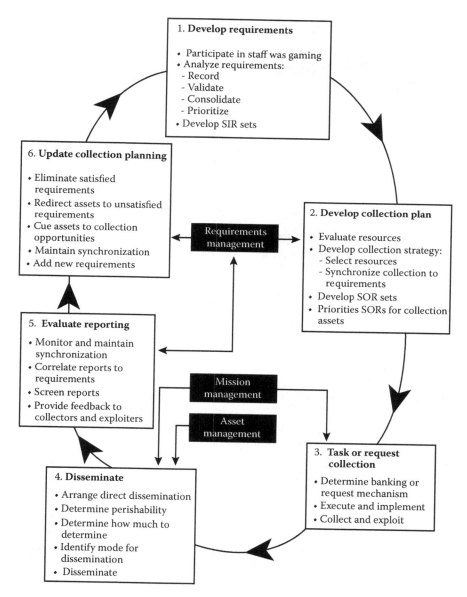

Figure 9.1 U.S. Army's collection management cycle.

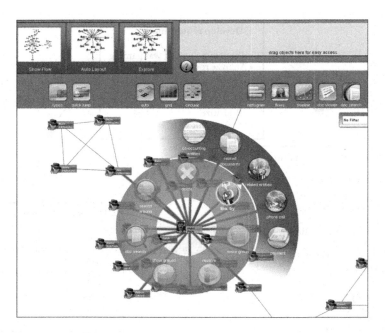

Figure 9.2 Palantir™ screenshot.

by DHS, NSA, FBI, CDC, the Marine Corps, the Air Force, and Special Operations Command; see Figure 9.2) and IBM's Analyst's Notebook™ (used by the U.S. Army; see Figure 9.3) with their associated relational databases have greatly boosted the research capabilities of the individual analyst.[2,3] The recently acquired ability to reach out from one's workstation and query thousands of terabytes of collected data has revolutionized the intelligence analyst's ability to do applied research.

Only after exhausting the information resources available from their workstations do analysts reach out to the collection manager to satisfy IRs.

Collection managers match intelligence requirements against collection assets/sources, then request, direct, and orchestrate collection assets/sources against collection targets in order to gain useful raw intelligence data to feed into the analysis process.

[2] Wikipedia, Palantir Technologies, https://en.wikipedia.org/wiki/Palantir_Technologies.
[3] Wikipedia, Analyst's Notebook, https://en.wikipedia.org/wiki/Analyst%27s_Notebook.

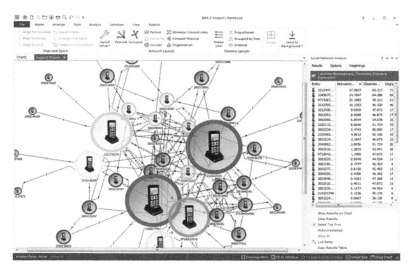

Figure 9.3   Analyst's Notebook™ screenshot.

COLLECTION PLANNING

There are several approaches to collection planning. That said, unfortunately today many analysts have no collection plan other than approaching the collection manager and stating, "These are my intelligence gaps, how can you help?"

One method for planning a collection strategy is to first prepare a list of expected data (and collection mechanisms) associated with your target and determine what would be the simplest to collect. The activity associated with the desired data (or target), which may include physical features of terrain or objects, human contacts or associations, target behavior, or natural and man-made occurrences. For example, if an analyst wants to know if a specific person lives at a certain address, the activity associated with the target is their "address," what

> **COLLECTION PLANNING TIPS**
> - **Start by having analyst and collection manager collaborate**
> - **Ask the questions**
>   - **What am I looking for?**
>   - **How will I know it, if I see it?**

121

the person "looks like," or "how they sound." To validate if they live at the address, an analyst could have an inexpensive gift delivered anonymously by a messenger, call their home phone number, or even set up 24-hour surveillance on the residence. These approaches to collecting the information are all possible; some are more efficient than others, but none are foolproof.

The collection manager and the intelligence analyst try to collaborate to identify the most revealing activity that satisfies IR, usually by asking the questions, "What am I looking for?" and "How will I know it if I see it?" The analyst works with the collection manager to identify key or essential elements that will provide the information needed with some level of confidence that it is valid.

Selecting Sensors and Sources

Some methods for selecting collection sources and sensors include the following:

- Past successes. Previous successful analysis of expected target sensor results and reliable source reporting matched to the customer's needs can determine what collection source/method best permits collection.
- Type of target. Larger, more fixed, easy-to-locate targets and subjects such as ports, industrial facilities, and garrisoned troop concentrations can be collected on using a few (or even one) commercial orbital satellite. However, observing a lone, highly mobile terrorist in an urban area

AUTHOR'S NOTES
- GPS tracking is becoming ever-more common in today's law enforcement activities.
- GPS-collected evidence was allowed and contributed to the successful conviction of Scott Peterson in his 2004 murder trial, in which Peterson was convicted of murdering his pregnant wife Laci.
- GPS evidence showed that Peterson returned to the scene of the crime multiple times while under investigation.
- Prosecutors say the GPS evidence was circumstantial but indicates Peterson behaved as if he were guilty by driving to San Francisco Bay in January 2003, possibly fearing someone would find the bodies.

may require multiple sensors and sources as well multiple types of sensors and sources to gain adequate coverage.

- What is new! Increasingly sophisticated identification and tracking sensors such as visual biometrics (e.g., using the shape of one's ear to make identifications) and global positioning system (GPS) trackers are coming into their own and are essential for drawing key conclusions, and therefore should be given priority.

Limitations on Collections

Multiple factors negatively affect collection efforts. The following list describes but a few:

- Available number of collection assets. Often there are far more collections requirements than assets capable of collecting the data.
- Limited money, time, and skilled professionals. Especially when dealing with cutting-edge sensors, there may be only one or two prototypes and qualified operators and analysts available to exploit collections.
- Sensor data overload. In Afghanistan and Iraq, the U.S. military and IC witnessed a huge increase in the amount of sensor data streaming back into the United States for analysis. The increase far outpaced the number of analysts available to properly screen and analyze the data.
- Authorization for collection. Many legal jurisdictional considerations and regulatory aspects control and often prohibit collection efforts (e.g., wiretap legislation, privacy considerations).
- Usable data. The format of the collect data must be usable or easily converted to a usable format. For example, imagery without the associated time and location metadata is virtually useless.

COLLECTION SOURCES AND DISCIPLINES

As mentioned above, usable data may be distributed directly from the collection platform to the requesting analyst; however, a significant portion of sensor and source data must first be processed into a usable form before it can be used in analysis.

There are many more intelligence disciplines that are involved in the post-processing of raw data than just collecting and exploiting the raw data. The following lists most of those disciplines:

- Human intelligence (HUMINT): Human operatives
- Imagery intelligence (IMINT): Satellites, aerial reconnaissance
- Measurement and signature intelligence (MASINT): Spectroscopy, directional acoustic measurement
    - Radar Intelligence (RADINT): Radar Signal Signature intelligence
    - Acoustic Intelligence (ACOUSTINT): Sound Signature intelligence
- Open-source intelligence (OSINT): Public information sources, Internet
- Signals intelligence (SIGINT): Radars, radios, cell phone transmissions/emissions
    - Electronic Intelligence (ELINT): Intelligence gathering by use of electronic sensors
    - Communications Intelligence (COMINT): Messages/voice information derived from intercepts
- Technical intelligence (TECHINT): Testing and analysis of capture equipment and materials

Raw collected information for U.S. government intelligence purposes is routed through the recognized intelligence collection disciplines listed previously.

Intelligence analysts use a broad range of information sources to derive their hypotheses and generate IRs. Jerome Clauser and Sandra Weir in their research on intelligence acquisition methodologies describe basic research foundations and the inductive and deductive models for performing intelligence analysis. Theoretically (as proposed by Clauser and Weir) there are four general categories of information sources used for intelligence gathering: People, physical objects, emanations, and records. The information provided by the sources is not intelligence if the information is still in its raw form and value has not been added to the information.[4]

---

[4] Jerome K. Clauser and Sandra M. Weir, Intelligence Research Methodology: An Introduction to Techniques and Procedures for Conducting Research in Defense Intelligence, Pennsylvania State College, 1975.

People

People are the primary source for in-depth information as gathered from subject experts and professionals. To a lesser extent, raw information is gathered from eyewitnesses who encountered firsthand accounts of any given situation. Verbal information is gathered from people, and at times, these sources provide more timely and accurate information than available documented information sources. Human source intelligence (HUMINT) is dependent on interpersonal communication. HUMINT sources include prisoners, intelligence operatives, confidential informants, and refugees who may be willing or forced to provide information.

Physical Objects

Physical objects as information sources provide a deeper understanding of situations and further substantiate verbal accounts. In situations where information sources from people are absent, objects provide a clue for deeper insights. IMINT falls under the "physical object" source. The images are captured from satellites or UAVs. Documented records show that IMINT from satellites during the first Gulf War, Enduring Freedom (Afghanistan), and Iraqi Freedom assisted combat operations by the United States, NATO, and Coalition Forces.

Emanations

Emanation sources provide a basis for scientific and technical analysis. For example, a bullet may be further technically examined to gather the make and model of the weapon it was fired. MASINT Measurement and signature intelligence (MASINT) and signals intelligence (SIGINT) are examples of ways to more thoroughly analyze emanations. MASINT information is obtained from technical sensors. MASINT encompasses smaller subclasses of intelligence such as RADINT (radar intelligence) and acoustic intelligence (ACOUSTINT). SIGINT also encompasses several narrower terms of intelligence, such as electronics intelligence (ELINT). SIGINT detects transmissions from electronic systems and provides information on the type and location of other electronic devices such as cell phones.

Documents/Records

Documented records, including electronic documents, databases, and the Internet, enable analysts to research and find specific information.

A dictionary is an example of documented records where analysts confirm the correct usage of words. IMINT and SIGINT can also be sources of documented records.

Intelligence from open sources (OSINT) was popularized when intelligence analysts realized that other information sources became "stove piped" over time. *Stove piping* is where most of the information for a specific subject is available only in isolated environments. OSINT is regarded as the core for all intelligence collections and analyses. Governments, as well as businesses, exploit open sources for intelligence.

Special Sources

Special sources is term used in intelligence circles that refers to a set of restricted sources, available only for government use. These special sources include, but are not limited to, espionage or human intelligence (HUMINT), intercepted communications or other signals (SIGINT), and spy satellite photos or other images (IMINT). These special sources can easily become stovepiped due to excessive classification and compartmentation.

COLLECTION OPERATIONS

Finally, after defining the collection requirements and selecting collection strategies, the intelligence organization needs to select a process for selecting resources to collect and then exploit the collected data for further analysis. These activities are referred to as *collection operations*. These tasks are often completed by IC specialists associated with the intelligence discipline. Isolated field intelligence operations may use one person, or a small group, to handle all facets of collection management.

Whether it is an individual or an IC collection staffing element, the responsible collection element develops the collection strategy taking into account the following concepts:

- Tipping and Cuing
- Redundancy
- Mix
- Integration[5]

---

[5] U.S. Department of the Army, FM 34-2 Collection Management and Synchronization Planning, 1994.

Tipping and Cuing

Tipping and cuing involves the use of one or more sensor systems to provide data that directs collection by other systems. For example, if you are looking for single low-profile watercraft at sea, requesting one collection asset to sweep the suspected target area electronically with a wide area surveillance system, such as a surface level search radar, reveals activity that triggers direct collection by a more accurate, pinpoint sensor system such as an unmanned aerial vehicle (UAV).

Redundancy

Redundancy involves the application of several identical collection assets to cover the same target. Using redundant tasking against high-priority targets increases the probability of success over using any one system. For example, several listening devices are placed in a suspect's home, office, and car to record and capture incriminating discussions.

Mix

Mix refers to planning for complementary coverage by a combination of assets from multiple disciplines. Sensor mix increases the probability of collection, reduces the risk of errors or deception, facilitates cuing, and provides more complete reporting. For example, thermal imagery from a UAV may indicate several hot spots in a jungle area suspected of housing a drug production facility. A police reconnaissance element observing the same hot spots may reveal that half of those hot spots are actually local villagers preparing meals and not drug production facilities.

Integration

Integration is the resource management aspect of collection strategy development. Barring a decision to use redundant coverage of a critical target, attempt to integrate new requirements into planned or ongoing missions. Integration helps avoid the common problem of undertasking very capable collectors. During limited periods of time, collection capability may exceed that of the tasking. The director of the collection element can resolve this by reevaluating each collection asset for excess capability, focusing excess collection capability on the most important of the remaining unfulfilled requirements, and finally redirecting assets to maximize support to the most important requirements, new or old.

Small Element Collection Management Operations

The small, multidisciplinary intelligence elements (such as a UAV operation cell) may experience certain advantages and difficulties in managing multiple phases of the intelligence process at the same time. By not being encumbered by a large bureaucracy and the associated obstacles to providing efficient customer support, the element will likely experience a greater efficiency. The limited staff will likely be forced to wear multiple hats and to fulfill all the requirements or collection management and other phases of the intelligence cycle. The net benefit is collection planning and tasking is done in one place; therefore, fewer scheduling issues are presented. Collected information does not have to leave the building/unit to be processed, exploited, or analyzed, and thus there are fewer outside communications, associated delays, and communication errors.

Today the amount of data circulated in the IC has become unmanageable and the problem gets bigger every day. Small multiple-discipline intelligence elements that handle the tasking, collection, processing, exploitation, analysis, and dissemination (TCPED) aspects of the intelligence process are critical to getting high-priority actionable intelligence to the end user in real-time.

The downside may be in the added expense required to locate and cross-train personnel in all the special skill disciplines required to handle greater portions of the intelligence cycle. The element will also be limited by sensors and sources associated with the element. For example, the analytical products from a UAV operations and analysis cell will be limited by the number and type of sensors operating on the UAV platform and the other intelligence communications links and other collaborative elements (if any) available to the associated analytical cell.

DEVELOPING AN OPEN SOURCE COLLECTION PLAN

In order to provide a realistic, but unclassified example, the book uses the Internet, an open source data provider commonly used by the intelligence community. Therefore, OSINT will be used exclusively to develop a collection plan for demonstration purposes. See the following for an example of how to construct a simplified OSINT collection plan.

Example: Open Source Collection Plan

Scenario: Recent media reports indicate that ISIS/ISIL is using Twitter to promote riots and terror-related activities. DHS officials have raised concerns about the possibility of ISIS/ISIL planning, coordinating, or even instigating terror acts or social unrest in the United States. See Figures 9.4 through 9.7.

You have been tasked to do an OSINT analysis of the following IR: "Are terrorist organizations (specifically ISIL) using social

Terrorists Love Twitter

Pat McGlynn
December 15, 2014

Terror groups around the world are taking to Twitter. They use it to advocate their positions and spread their Jihadist ideas and promote their brand. Recruitment and fundraising is also a goal.

Figure 9.4 Terrorists love Twitter; conceptual news article.

Simplified open source data collection plan worksheet

Select indicators and information to collect and identify for each one the data collection methods you will most likely use and the schedule for your data collection.

Information requirements:

Are terrorist organizations (specifically ISIL) using social networks (specifically Twitter) to plan or encourage terrorism in the United States?

Information/data	Indicator(s)	Data collection method	How will data be validated?
Identify the information/data you are looking for and write them below	*Identify which indicator(s) to be measured to find the desired information/data and write them below*	*Identify which type of OSINT data collection method will be conducted (e.g., search engine, social network search)*	*Describe the validation methodology*
ISIL-related threatening posts on Twitter	• Positive validated returns for ISIL threats on the United States • Determine baseline • Determine trend	Topsy.com: Social media Analytics online application. Allows search by keyword, time and place, set alerts, and analyze sentiment for every tweet ever made	Cross-reference results using socialmention.com and random Google searches

Figure 9.5 Simplified open source data collection plan.

129

networks (specifically Twitter) to plan or encourage terrorism in the United States?"

Instructions: Develop a collection plan describing how you will identify, collect, and validate this IR, as illustrated in Figure 9.5.

Collection Planning Steps:

1. Analyze IR: "What am I looking for, and how will I know it if I see it?" For example: Threatening posts on Twitter, keyword searches for ISIS/ISIL using phrasing from previous posts, and so on.

2. Do I already have the answer: Yes/No. If "no," look to see if the answer has already been generated.

Figure 9.6 Example #1, Jihadist Twitter posting. (Courtesy of MEMRI, www.memri.org.)

- If it has, the analyst needs only to validate that it is still accurate and current.
- If it checks out, the information is distributed to the end user.

3. Prepare a list of expected data and associated collection mechanisms with your IR and determine what would be the simplest to collect. For example, associated icons, Jihadist flags, collection

Figure 9.7 Example #2, Jihadist Twitter posting. (Courtesy of Twitter.com.)

mechanism: "Topsy.com," and so on.

4. Determine the collection strategy:
   - What has worked in the past?
   - What collection mechanisms are new and promising?
   - What is available?
5. What are the processing and validation requirements? For example, process to determine baseline activity, analyze for trends, validate results using Socialmention.com, and so on.
6. Assign and schedule resources.

Note: Since the "simplified" example above only used one collection mechanism/platform, there was no tipping and cuing, redundancy, mix, or integration of collection mechanism/platforms. However, there are other readily available online social media analytic applications. These social media analytic applications could be applied to the example task in parallel to provide tipping and cuing, redundancy, mix, or integration, and very likely higher product confidence levels. A few of the social media analytic applications that could have been used include Social Analytics (socanalytics.com), SproutSocial.com, Google Analytics, and so on.

CHAPTER SUMMARY

This chapter described the collection process, referring to a step in the formal intelligence cycle process. In many cases, the information needed by the analyst is either already available or is already being sought by collection assets. If not, the analyst may request collection on the subject/problem set, or if this is not possible, identify the "information gap" in their final intelligence product. Success, or failure, of the analysis process rests often on the quality and quantity of collection results.

A major aspect of the collection process is basic research, matching intelligence gaps or needs to available sources of information, with the results to be molded into usable intelligence.

Collection Management

Collection management is the process of managing and organizing the collection of intelligence from various sources. Analysts initially look to see if the answer to the intelligence requirement has already been generated. If it has, the analyst only needs to validate that it is still accurate and current. If it checks out, then the information is distributed to the end user. If the answer is not current or is no longer valid, the analyst uses research to answer the IR using existing intelligence and readily available data sources.

Traditional Methods
In the not-too-distant past, analysts would go to their own files or collections of data, also known as an "analyst's shoebox" to start their research. Even though the tools have improved, the conceptual process is the same—it is still basic applied research.

Modern Methods
The U.S. IC has significantly benefited from algorithm-networked search engines (much like Internet search engines Yahoo™ and Google™). Only after exhausting the information resources available from their workstations do analysts reach out to the collection manager to satisfy IRs.

Collection managers match intelligence requirements against collection assets/sources then request, direct, and orchestrate collection assets/sources against collection targets in order to gain useful raw intelligence data to feed into the analysis process.

Collection Planning

One method for planning a collection strategy is to first prepare a list of expected data (and collection mechanisms) associated with your target and determine what would be the simplest to collect. The activity associated with desired data (or target), which may include physical features of terrain or objects, human contacts or associations, target behavior, or natural and man-made occurrences.

The collection manager and the intelligence analyst try to collaborate to identify the most revealing activity that satisfies the IR. Usually by asking the questions "What am I looking for?" and "How will I know it if I see it?", the analyst works with the collection manager to identify key or essential elements that will provide the information needed with some level of confidence that it is valid.

Selecting Sensors and Sources
Some methods for selecting collection sources and sensors:

- Past successes
- Type of target
- What is new

Limitations on Collections

Multiple factors negatively affect collection efforts. The following list describes but a few:

- Available number of collection assets
- Limited money, time, and skilled professionals
- Sensor data overload
- Authorization for collection
- Usable data

Collection Sources and Disciplines

There are multiple intelligence disciplines that post-process raw data more than collect it. The following lists most of those disciplines:

- Human intelligence (HUMINT): Human operatives
- Imagery intelligence (IMINT): Satellites, aerial reconnaissance
- Measurement and signature intelligence (MASINT): Spectroscopy, directional acoustic measurement
  - Radar Intelligence (RADINT): Radar Signal Signature intelligence
  - Acoustic Intelligence (ACOUSTINT): Sound Signature intelligence
- Open-source intelligence (OSINT): Public information sources, Internet
- Signals intelligence (SIGINT): Radars, radios, cell phone transmissions/emissions
  - Electronic Intelligence (ELINT): Intelligence gathering by use of electronic sensors
  - Communications Intelligence (COMINT): Messages/voice information derived from intercepts
- Technical intelligence (TECHINT): Testing and analysis of capture equipment and materials

Special Sources

Special sources is a term used in intelligence circles that refers to a set of restricted sources available only for government use. These special sources include, but are not limited to, espionage or human intelligence (HUMINT), intercepted communications or other signals (SIGINT), and spy satellite photos or other images (IMINT). These special sources can easily become stovepiped due to excessive classification and compartmentation.

Collection Operations

Finally, after defining the collection requirements and selecting collection strategies, the intelligence organization needs to select a process for selecting resources to collect then exploit the collected data for further analysis. These activities are referred to as collection operations. Whether it is an individual or an IC collection staffing element, the responsible collection element develops the collection strategy taking into account the following concepts:

- Tipping and Cuing
- Redundancy
- Mix
- Integration[6]

Small Element Collection Management Operations

The small, multidisciplinary intelligence elements (such as a UAV operations cell) may experience certain advantages and difficulties in managing multiple phases of the intelligence process at the same time. By not being encumbered by a large bureaucracy and the associated obstacles to providing efficient customer support, the element will likely experience a greater efficiency. The limited staff will likely be forced to wear multiple hats and to fulfill all the requirements or collection management and other phases of the intelligence cycle. The net benefit is collection planning and tasking is done in one place; therefore, there are fewer scheduling issues. Collected information does not have to leave the building/unit to be processed, exploited, or analyzed; and thus, there are fewer outside communications, associated delays, and communication errors.

---

[6] U.S. Department of the Army, FM 34-2 Collection Management and Synchronization Planning, 1994.

10

Analytical Tradecraft

INTRODUCTION

The word *tradecraft* is associated with clandestine intelligence services who use it to describe the special skills and methods required in the performance of the spy trade. At one time within the intelligence community, the term *tradecraft* referred exclusively to the techniques used in espionage (e.g., dead drops, micro dots, listening devices). Over the years, especially after the Cold War, the term has evolved to include other intelligence activities.

Analytical tradecraft refers to the body of specific methods used for intelligence analysis. The purpose of analytical tradecraft improves the quality of the product and adds value for the intelligence product consumer. Utilizing tradecraft principles and practices enhances the end product, providing the analyst with needed consumer feedback to clarify "those questions that most need answering," thus focusing the analyst and assisting in managing a deluge of information, discerning trends, and identifying attempts at deception.

On June 21, 2007, the Director of National Intelligence (DNI) signed and implemented Intelligence Community Directive (ICD) Number 203, Analytic Standards, governing the production and evaluation of intelligence analysis and analytical products. ICD 203 states the mission and obligation of all analytic elements of the Intelligence Community (IC) to meet the highest standards of integrity and rigorous analytical thinking.[1]

---

[1] Office of the Director of National Intelligence, Analytic Standards, Intelligence Community Directive 203 (ICD 203), June 21, 2007.

Various congressional commissions as well as other studies in the past to the present identified intelligence shortcomings and recommended fixes. The brunt of these reports have prodded the analytic community to develop and implement new tools and processes to better produce and interpret intelligence products. Analytic Tradecraft Standards represent the IC's analytic transformation efforts to improve support to a wide range of intelligence customers.[2,3]

The constantly changing threat profiles and the evermore complex methods analysts use to make sense of these threats have driven the IC to develop tradecraft and promulgate standards for intelligence analysis and production. This chapter identifies efforts by the IC to implement analytical standards and tradecraft. Additionally, it identifies several analytical techniques used by the IC and identifies the issues and problem sets where they are most often applied.

ANALYTICAL METHODS TECHNIQUES

By the time the analyst is ready to analyze the data collected, he or she has explored and created an intelligence question, developed a plan for answering the question, established a plan to acquire information relevant to the question, collected information based on that plan, and selected relevant information that addressed the question. It is now time to create an assessment based upon the collected information that addresses the intelligence question. So, the question becomes, "How do I create an intelligence assessment?"

Even if you carefully read through all the collected information, as important as that is, it is not enough. Seldom does the correct answer jump out from the collected data. The answers are fragmented and scattered like parts of a 10,000-piece puzzle with half the pieces missing or damaged. Using the collected information, some of which has to be exploited first by translation or other technical means, to be properly understood, the analyst examines each piece of data individually and as a whole to create a meaningful and accurate assessment.

---

[2] U.S. Government, *National Commission on Terrorist Attacks Upon the United States, http:// govinfo.library.unt.edu/911/hearings/hearing3/witness_emerson.htm*, retrieved 2015-10-23.

[3] U.S. Government, Commission on the Intelligence Capabilities of the United States Regarding Weapons of Mass Destruction, *http://govinfo.library.unt.edu/wmd/about.html*, retrieved 2015-10-23.

Extracting the meaning of collected information to create an assessment, which is disseminated as intelligence, is the ultimate purpose of analysis. Information will be provided in this chapter to aid you in developing and focusing your mental framework in

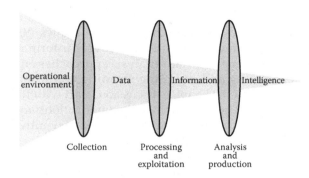

Figure 10.1 Relationship of data, information, and Intelligence.

preparation for this crucial task. See Figure 10.1.

This chapter encourages you to mentally engage with the topics described that affect your thinking and reflect upon those topics, considering your own behaviors and capabilities. As you will see, a recurring theme about "thinking" and its importance to motivation and intellectual engagement relative to the topic.

Sherman Kent of Yale University pioneered many of the methods of intelligence analysis. Kent, often described as the father of intelligence analysis, identifies two steps after all the information has been acquired:

1. Critical evaluation of the data thus assembled
2. Study of the evaluated data with the intent of finding some inherent meaning[4]

Evaluating information and determining the meaning of information has always been an integral part of the practice of data and intelligence analysis. However, as the volume of information has increased, the issues have become more complex and the meanings subtler. Determining meaning has rapidly become more burdensome and intellectually difficult. Consequently, there has been an increasing amount of attention in intelligence literature on understanding traditional analysis methods and techniques, as well as the development of new methods and techniques to supplement or replace what has been used.

---

[4] Sherman Kent, *Strategic Intelligence for American World Policy*, Princeton University Press, 1949.

These analytical methods and techniques are often referred to as structured analytic methods or techniques (SATs). This chapter will introduce a few SATs and also provide information for you to consider in choosing appropriate analysis approaches and techniques to aid you in evaluating and assigning meaning to information.

To begin the chapter discussion, start with the role of SATs in understanding information to include the functions and types of thinking that occur in the cognitive domain, as well as cognitive factors that impact the quality of thinking during analysis.

In subsequent chapters, additional analytic approaches will be introduced to assist in organizing information and assign meaning to it, arranging your information, and formulating and evaluating hypotheses.

This chapter does not provide a comprehensive list of the tradecraft analytical techniques used by intelligence officers to conduct analysis. It does, however, highlight how structured analytic techniques can help one challenge judgments, identify mental mindsets, stimulate creativity, and

ANALYTICAL TRADECRAFT TIPS

- First identify the relevant and diagnostic information that is acquired through open source and clandestine means.
- Then choose an appropriate SAT which adequately *interprets gathered information* and considers a range of alternative explanations and outcomes to ensure potentially relevant hypotheses are NOT dismissed and supporting information opportunities to warn potentially missed.
- *Use diagnostic techniques* to actively review the accuracy of mind sets by applying structured analytic techniques that will make those mental models more explicit and expose key assumptions.
- *Use contrarian techniques* to challenge all assumptions and current thinking by adding a diversity of knowledge and beliefs.
- *Use imaginative thinking techniques* to develop new insights, develop different perspectives, develop alternative outcomes, or predict future events.

manage uncertainty. In short, incorporating regular use of techniques such as these can enable one to structure thinking for difficult questions.

SATs

There are various definitions for SATs and much debate about the value of using them, both for individual analysts and for analytic groups. While the debate continues, there has been little systematic research on the application of SATs to intelligence analysis. Opinions vary, but many agree that the use of SATs are not widespread among analysts. Even the proponents of SATs acknowledge that the most frequently used way of conducting analysis is

- *The Intuitive Method* (also known as "read a bunch of stuff, think about it for a bit, and then write something") remains the most popular method for producing intelligence analysis.[5]
- *The traditional CIA method of analysis* differs slightly; Read as much as you have time to read that day, think about it, suck an answer out your thumb, and write it down in as crisp a manner as possible.[6]
- Traditional intelligence assessment methodology has always been historiographical; strictly descriptive.[7]

Benefits of Using SATs

Structured techniques are used to mitigate the adverse impact on analysis caused by cognitive limitations and pitfalls. The most distinctive characteristic is that structured techniques externalize and decompose analytical thinking in a manner that enables it to be reviewed and critiqued piece by piece, or step by step, by other knowledgeable analysts. These techniques can be used by the average analyst who lacks advanced training in statistics, math, or the hard sciences. For most analysts, training in

---

[5] Kristan J. Wheaton, *Top 5 Intelligence Analysis Methods* (list), Sources and Methods BlogSpot, http://sourcesandmethods.blogspot.com, retrieved 2015.

[6] Stephen Marrin, Intelligence analysis: Structured methods or intuition?, *American Intelligence Journal*, Vol. 25, 2007.

[7] Timothy J. Smith, Predictive warning: Teams, networks, and scientific method, in *Analyzing Intelligence: Origins, Obstacles, and Innovations*, Georgetown University Press, 2008.

structured analytic techniques is obtained only within the intelligence community.[8]

Due to perceived shortcomings in the results of intuitive analysis, the amount of writing and development focused on SATs has grown. According to proponents, the benefits associated with the use of SATs are

- SATs are the enablers of collaboration. They are the process by which effective collaboration occurs.[9]
- The primary value of analytic techniques or structured methods is that they provide a way to account for the analytic judgment: an analytic "audit trail," as it were.[10]

> **SAT TIPS**
>
> - There is *no* magic formula for always making the right analytic judgment
> - However, SATs are well-established procedures for reducing the frequency and severity of analytical errors
> - SATs enable collaboration by
>   - Documenting and externalizing analysis to allow a thought exchange process
>   - Decomposing analysis into steps for external review by other knowledgeable analysts

There exists a diversity of opinions on the uses of SATs in intelligence production. It can be correctly inferred that some SATs are more suitable for certain types of analysis or are more pertinent depending on the issues being addressed. As an analyst, you are the intended beneficiary of these many SATs and can select those that will benefit your analysis from all of those available.

---

[8] Richards J. Heuer, Taxonomy of Structured Analytic Techniques, paper presented at the International Studies Association Annual Convention, 2008.

[9] Richards J. Heuer, The Evolution of Structured Analytic Techniques, Speech presented to the National Academy of Science, Washington, D.C., December 8, 2009.

[10] Stephen Marrin, Intelligence analysis: Structured methods or intuition?, *American Intelligence Journal*, Vol. 25, 2007.

SAT Groupings

This chapter explores four analytical tradecraft groupings of SATs. Pattern recognition, diagnostic, contrarian, and imaginative. In fact, many of the techniques will use some combination of these functions. Analysts will want to select the tool that best accomplishes the specific task they set out for themselves. Although application of these techniques alone is no guarantee of analytic precision or accuracy of judgments, it does improve the sophistication and credibility of intelligence assessments as well as their usefulness to policymakers. As Richards Heuer Jr. notes in his own work on cognitive bias, "analysis can be improved."[11]

Pattern Recognition Techniques

Pattern recognition techniques array information in order to enhance the interpretation and recognition of patterns or relationships. As you read through the various pattern recognition techniques listed, notice that each technique endeavors to organize and display the data in such a way that the analyst can better comprehend the information as individual pieces, in association with a larger group, or in the aggregate. The following is a list of the more commonly used pattern recognition techniques by the business community, IC, and criminal forensic groups:

- Classic Pattern Recognition
- Social Network Analysis
- Trend Analysis
- Five Force Analysis
- Strength, Weakness, Opportunity, Threat (SWOT) Analysis
- Geospatial Analysis
- Timeline Analysis
- Cost–Benefit Analysis (CBA)
- Sorting
- Event Trees and Fault Trees

Pattern Recognition

Pattern recognition is the arraying of information so as to enhance the recognition of patterns or relationships (illustrated in Figure 10.2).

---

[11] Richards J. Heuer Jr., *Psychology of Intelligence Analysis*, Military Bookshop, 2010.

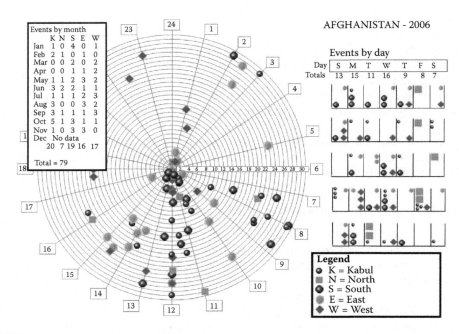

Figure 10.2 Pattern-analysis plot sheet. (From FM 3-24.2, Tactics in Counterinsurgency.)

The U.S. military routinely uses a form of pattern analysis to determine event patterns and predict potential hazards. The military application of pattern analysis looks at events or actions over a period of time in a defined location or area. It is used to discover likely patterns or similarities that lead to a logical conclusion, that the action or event will occur again in the same location or timeframe. The two most common forms are coordinates register and pattern-analysis plot sheet.[12] See Figure 10.2 for an example of a completed pattern-analysis plot sheet.

Another example of using pattern analysis is crime scene bloodstain pattern analysis. The blood drops behave in predictable ways when they strike a surface or when a force acts upon them (Figure 10.3). The shape and size of the puddle depends on the amount of liquid, the height of the container, and whether you spill on carpet, wood, linoleum, or some other

---

[12] Headquarters Department of Army, *Tactics in Counterinsurgency*, Field Manual, FM 3-24.2, April 2009.

142

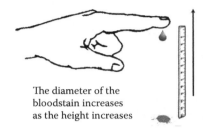

The diameter of the bloodstain increases as the height increases

Figure 10.3 How bloodstain analysis works.

surface. In general, more liquid, or a fall from a greater height, will make a larger puddle.[13] See Figure 10.3 for an example of pattern analysis of blood drops.

Social Network Analysis

Social network analysis is an analytical technique which describes and maps relationships between individuals, groups, organizations, or resources. This analytical technique attempts to answer the question "who knows whom?" (example in Figure 10.4).

Social network analysis is used to model emerging and informal communication patterns in an organization by mapping these relationships. With this insight, analysts can predict behavior and decision-making within a social organization and evaluate specific courses of action that could influence the members of a social network in a desirable way."[14] A visualization of a social network is depicted in Figure 10.4. Social network analysis is covered in greater detail later in the text.

Trend Analysis

Trend analysis (illustrated in Figure 10.5) is the analysis of changes over time, and is used primarily in marketing, business planning, and tactical and strategic operations planning and assessment, at national and corporate levels around the world. It includes a number of submethodologies: historical trend analysis, content analysis, cyclical pattern analysis, and the use of expert opinions called Delphi processes. It is not designed to be used as a standalone method, but it can be useful when combined with other approaches.[15]

---

13 Shanna Freeman and Nicholas Gerbis, How bloodstain pattern analysis works, How Stuff Works Website, http://science.howstuffworks.com/bloodstain-pattern-analysis1.htm, retrieved 2015.
14 L. E. Weaver, eds. K.J. Wheaton, E.E. Mosco, and D.E. Chido, *The Analyst's Cookbook*, Volume I, Mercyhurst College Institute of Intelligence Studies Press, 2006.
15 Z. Hill, eds. K.J. Wheaton, E.E. Mosco, and D.E. Chido, *The Analyst's Cookbook. Volume I*, Mercyhurst College Institute of Intelligence Studies Press, *2006*.

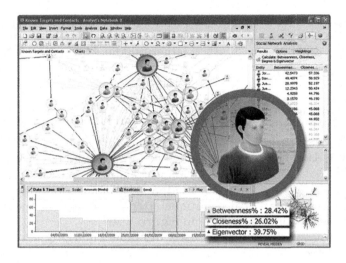

Figure 10.4 Social network analysis. (Courtesy of i2 Analyst's Notebook.)

Note: In reference to Figure 10.5, CBS News states that the United States–led military coalition in Afghanistan incorrectly reported a decline in Taliban attacks in the previous year (2012), and officials later corrected themselves, saying that there was actually no change in the number of attacks on international troops from 2011 to 2012.[16]

AUTHOR'S NOTE

Trend analysis, like all analysis, is susceptible to erroneous inputs and subsequent erroneous outputs.

The basis (rather than the data) of Figure 10.5 I call into question. Why use a drop in the number of Taliban-initiated attacks as a metric of success? Wouldn't the number of successful attacks be better metrics, or attacks which cause coalition casualties? Would not five attacks, each of which caused casualties, deserve greater consideration than 50 ineffective attacks that caused zero casualties?

Analysts must consider the validity of the data they are collecting for trend analysis and ensure it truly measures what they want to measure.

---

[16] CBS News website, Taliban attacks did not drop in 2012 after all, U.S. military says, http://www.cbsnews.com/news/taliban-attacks-did-not-drop-in-2012-after-all-us-military-says, retrieved December 2015.

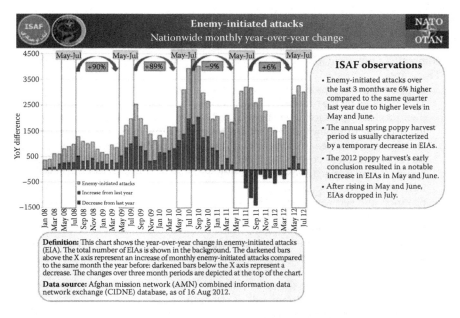

Figure 10.5   Enemy-initiated attacks, May–July, 2008 to 2012, in Afghanistan.

Five Forces Analysis

Harvard Business College Professor Michael E. Porter proposed a model to explain business strategy. This model claims that five forces influence every market and industry. The five forces are threat of new entrants, power of suppliers, power of buyers (customers), threat of substitutes, and market competitors. Although designed

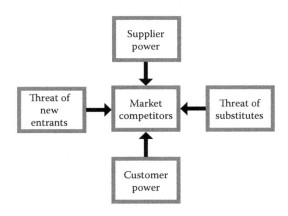

Figure 10.6   Five forces analysis.

for business purposes, its ability to provide insight in other competitive environments (e.g., opposing criminal organizations, cartels, rival terror groups) is quite helpful. See Figure 10.6.

METHOD

Five forces analysis assumes that there are five important forces that determine competitive power in a business situation (or other competitive environments). These are

1. **Supplier Power:** This assesses how easy it is for suppliers to drive up prices. This is driven by the number of suppliers of each key input, the uniqueness of their product or service, their strength and control over you, the cost of switching from one to another, and so on. The fewer the supplier choices you have, and the more you need suppliers' help, the more powerful your suppliers are.
2. **Buyer Power:** Here you ask yourself how easy it is for buyers to drive prices down. Again, this is driven by the number of buyers, the importance of each individual buyer to your business, the cost to them of switching from your products and services to those of someone else, and so on. If you deal with few powerful buyers, then they are often able to dictate terms to you.
3. **Competitive Rivalry:** Which gauges the number and capability of your competitors. If you have many competitors, and they offer equally attractive products and services, then you'll most likely have little power in the situation, because suppliers and buyers will go elsewhere if they don't get a good deal from you. On the other hand, if no one else can do what you do, then you can often have tremendous strength.
4. **Threat of Substitution:** This is affected by the ability of your customers to find a different way of doing what you do—for example, if you supply a unique software product that automates an important process, people may substitute by doing the process manually or by outsourcing it. If substitution is easy and substitution is viable, this weakens your power.
5. **Threat of New Entry:** Power is also affected by the ability of people to enter your market. If it costs little in time or money to enter your market and compete effectively, if there are few economies of scale in place, or if you have little protection for your key technologies, then new competitors can quickly enter your market and weaken your position. If you have strong and durable barriers to entry, then you can preserve a favorable position and take fair advantage of it.

While the five forces analysis originally serves as a business model, its unique analysis of competition has a number of applications. The political (or other competitive) environment surrounding a government (criminal/terror) organizational structure exemplifies a beneficial non-industry use. By adjusting the ultimate goal of the target from maximizing profit to suit the specific circumstances, the five forces method yields insightful analysis of virtually any environment.[17]

---

[17] Michael E. Porter, The five competitive forces that shape strategy, *Harvard Business Review,* January 2008.

Strengths, Weaknesses, Opportunities, and Threats (SWOT) Analysis

SWOT is a useful analytical technique for conducting an environmental scan to determine an organization's internal and external situation. SWOT analysis (also known as the SWOT matrix, see matrix below) helps strategists focus on the key issues that must be addressed in order to enhance a mission's, project's, or organization's success.

It is especially useful in analyzing an entity's current situation in a short period of time.

	METHOD	
Note: Remember that the purpose of performing a SWOT is to reveal positive forces that work together and potential problems that need to be recognized and possibly addressed.		
	STRENGTHS 1. 2. 3. 4.	WEAKNESSES 1. 2. 3. 4.
OPPORTUNITIES 1. 2. 3. 4.	Opportunity/Strength (O/S) Strategies (Use the strengths to take advantage of opportunities) 1. 2.	Opportunity/Weakness (O/W) Strategies (Overcome weaknesses by taking advantage of opportunities) 1. 2.
THREATS 1. 2. 3. 4.	Threat/Strength (T/S) Strategies Use strengths to avoid threats 1. 2.	Threat/Weakness (T/W) Strategies (Minimize weaknesses and avoid threats) 1. 2.

Geospatial Analysis

Geospatial analysis is the gathering, display, and manipulation of imagery, GPS (see Figure 10.7), satellite photography and historical data, described explicitly in terms of geographic coordinates or implicitly, in other terms (e.g., street address, postal code) as they are applied to geographic models.

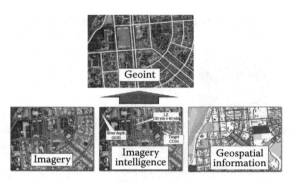

Figure 10.7　Geospatial Information as a Component of GEOINT. (Courtesy of National Geospatial-Intelligence Agency.)

Geospatial analysis is helpful and enhances most analytical processes, providing additional insight and context, it is critical to targeting analysis. See Figure 10.7 for an example of a geospatial product combining raw imagery, imagery intelligence, and geospatial information.

Timeline Analysis

Timeline analysis is an excellent technique for revealing patterns and relationships among data. This technique supports trend analyses, and situational assessments.[18] Timeline analysis uses a graphic representation showing the passage of time as a line to assist the analyst in visualizing events, associating time(s) (or time periods) and placing them in a chronological order.

Timeline analysis depicts events as they unfold over time (Figure 10.8), allowing analysts to understand cause and effect, identify patterns, and decide upon appropriate courses of action. Entities can be tracked over time to identify their associations with an event or incident. See Figure 10.8.

---

[18]　E.L. Williams-Taliaferro, eds. K.J. Wheaton, E.E. Mosco, and D.E. Chido, *The Analyst's Cookbook, Volume I*, Mercyhurst College Institute of Intelligence Studies Press, 2006.

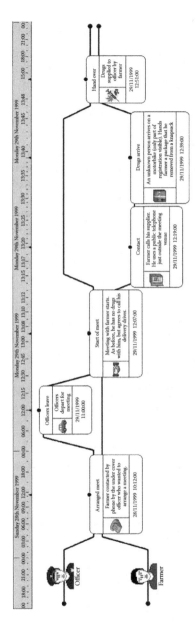

Figure 10.8   Example of timeline analysis. (Courtesy of 12 Analyst's Notebook.)

Cost–Benefit Analysis (CBA)

CBA is a framework for assessing and comparing the costs and benefits of an activity, project, or policy over a particular period of time. It uses a systematic approach to estimating the strengths and weaknesses of alternatives that satisfy transactions, activities, or functional requirements.

Broadly, CBA has two purposes:

1. To determine the soundness of a decision (justification/feasibility).
2. To provide a basis for comparing projects/decisions. It involves comparing the total expected cost (labor hours, dollars, resources, human lives, etc.) of each option against the total expected benefits, to see whether the benefits outweigh the costs, and by how much.

The technique is frequently used in the public sector to analyze policies affecting public projects in the areas of transportation, health, criminal justice, defense, education, and the environment.[19]

AUTHOR'S NOTE

Observe that each of the pattern recognition techniques presented in this chapter are designed to array the data to aid the analyst's efforts to

- Interpret the information presented.
- Comprehend and express the meaning or significance of a wide variety of experiences, situations, data, events, judgments, conventions, beliefs, rules, procedures, or criteria.

METHOD

1. Briefly describe an activity/project/policy that require a cost and benefits analysis over a period of time.
2. Provide a list and description of alternatives that you intend to consider.
3. Identify the factors/aspects for each alternative which you intend compare/ weigh in order to reach a conclusion. Include some justification/rationale for using the particular factors/aspects which were chosen.

(Continued)

---

[19] E. Pate, eds. K.J. Wheaton, E.E. Mosco, and D.E. Chido, *The Analyst's Cookbook, Volume I,* Mercyhurst College Institute of Intelligence Studies Press, 2006.

METHOD

---

4. Select (or develop, if one does not exist) a mechanism to collect the "cost" over the given time period for each alternative.
5. Select (or develop, if one does not exist) a mechanism to define the associated benefit(s) for each alternative.
6. Array the "cost(s)" versus "benefit(s)" for each alternative and make a selection.
7. Identify your final recommendation along with your justification for making the recommendation.

AUTHOR'S NOTE

In 1945, a CBA was performed as part of the deliberation process as to whether or not the U.S. should use the atomic bomb on Japan. Contributing to the discussion was the Joint Chiefs of Staff estimate that the invasion and occupation of Japan could cost America 1.2 million casualties, with 267,000 deaths.

C. N. Trueman, *Operation Downfall*, historylearningsite.co.uk., *The History Learning Site*, 19 May 2015.

Sorting

Sorting is a basic structuring technique for grouping information to develop insight to facilitate analysis. It involves any process of arranging items systematically. The purpose of sorting information is to optimize its usefulness for specific tasks. In general, there are two ways of grouping information: By category, for example, a catalogue where items are compiled together under headings such as "terror group," "military," "criminal organization," or by name, location, or time; and by the intensity of some property, such as size, for example, from the smallest to largest. Sorting can be used to describe a variety of categories of ordered information.

Often information is sorted using different methods at different levels of abstraction, for example, some telephone directories are sorted by location, by category (business or residential), and then alphabetically. New media still subscribes to these basic sorting methods, for example, a Google search returns a list of webpages in a hierarchical list based on its own scoring system for how closely they match the search criteria (from closest match downwards).

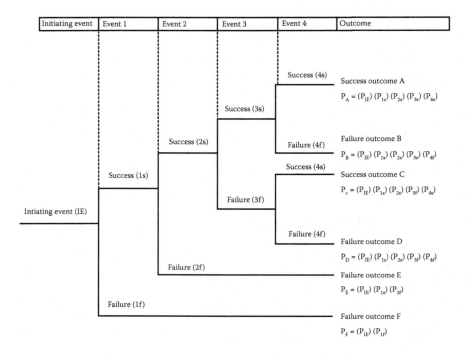

Figure 10.9 Example of event tree analysis.

This technique is most useful for reviewing massive data stores that pertain to an intelligence challenge.[20]

Event Trees and Fault Trees

The graphical depiction of a potential temporal sequence of events, including potential junctures within the event sequence is shown in Figure 10.9. Event trees and fault trees are often confused. Event trees can handle better notions of continuity (logical, temporal, and physical), whereas fault trees are most powerful in identifying and simplifying failure scenarios. Fault trees lay out relationships among events whereas event trees lay out sequences of events linked by conditional probabilities. See Figure 10.9.

Event tree analysis and fault tree analysis are closely linked. Fault trees are often used to quantify system events that are part of event tree sequences.

---

[20] Defense Intelligence Agency (DIA), Anonymous, *A Tradecraft Primer: Basic Structured Analytic Techniques,* 2nd ed., 2009.

The logical processes employed to evaluate event tree sequences and quantify the consequences are the same as those used in fault tree analyses.[21]

The following table outlines various analytical issues/problems and the more appropriate pattern recognition techniques analysts can select from to assist in resolving the issue.

Analysis issue/problem	Trend analysis*	(SWOT) strengths, weaknesses, opportunities, and threats	Five forces analysis	Social network analysis	Classic pattern recognition	Geospatial analysis*	Timeline analysis	Cost benefit analysis (CBA)	Sorting	Event trees and fault trees
Tactical and strategic operations planning and assessment	X	X	X	X	X	X	X	X	X	X
Current situation in a short period of time		X				X				
Political (or other competitive) environment surrounding a government (or criminal/terror) organizational entity		X	X					X		X
Modeling organizational communication patterns				X						
Determining event patterns and predict potential hazards	X				X	X	X	X		
Understanding cause and effect and identifying patterns							X			X
Performing targeting analysis					X	X				
Determining soundness of a decision		X						X		
Providing a basic for comparing projects/decisions		X						X		
When absorbing and evaluating a large amount of data									X	
Tracking events to monitor and evaluate changes	X									
Weighing validity of sources/information	X	X	X	X	X	X	X	X	X	X
Checking/rechecking key assumptions		X	X					X		

Note: "*" Technique not designed to be used as a standalone method; is most useful when combined with other analytical approaches.

Diagnostic Techniques

Diagnostic techniques are primarily aimed at making analytic arguments, assumptions, or intelligence gaps more transparent. They challenge the

---

[21] Defense Intelligence Agency (DIA), Anonymous, *A Tradecraft Primer: Basic Structured Analytic Techniques*, 2nd ed., 2009.

analyst to rethink the basis upon which he or she has made judgments. Four diagnostic techniques used to change or validate the analyst's mindset:

- Key Assumptions Check
- Quality of Information Check
- Indicators or Signposts of Change
- Analysis of Competing Hypotheses (ACH)

Key Assumptions Check

The key assumptions check technique lists and reviews the key working assumptions on which fundamental judgments rest.

A key assumption is any hypothesis that analysts have accepted to be true and which forms the basis of the assessment. For example, military analysis may focus exclusively on analyzing key technical and military variables (sometimes called factors) of a military force and "assume" that these forces will be operated in a particular environment (desert, open plains, arctic conditions, etc.). Postulating other conditions or assumptions, however, could dramatically impact the assessment.

Historically, U.S. analysis of Soviet Warsaw Pact operations against NATO had to "assume" a level of non-Soviet Warsaw Pact reliability (e.g., would these forces actually fight?). In this case, there was a high degree of uncertainty and depending on what level of reliability one assumed, the analyst could arrive at very different conclusions about a potential Soviet offensive operation. Additionally, when economists assess the prospects for foreign economic reforms, they may consciously, or not, assume a degree of political stability in those countries or the region that may or may not exist in the future. Likewise, political analysts reviewing a developing country's domestic stability might unconsciously assume stable oil prices when this key determinant of economic performance and underlying social peace might fluctuate. All of these examples highlight the fact that analysts often rely on stated and unstated assumptions to conduct their analysis. The goal is not to undermine or abandon key assumptions; rather, it is to make them explicit and identify what information or developments would demand reassessing.[22]

A "key assumptions" check is most useful at the beginning of an analytic project. An individual analyst or a team can spend an hour or two articulating and reviewing the key assumptions. Reassessing assumptions

---

[22] U.S. Government, Central Intelligence Agency (CIA), A Tradecraft Primer: Structured Analytic Techniques for Improving Intelligence Analysis, March 2009.

may also be valuable at any time prior to finalizing judgments, to insure that the assessment does not rest on flawed premises. Identifying hidden assumptions can be one of the most difficult challenges an analyst faces, as they are ideas held often subconsciously, to be true and therefore, seldom examined and almost never challenged.[23]

METHOD	QUESTIONS TO ASK
Checking for key assumptions requires analysts to consider how their analysis depends on the validity of certain premises, which they do not routinely question or believe to be in doubt. A four-step process will help analysts: 1. Review what the current analytic line on this issue appears to be and write it down for all to see. 2. Articulate all the premises, both stated and unstated in finished intelligence, which are accepted as true for this analytic line to be valid. 3. Challenge each assumption, asking why it "must" be true and whether it remains valid under all conditions. 4. Refine the list of key assumptions to contain only those that "must be true" to sustain your analytic line; consider under what conditions or in the face of what information these assumptions might not hold.	• How much confidence exists that this assumption is correct? • What explains the degree of confidence in the assumption? • What circumstances or information might undermine this assumption? • Is a key assumption more likely a key uncertainty or key factor? • Could the assumption have been true in the past but less so now? • If the assumption proves to be wrong, would it significantly alter the analytic line? How? • Has this process identified new factors that need further analysis?

Quality of Information Check

The quality of information check technique evaluates completeness and soundness of available information sources.

Weighing the validity of sources is a key feature of any critical thinking. Moreover, establishing how much confidence one puts in analytic judgments should ultimately rest on how accurate and reliable the information base is. Hence, checking the quality of information used in intelligence analysis is an ongoing, continuous process.

---

[23] U.S. Government, Central Intelligence Agency (CIA), A Tradecraft Primer: Structured Analytic Techniques for Improving Intelligence Analysis, March 2009.

Having multiple sources on an issue is not a substitute for having good information that has been thoroughly examined. Analysts should perform periodic checks of the information base for their analytic judgments. Otherwise, important analytic judgments can become anchored to weak information, and any "caveats" attached to those judgments in the past can be forgotten or ignored over time.

If a major analytic assessment is planned, analysts should individually or collectively review the quality of their information and refresh their understanding of the strengths and weaknesses of past reporting on which an analytic line of reasoning rests. Without understanding the context and conditions under which critical information has been provided, it will be difficult for analysts to assess the information's validity and establish a confidence level in an intelligence assessment.[24]

METHOD

An analyst or a team might begin a quality of information check by developing a database in which information is stored according to source type and date, with additional notations indicating strengths or weaknesses in those sources. Ideally, analysts would have a retrieval and search capability on the database so that periodic reviews are less labor-intensive and result in a more complete review of all sources used in past analysis. For the information review to be fully effective, analysts will need as much background information on sources as is feasible. Knowing the circumstances in which reporting was obtained is often critical to understanding its validity. With the data in hand, analysts can then

- Review systematically all sources for accuracy.
- Identify information sources that appear most critical or compelling.
- Check for sufficient and strong corroboration of critical reporting.
- Reexamine previously dismissed information in light of new facts or circumstances that cast it in a different light.
- Ensure that any recalled reporting is identified and properly flagged for other analysts; analysis based on recalled reporting should also be reviewed to determine if the reporting was essential to the judgments made.
- Consider whether ambiguous information has been interpreted and caveated properly.
- Indicate a level of confidence that analysts can place in sources, which are likely to figure in future analytic assessments.

---

[24] U.S. Government, Central Intelligence Agency (CIA), *A Tradecraft Primer: Structured Analytic Techniques for Improving Intelligence Analysis*, March 2009.

Indicators or Signposts of Change

The indicators or signposts of change technique periodically reviews a list of observable events or trends to track events, monitor targets, spot emerging trends, and warn of unanticipated change.

An analyst or team can create an indicators or signposts list of observable events that one would expect to see if a postulated situation is developing, which may include: economic reform, military modernization, political instability, or democratization. Constructing the list might require only a few hours or as much as several days to identify the critical variables associated with the targeted issue. The technique can be used whenever an analyst needs to track an event over time to monitor and evaluate changes. However, it can also be a very powerful aid in supporting other structured methods explained later in this book. In those instances, analysts would be watching for mounting evidence to support a particular hypothesis, low-probability event, or scenario.

When there are sharply divided views on an issue, an indicators or signposts list can also "depersonalize" the argument by shifting analytic attention to a more objective set of criteria. Using an indicators list can clarify substantive disagreements, once all sides agree on the set of objective criteria used to measure the topic under study.[25]

METHOD

Whether used alone, or in combination with other structured analysis, the process is the same:
- Identify a set of competing hypotheses or scenarios.
- Create separate lists of potential activities, statements, or events expected for each hypothesis or scenario.
- Regularly review and update the indicators lists to see which are changing.
- Identify the most likely or most correct hypotheses or scenarios based on the number of changed indicators that are observed.

Developing two lists of indicators for each hypothesis or scenario may prove useful to distinguish between indicators that a development is or is not emerging. This is particularly useful in a "what if?" analysis, when it is important to make a case that a certain event is unlikely to happen.

---

[25] U.S. Government, Central Intelligence Agency (CIA), *A Tradecraft Primer: Structured Analytic Techniques for Improving Intelligence Analysis*, March 2009.

Analysis of Competing Hypotheses (ACH)

The ACH technique identifies and defines alternative explanations (hypotheses) and the evaluation of all evidence that will reject rather than confirm hypotheses.

Analysis of Competing Hypotheses (ACH) has proved to be a highly effective technique when there is a large amount of data to absorb and evaluate. While a single analyst can use ACH, it is most effective with a small team that can challenge each other's evaluation of the evidence. Developing a matrix of hypotheses and loading collected information into the matrix can be accomplished in a relatively short period of time. If the data must be reassembled, the initial phases of the ACH process may require additional time. Sometimes a facilitator or someone familiar with the technique can lead new analysts through this process for the first time.

ACH is particularly appropriate for controversial issues when analysts want to develop a clear record that shows what theories they have considered and how they arrived at their judgments. Developing the ACH matrix allows other analysts or policymakers to review their analysis and identify areas of agreement and disagreement. Evidence can also be examined more systematically. This makes the technique ideal for considering the possibility of deception and denial.[26]

METHOD

ACH demands that analysts explicitly identify all the reasonable alternative hypotheses, then array the evidence against each hypothesis, rather than evaluating the plausibility of each hypothesis one at a time. In order to be effective initially, the process must

- Ensure that all the information and argumentation is evaluated and given equal treatment or weight when considering each hypothesis.
- Prevent the analyst from premature closure on a particular explanation or hypothesis.
- Protect the analyst against innate tendencies to ignore or discount information that does not fit comfortably with the preferred explanation at the time.

(Continued)

---

[26] U.S. Government, Central Intelligence Agency (CIA), *A Tradecraft Primer: Structured Analytic Techniques for Improving Intelligence Analysis,* March 2009.

METHOD

To accomplish this, the process should follow these steps:

- Brainstorm among analysts with different perspectives to identify all possible hypotheses.
- List all significant evidence and arguments relevant to all the hypotheses.
- Prepare a matrix with hypotheses across the top and each piece of evidence on the side.*
- Determine whether each piece of evidence is consistent, inconsistent, or not applicable to each hypothesis.
- Refine the matrix and reconsider the hypotheses; in some cases, analysts will need to add new hypotheses and reexamine the information available.
- Focus on disproving hypotheses rather than proving them.
- Tally the pieces of evidence that are inconsistent and consistent with each hypothesis to see which explanations are the weakest and strongest.
- Analyze how sensitive the ACH results are to a few critical items of evidence; should those pieces prove to be wrong, misleading, or subject to deception, how would it impact an explanation's validity?
- Ask what evidence is not being seen but would be expected for a given hypothesis to be true. Is denial and deception a possibility?
- Report all the conclusions, including the weaker hypotheses that should still be monitored as new information becomes available.
- Establish the relative likelihood for the hypotheses and report all the conclusions, including the weaker hypotheses that should still be monitored as new information becomes available.
- Identify and monitor indicators that would be both consistent and inconsistent with the full set of hypotheses. In the latter case, explore what could account for inconsistent data.

Note: The "diagnostic value" of the evidence will emerge as analysts determine whether a piece of evidence is found to be consistent with only one hypothesis, or could support more than one or indeed all hypotheses. In the latter case, the evidence can be judged as unimportant to determining which hypothesis is more likely correct.

Analysis issue/problem \ Analytical technique	Key assumptions check	Quality of information check*	Indicators or signposts of change	Analysis of competing
Tactical and strategic operations planning and assessment	X	X	X	X
Current situation in a short period of time		X		
Political (or other competitive) environment surrounding a government (or criminal/terror) organizational entity	X	X		
Modeling organizational communication patterns		X	X	
Determining event patterns and predict potential hazards		X	X	
Understanding cause and effect and identifying patterns	X	X		
Performing targeting analysis	X	X		
Determining soundness of a decision	X	X		
Providing a basic for comparing projects/decisions		X		
When absorbing and evaluating a large amount of data		X		X
Tracking events to monitor and evaluate changes		X	X	
Weighing validity of sources/information	X	X	X	X
Checking/rechecking key assumptions	X	X	X	X
Challenging mind-sets with two existing dominant views		X		
Recognizing impact of seemingly low probability events		X		
Challenging an analytic consensus or a key assumption	X	X		X
Challenging a strong mind-set that an event will NOT happen or confidently made forecast may NOT be justified	X	X		
Stimulating new thinking on a problem/issue		X		
Identifying all the critical, external factors that could influence how a particular situation will develop	X	X	X	
Trying to see a situation from perspective of another individual or group	X	X		
Situation is viewed as "too complex" or the outcomes as "too uncertain" to trust a single outcome asessment	X	X	X	

The following table outlines various analytical issues/problems and the more appropriate diagnostic techniques analysts can select in order to assist in resolving the issue.

Note: These techniques are not designed to be used as a standalone methods. They are most useful when combined with other analytical approaches.

Contrarian Techniques

Contrarian techniques explicitly challenge current thinking by adding a diversity of knowledge and beliefs to the analysis process. Four common contrarian techniques used to challenge the analyst's perceptions are

- Devil's Advocacy
- Team A/Team B
- High-Impact/Low-Probability Analysis
- "What If?" Analysis

Devil's Advocacy

The devil's advocacy technique challenges a single, strongly held view or consensus by building the best possible case for an alternative explanation.

METHOD

To challenge the prevailing analytic line, the devil's advocate must

- Outline the mainline judgment and key assumptions and characterize the evidence supporting that current analytic view.
- Select one or more assumptions, stated or implied, that appear the most susceptible to challenge.
- Review the information used to determine whether any is of questionable validity, whether deception is possibly indicated, or whether major gaps exist.
- Highlight the evidence that could support an alternative hypothesis or that contradicts the current thinking.
- Present the findings that demonstrate flawed assumptions, poor quality evidence, or possible deception at work.
- Consider drafting a separate contrarian paper that lays out the arguments for a different analytic conclusion if the review uncovers major analytic flaws.
- Be sure that any products generated clearly lay out the conventional wisdom and are identified as an explicitly "devil's advocate" project; otherwise, the reader can become confused as to the current official view on the issue.

Devil's advocacy is most effective when challenging analytic consensus or key assumptions regarding a critically important intelligence question. On those issues that one cannot afford to get wrong, devil's advocacy can provide further confidence that the current analytic line will hold up to close scrutiny. Analysts can often assume the role of the devil's advocate if they have some doubts about a widely held view, or a manager might designate a courageous analyst to challenge the prevailing wisdom in order to reaffirm the group's confidence in those judgments. In some cases, analysts can review a key assumption of a critical judgment in the course of their work, or more likely, a separate analytic product can be generated that arrays all the arguments and data that support a contrary hypothesis. When analysts have worked on an issue for a long period of time, it is probably wise to assume that a strong mindset exists that deserves the closer scrutiny provided by devil's advocacy.[27]

Team A/Team B

Use of separate analytic teams that contrast two (or more) strongly held views or competing hypotheses.

A Team A/Team B approach is different from devil's advocacy, where the purpose is to challenge a single dominant mindset. Team A/Team B recognizes that there may be competing and possibly equally strong mindsets held on an issue that need to be clarified. Sometimes analysts confuse the two techniques by drafting a Team B exercise that is really a devil's advocacy exercise.

If there are at least two competing views within an analytic cell or perhaps competing opinions within the policymaking community on a key issue, then Team A/Team B analysis can be the appropriate technique to use. Developing a full-blown Team A/Team B exercise requires a significant commitment of analytic time and resources, so consideration should be given to whether the analytic issue merits this kind of attention.

A longstanding policy issue, a critical decision that has far-reaching implications, or a dispute within the analytic community that has obstructed effective cross-agency cooperation would be grounds for using Team A/Team B. If those circumstances exist, analysts will need to review all of the data to develop alternative papers that can capture the essential differences between the two viewpoints.[28]

---

[27] U.S. Government, Central Intelligence Agency (CIA), *A Tradecraft Primer: Structured Analytic Techniques for Improving Intelligence Analysis*, March 2009.

[28] U.S. Government, Central Intelligence Agency (CIA), *A Tradecraft Primer: Structured Analytic Techniques for Improving Intelligence Analysis*, March 2009.

METHOD	
Analysis Phase	**Debate Phase**
A Team A/Team B exercise can be conducted on an important issue to • Identify the two (or more) competing hypotheses/points of view. • Form teams/designate individuals to develop the best case that can be made for each hypothesis. • Review all information that supports their respective positions. • Identify missing information that would buttress their hypotheses. • Structure each argument with an explicit presentation of key assumptions or key pieces of evidence.	An oral presentation of the alternative arguments and rebuttals in parallel fashion can then be organized for the benefit of other analysts: • Set aside time for an oral presentation of the alternative team findings; this can be an informal brainstorming session or a more formal "debate." • Have an independent "jury of peers" listen to the oral presentation, prepared to question the teams regarding their assumptions, evidence, or logic. • Allow each team to present their case, challenge the other team's arguments, and rebut the opponent's critique of its case. • Let the jury consider the strength of each presentation and recommend possible next steps for further research and collection efforts.

High-Impact/Low-Probability Analysis

High-impact/low-probability analysis highlights a seemingly unlikely event that would have major policy consequences if it happened.

High-impact/low-probability analysis is a contrarian technique that sensitizes analysts to the potential impact of seemingly low probability events that would have major repercussions on U.S. interests. Use of this technique is advisable when analysts and policymakers are convinced that an event is unlikely but they have not given much thought to the consequences of its occurrence. In essence, this can be a warning that the intelligence and policy communities must be alert to an unexpected but not impossible event. For example, the fall of the Shah, the collapse of the Soviet Union, and the reunification of Germany were all considered low-probability events at one time. Analysts might have benefited from considering the consequences of such events and how they might have plausibly occurred.[29]

METHOD

If there is a strongly held view that an event is unlikely, postulating precisely the opposite should not be difficult.
- Define the high-impact outcome clearly. This potential outcome is what will justify examining what most analysts believe to be a very unlikely development.
- Devise one or more plausible explanations for "pathways" to the low probability outcome. This should be as precise as possible, as it can help identify possible indicators for later monitoring.
- Insert possible triggers or changes in momentum, if appropriate. These can be natural disasters, sudden health problems of key leaders, or new economic or political shocks that might have occurred historically or in other parts of the world.
- Brainstorm with analysts having a broad set of experiences to aid the development of plausible but unpredictable triggers of sudden change.
- Identify for each pathway a set of indicators or "observables" that would help you anticipate that events were beginning to play out this way.
- Identify factors that would deflect a bad outcome or encourage a positive outcome.

"What If" Analysis

"What if" analysis assumes that an event has occurred with potential (negative or positive) impact and explains how it might occur.

"What if" analysis is another contrarian technique for challenging a strong mindset that an event will not happen or that a confidently made forecast may not be entirely justified. It is similar to a high-impact/low-probability analysis, but it does not dwell on the consequences of the event as much as it accepts the significance, and moves directly to explaining how it might occur.[30]

---

[29] U.S. Government, Central Intelligence Agency (CIA), *A Tradecraft Primer: Structured Analytic Techniques for Improving Intelligence Analysis*, March 2009.

[30] U.S. Government, Central Intelligence Agency (CIA), *A Tradecraft Primer: Structured Analytic Techniques for Improving Intelligence Analysis*, March 2009.

METHOD

Like other contrarian methods, "What if" analysis must begin by stating clearly the conventional analytic line and then pausing to consider what alternative outcomes are too important to dismiss, even if unlikely. Brainstorming over a few days or weeks can develop one or more plausible scenarios by which the unlikely event occurs:

- Assume the event has happened.
- Select some triggering events that permitted the scenario to unfold to help make the "what if" more plausible; for example, analysts might postulate the death of a leader, a natural disaster, or some economic event that would start a chain of other events.
- Develop a chain of argumentation based as much on logic as evidence to explain how this outcome could have occurred.
- "Think backward" from the event in concrete ways. Do this by specifying what must actually occur at each stage of the scenario is often very useful.
- Identify one or more plausible pathways or scenarios to the unlikely event. Very often more than one will appear possible.
- Generate a list of indicators or "observables" for each scenario that would help to detect the beginnings of the event.
- Consider the scope of the positive and negative consequences of each scenario and the relative impacts of either.
- Monitor the indicators developed on a periodic basis.

The following table outlines various analytical issues/problems and the more appropriate contrarian techniques analysts can select from to assist in resolving the issue.

Analysis issue/problem	Devil's advocacy	Team A/Team B	High-impact/ low-probability analysis	What if? Analysis
Tactical and strategic operations planning and assessment	X	X	X	X
Weighing validity of sources/information	X	X	X	X
Checking/rechecking key assumptions	X	X	X	X
Challenging mind-sets with two existing dominant views	X			
Recognizing impact of seemingly low probability events			X	
Challenging a strong mind-set that an event will NOT happen or confidently made forecast may NOT be justified				X

Imaginative Thinking Techniques

Imaginative thinking techniques are focused on developing new insights, developing different perspectives or alternative outcomes, or predicting future events. The following are four imaginative thinking techniques used by the intelligence community:

- Brainstorming
- Outside-In Thinking
- Red Team Analysis
- Alternative Futures Analysis

Brainstorming

Brainstorming is an unrestrained group process designed to generate new ideas and concepts.

Brainstorming is a widely used technique for stimulating new thinking and it can be applied to virtually all of the other structured analysis techniques as an aid to thinking. Typically, analysts will brainstorm when they begin a project to help generate a range of hypotheses about their issue.

Brainstorming, almost by definition, involves a group of analysts meeting to discuss a common challenge. A modest investment of time at the beginning of, or at critical points of, a project can be advantageous in defining different perspectives to help structure a problem. This group process allows others to build on an initial idea suggested by a member of the brainstorming session.

An individual analyst also can brainstorm to produce a wider range of ideas than a group might generate without regard for other analysts' egos, opinions, or objections. However, an individual will not have the benefit of others' perspectives to help develop the ideas as fully. Moreover, an individual may have difficulty breaking free of his or her cognitive biases without the benefit of a diverse group.[31]

---

[31] U.S. Government, Central Intelligence Agency (CIA), *A Tradecraft Primer: Structured Analytic Techniques for Improving Intelligence Analysis*, March 2009.

METHOD

Paradoxically, brainstorming should be a very structured process to be most productive. An unconstrained, informal discussion might produce some interesting ideas, but usually a more systematic process is the most effective way to break down mindsets and produce new insights. In particular, the process involves a divergent thinking phase to generate and collect new ideas and insights, followed by a convergent phase in which ideas are grouped and organized around key concepts. Some simple rules to be followed include but are not limited to

- Never censor an analyst's ideas no matter how unconventional they might sound.
- Find out what prompted the thought, as it might contain the seeds of an important connection between the topic and an unstated assumption.
- Give yourself enough time to do brainstorming correctly. It usually takes one hour to set the "rules" of the game, get the group comfortable, and exhaust the conventional wisdom on the topic. Only then will the truly creative ideas begin to emerge.
- Involve at least one "outsider" in the process. The outsider should be someone who does not share the same educational background, culture, technical knowledge, or mindset as the core group but has some familiarity with the topic.

DIVERGENT THINKING PHASE

- Distribute Post-it notes and pens or markers to all participants. Typically, 10–12 people works best.
- Pose the problem in terms of a "focal question." Display it in one sentence on a large easel or whiteboard.
- Ask the group to write down responses to the question using key words that will fit on the small Post-it note.
- Stick all the notes on a wall for all to see and treat all ideas the same.

CONVERGENT THINKING PHASE

- Ask the participants as a group to rearrange the notes on the wall according to their commonalities or similar concepts. No talking is permitted. Some notes may be moved several times as notes begin to cluster. Copying some notes is permitted to allow ideas to be included in more than one group.
- Select a word or phrase that characterizes each grouping or cluster once all the notes have been arranged.

(Continued)

METHOD
• When a pause follows the initial flow of ideas, the group is reaching the end of their conventional thinking and the new divergent ideas are then likely to emerge. • End the "collection stage" of the brainstorming after two or three pauses.	• Identify any notes that do not easily fit with others and consider them either useless noise or the beginning of an idea that deserves further attention. • Assess what the group has accomplished in terms of new ideas or concepts identified or new areas that need more work or further brainstorming. • Instruct each participant to select one or two areas that deserve the most attention. Tabulate the votes. • Set the brainstorming group's priorities based on the voting and decide on the next steps for analysis.

Outside-In Thinking

Outside-in thinking is used to identify the full range of basic forces, factors, and trends that would indirectly shape an issue.

Analysts find this technique most useful in the conceptualization of an analytic project, when the goal is to identify all the critical, external factors that could influence how a particular situation will develop. It would work well for a group of analysts responsible for a range of functional or regional issues. When assembling a large database that must identify a number of information categories or database fields, this technique can aid in visualizing the entire set of categories that might be needed in a research effort. Often analysts realize only too late that some additional information categories will be needed and then must go back and review all previous files and recode the data. With a modest amount of effort, outside-in thinking can reduce the risk of missing important variables early in the analytic process.[32]

---

[32] U.S. Government, Central Intelligence Agency (CIA), *A Tradecraft Primer: Structured Analytic Techniques for Improving Intelligence Analysis*, March 2009.

METHOD

The process begins by developing a generic description of the problem or the phenomenon under study. Once this has been completed, analysts should:

- List all the key forces (social, technological, economic, environmental, and political) that could have an impact on the topic, but over which one can exert little influence (e.g., globalization, social stress, the Internet, or the global economy).
- Focus next on key factors over which an actor or policymaker can exert some influence. In the business world this might be the market size, customers, the competition, suppliers or partners; in the government domain, it might include the policy actions or the behavior of allies or adversaries.
- Assess how each of these forces could affect the analytic problem.
- Determine whether these forces actually do have an impact on the particular issue based on the available evidence.

Red Team Analysis

Red Team analysis models the behavior of an individual or group by trying to replicate how an adversary would think about an issue. Red Team analysis is difficult. It requires significant time to develop a team of qualified experts who can think like the adversary. The team has to distance itself from the normal analysis and work as though living in the target's world. Without a sophisticated understanding of the culture, operational environment, and personal histories of the foreign group, analysts will not be able to behave or think like the enemy. Analysts can never truly escape their own experiences and mindsets. This technique can at least prevent them from falling into mirror-imaging unconsciously.

The novel feature of Red Team analysis is its presentation.

- The analysis is often in a "first person" format, that is, drafted as memos to or from a leader or group.
- Red Team analysis avoids the use of caveats or qualifications and assumes that the recipient understands that the paper is aimed more at provoking thought or challenging the conventional understanding of how an adversary thinks.
- Such papers are rarely coordinated among other experts and do not purport to represent the consensus view on an issue.

Frequently, analysts face the challenge of forecasting how a foreign leader or decision-making group may behave when it is clear that there is a risk of falling into a "mirror-image" problem. That is, analysts can

169

sometimes impute to a foreign actor the same motives, values, or understanding of an issue that they hold. Traditional analysis sometimes assumes that foreign leaders or groups will behave "rationally" and act as the analysts would if faced with the same threats or opportunities. History has shown that foreign leaders often respond differently to events because of different cultural, organizational, or personal experiences.

Red Team analysis tries to consciously place analysts in the same cultural, organizational, and personal setting (putting them in their shoes) in which the target individual or group operates. Whereas analysts normally work from the position of the "blue" (friendly forces), a "red" team of analysts attempts to work in the environment of the hostile forces.

Red Team papers do not plot out all possible courses of action but seek to give a prediction based on the target's special personal, organizational, or cultural experiences.[33]

METHOD

On issues that lend themselves to Red Team analysis, a manager needs to build a team of experts with in-depth knowledge of the operating environment, the target's personality, and the style of thinking used. The team should be populated not just with those who understand the language, but also with people who might have experienced the culture, share the ethnic background, or have worked in a similar operational environment. Once established and separated from traditional analysis, the team members should:
- Put themselves in the adversary's circumstances and react to foreign stimuli as the target would.
- Develop a set of "first-person" questions that the adversary would ask, such as, "How would I perceive incoming information; what would be my personal concerns; or to whom would I look for an opinion?"
- Draft a set of policy papers in which the leader or group makes specific decisions, proposes recommendations, or lays out courses of actions. The more these papers reflect the cultural and personal norms of the target, the more they can offer a different perspective on the analytic problem.

Alternative Futures Analysis
Alternative futures analysis systematically explores multiple ways a situation can develop when there is high complexity and uncertainty.

---

[33] U.S. Government, Central Intelligence Agency (CIA), *A Tradecraft Primer: Structured Analytic Techniques for Improving Intelligence Analysis*, March 2009.

Alternative futures analysis (often referred to as scenarios) is most useful when a situation is viewed as too complex or the outcomes as too uncertain to trust a single outcome assessment. First, analysts must recognize that there is high uncertainty surrounding the topic in question. Second, they, and often their customers, recognize that they need to consider a wide range of factors that might bear on the question. And third, they are prepared to explore a range of outcomes and are not wedded to any preconceived result. Depending on how elaborate the futures project, the effort can amount to considerable investment in time, analytic resources, and money. A team of analysts can spend several hours or days organizing, brainstorming, and developing multiple futures. Alternatively, a larger-scale effort can require preparing a multi-day workshop that brings together participants (including outside experts). Such an undertaking often demands the special skills of trained scenario-development facilitators and conferencing facilities.

This technique is in sharp contrast to contrarian techniques, which attempt to challenge the analysts' high confidence and relative certitude about an event or trend. Instead, multiple futures development is a divergent thinking technique that uses the complexity and uncertainty of a situation to describe multiple outcomes or futures that the analyst and policymaker should consider, rather than to predict one outcome.[34]

METHOD

Although there are a variety of ways to develop alternative futures, the most common approach used in both the public and private sectors involves the following steps:

- Develop the "focal issue" by systematically interviewing experts and officials who are examining the general topic.
- Convene a group of experts (both internal and external) to brainstorm about the forces and factors that could affect the focal issue.
- Select by consensus the two most critical and uncertain forces and convert these into axes or continua with the most relevant endpoints assigned.
- Establish the most relevant endpoints for each factor, e.g., if economic growth were the most critical, uncertain force, the endpoints could be "fast" and "slow" or "transformative" and "stabilizing" depending on the type of issue addressed.
- Form a futures matrix by crossing the two chosen axes. The four resulting quadrants provide the basis for characterizing alternative future worlds.

(Continued)

---

[34] U.S. Government, Central Intelligence Agency (CIA), *A Tradecraft Primer: Structured Analytic Techniques for Improving Intelligence Analysis*, March 2009.

METHOD
• Generate colorful stories that describe these futures and how they could plausibly come about. Signposts or indicators can then be developed.   • Participants, especially policymakers, can then consider how current decisions or strategies would fare in each of the four worlds and identify alternative policies that might work better either across all the futures or in specific ones. By anticipating alternative outcomes, policymakers have a better chance of either devising strategies flexible enough to accommodate multiple outcomes or of being prepared and agile in the face of change.

Example of Alternative Futures

Figure 10.10 captures four potential futures. The exercise is constructed to aid analysts in understanding how foreign insurgents might carry out

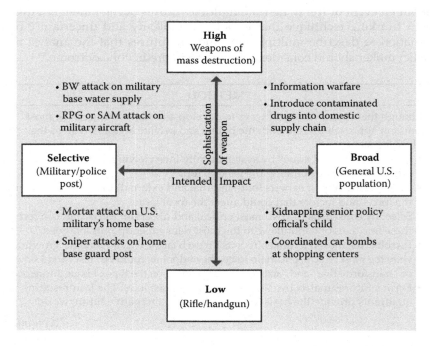

Figure 10.10 Example of using alternative futures analysis to define potential threats to the homeland. (Courtesy of CIA Tradecraft Primer.)

an attack on the United States. A brainstorming exercise helped analysts identify two key uncertainties (the sophistication of weapons used by the insurgents and the intended impact of the attack) and arrayed these factors on a graph as the "x" and "y" axes. The four resulting quadrants in the 2 × 2 matrix allowed analysts to visualize potential targets from the various combinations (low to high sophistication of weapons and selective to broad intended impact of an attack). For example, if a group possessed highly sophisticated weapons and intended a broad attack on the United States, potential targets could include computer networks and domestic drug supplies. Having filled in a quadrant, analysts can then turn to devising likely indicators or signposts of such a future.

The table outlines various analytical issues/problems and the more appropriate imaginative techniques analysts can select from to assist in resolving the issue.

Analysis issue/problem / Analytical technique	Brainstorming	Outside-in thinking	Red team analysis	Alternative futures analysis
Tactical and strategic operations planning and assessment	X	X	X	X
Current situation in a short period of time	X	X	X	
Political (or other competitive) environment surrounding a government (or criminal/terror) organizational entity	X	X	X	X
Modeling organizational communication patterns	X			
Determining event patterns and predict potential hazards		X		
Understanding cause and effect and identifying patterns		X		
Performing targeting analysis	X	X		
Determining soundness of a decision	X	X		
Weighing validity of sources/information	X	X	X	X
Checking/rechecking key assumptions	X	X	X	X
Challenging mind-sets with two existing dominant views	X	X		
Recognizing impact of seemingly low probability events	X	X		
Challenging an analytic consensus or a key assumption	X	X		
Challenging a strong mind-set that an event will NOT happen or confidently made forecast may NOT be justified	X	X		
Stimulating new thinking on a problem/issue	X	X		
Identifying all the critical, external factors that could influence how a particular situation will develop		X		
Trying to see a situation from perspective of another individual or group			X	
Situation is viewed as "too complex" or the outcomes as "too uncertain" to trust a single outcome assessment				X

Choosing a Suitable SAT

When considering the application of a particular SAT, the analyst should first develop an understanding of the characteristics of the intelligence issue. Some intelligence issues relate to a future state of affairs. The question, then, is: Is the future defined as tomorrow, next month, next year, or next decade? Additionally, other intelligence issues deal with the actions and decisions of individuals, groups, nations or international entities, and these characteristics may affect your choice of SATs. While understanding the nature of the issue is necessary, it is not enough to make an appropriate choice about the SATs to use. To select appropriate SATs, you should also consider whether the SAT helps you assign meaning to individual pieces of information, the aggregation of information, or both.

In addition, it is essential to consider the nature of the cognition that you are trying to aid by using the SAT. This requires an understanding of the cognition associated with analysis, as well as what aspects of cognition are aided by specific SATs.

As mentioned earlier in this chapter, a great deal of emphasis has been placed on the use of SATs. Johnston states, "Although well over 160 analytic methods are available to intelligence analyst, few methods specific to the domain of intelligence analysis exist."[35] However, Johnston did not specifically identify these 160-plus techniques, nor has the intelligence literature. Both the CIA and DIA have in-house training courses on SATs for their analysts.

Many classifications of SATs have been done. For example, Richards Heuer Jr. describes eight types: idea generation, scenarios and indicators, hypothesis generation and testing, assessment of cause and effect, challenge analysis, conflict management, and decision support. Heuer's 2010 book, *Structured Analytic Techniques for Intelligence Analysis*, describes 50 different techniques.[36]

The text uses only a sampling of SATs from the intelligence literature (i.e., DIA, CIA courses, and some others) grouped into four general categories: Pattern recognition, diagnostic, contrarian, and imaginative.

It goes without saying, there is not a direct one-for-one mapping of the cognitive factors and the SATs. In addition, many SATs address multiple aspects of thinking and some are designed for individual use, some for group use. However, the book contains multiple matrix tables that identify the more appropriate techniques for given analytical issues/problems.

CHAPTER SUMMARY

This chapter described what is meant by the term *analytical tradecraft*. *Analytical tradecraft* refers to the body of specific methods used for intelligence analysis. The purpose of analytical tradecraft improves the quality of

---

[35] Rob Johnston, *Analytic Culture in the U.S. Intelligence Community: An Ethnographic Study*, Center for the Study of Intelligence, 2005.

[36] Richards J. Heuer Jr. and Randolph H. Pherson, *Structured Analytic Techniques for Intelligence Analysis*, CQ Press College, 2010.

the product and adds value for the intelligence product consumer. Utilizing tradecraft principles and practices enhances the end product, providing the analyst needed consumer feedback to clarify "what questions most need answering"; focus the analyst; and assist in managing a deluge of information, discern trends, and identify attempts at deception.

Various congressional commissions as well as other studies have prodded the analytic community to develop and implement new tools and processes to better produce and interpret intelligence products. Analytic tradecraft standards represent the IC's analytic transformation efforts to improve support to a wide range of intelligence customers.[37,38]

The constantly changing threat profiles and the evermore complex methods analysts use to make sense of these threats have driven the IC to develop tradecraft and promulgate standards for intelligence analysis and production. This chapter identifies efforts by the IC to implement analytical standards and tradecraft. Additionally, it identifies several analytical techniques used by the IC and the issues/problem sets where they are most often applied.

Analytical Methods Techniques

Extracting the meaning of collected information to create an assessment, which is disseminated as intelligence, is the ultimate purpose of analysis. Information in this chapter will aid in developing and focusing your mental framework in preparation for this crucial task.

This chapter encourages you to mentally engage with the topics described that affect your thinking and reflect upon those topics, considering your own behaviors and capabilities. You will see a recurring theme about "thinking" and its importance to motivation and intellectual engagement relative to the topic.

Sherman Kent identifies two steps after all the information has been acquired:

1. Critical evaluation of the data thus assembled
2. Study of the evaluated data with the intent of finding some inherent meaning[39]

---

[37] US Government, *National Commission on Terrorist Attacks upon the United States, http:// govinfo.library.unt.edu/911/hearings/hearing3/witness_emerson.htm,* retrieved 2015-10-23.

[38] US Government, Commission on the Intelligence Capabilities of the United States Regarding Weapons of Mass Destruction, *http://govinfo.library.unt.edu/wmd/about.html,* retrieved 2015-10-23.

[39] Sherman Kent, *Strategic Intelligence for American World Policy,* Princeton University Press, 1949.

Determining meaning has rapidly become more burdensome and intellectually difficult. Consequently, there has been an increasing amount of attention in the intelligence literature on understanding traditional analysis methods and techniques, as well as the development of new methods and techniques to supplement or replace what has been used.

These analytical methods/techniques are often referred to as structured analytic methods or techniques (SATs). This chapter introduced a few SATs and also provided information for you to consider in choosing appropriate analysis approaches and techniques to aid you in evaluating and assigning meaning to information.

ANALYTICAL TRADECRAFT TIPS

- First identify the relevant and diagnostic information that is acquired through open source and clandestine means.
- Then choose an appropriate SAT which adequately *interprets gathered information* and considers a range of alternative explanations and outcomes to ensure potentially relevant hypotheses are *not* dismissed and supporting information opportunities to warn potentially missed.
- *Use diagnostic techniques* to actively review the accuracy of mind sets by applying structured analytic techniques that will make those mental models more explicit and expose key assumptions.
- *Use contrarian techniques* to challenge all assumptions and current thinking by adding a diversity of knowledge and beliefs.
- *Use imaginative thinking techniques* to develop new insights, develop different perspectives, develop alternative outcomes, or predict future events.

SATs

There are various definitions for what constitutes a SAT and much debate about the value of using them, both for individual analysts and for analytic groups. While the debate continues, there has been little systematic research on the application of SATs to intelligence analysis. Opinions vary, but many agree that use is not widespread among IC analysts. Even the proponents of SATs acknowledge that the most frequently used way of doing analysis is

- *The Intuitive Method* (also known as read a bunch of stuff, think about it for a bit, and then write something) remains the most popular method for producing intelligence analysis.[40]
- *The traditional CIA method of analysis*: Read as much as you have time to read that day, think about it, suck an answer out your thumb, and write it down in as crisp a manner as possible.[41]
- Traditional intelligence assessment methodology has always been historiographical ... strictly descriptive.[42]

Benefits of Using SATs

Structured techniques are used to mitigate the adverse impact on analysis caused by cognitive limitations and pitfalls. The most distinctive characteristic is that structured techniques externalize and decompose analytical thinking in a manner that enables it to be reviewed and critiqued piece by piece, or step by step, by other knowledgeable analysts. These techniques can be used by the average analyst who lacks advanced training

SAT TIPS

- There is *no* magic formula for always making the right analytic judgment
- However, SATs are well-established procedures for reducing the frequency and severity of analytical errors
- SATs enable collaboration by
  - Documenting and externalizing analysis to allow a thought exchange process
  - Decomposing analysis into steps for external review by other knowledgeable analysts

---

[40] Kristan J. Wheaton, Top 5 intelligence analysis methods (list), Sources and Methods BlogSpot, http://sourcesandmethods.blogspot.com, retrieved 2015.

[41] Stephen Marrin, Intelligence analysis: Structured methods or intuition?, *American Intelligence Journal*, Vol. 25, 2007.

[42] Timothy J. Smith, *Predictive Warning: Teams, Networks, and Scientific Method, in Analyzing Intelligence: Origins, Obstacles, and Innovations*, Georgetown University Press, 2008.

in statistics, math, or the hard sciences. For most analysts, training in structured analytic techniques is obtained only within the Intelligence Community.[43]

There exist a diversity of opinions on the usage of SATs in intelligence production, but you can correctly infer that some SATs are more suitable for certain types of analysis or are more pertinent depending on the issues being addressed.

SAT Groupings

This chapter explored four analytical tradecraft groupings of SATs: pattern recognition, diagnostic, contrarian, and imaginative. In fact, many of the techniques will do some combination of these functions. However, analysts will want to select the tool that best accomplishes the specific task they set out for themselves. Although application of these techniques alone is no guarantee of analytic precision or accuracy of judgments, it does improve the sophistication and credibility of intelligence assessments as well as their usefulness to policymakers. As Richards Heuer notes in his own work on cognitive bias, "analysis can be improved."[44]

Pattern Recognition Techniques

Pattern recognition techniques array information so as to enhance the interpretation and recognition of patterns or relationships. As you read through the various pattern recognition techniques listed, notice that each technique endeavors to organize and display the data in such a way that the analyst can better comprehend the information as individual pieces, in association with a larger group or in the aggregate. The following is a list of the more commonly used pattern recognition techniques by the business community, IC, and criminal forensic groups:

- Classic Pattern Recognition
- Social Network Analysis
- Trend Analysis
- Five Force Analysis
- Strength, Weakness, Opportunity, Threat (SWOT) Analysis
- Geospatial Analysis

---

[43] Richards J. Heuer Jr., Taxonomy of Structured Analytic Techniques, paper presented at the International Studies Association 2008 Annual Convention, 2008.

[44] Richards J. Heuer Jr., *Psychology of Intelligence Analysis*, Military Bookshop, 2010.

- Timeline Analysis
- Cost–Benefit Analysis (CBA)
- Sorting
- Event Trees and Fault Trees

Classic Pattern Recognition

Classic pattern recognition is the arraying of information so as to enhance the recognition of patterns or relationships.

Social Network Analysis

Social network analysis is an analytical technique that describes and maps relationships between individuals, groups, organizations, or resources. This analytical technique attempts to answer the question "who knows whom?"

Trend Analysis

Trend analysis, analysis of changes over time, is used primarily in marketing, business planning, and tactical and strategic operations planning and assessment at national and corporate levels around the world. It includes a number of submethodologies: Historical trend analysis, content analysis, cyclical pattern analysis, and the use of expert opinions called Delphi processes. It is not designed to be used as a standalone method, but it can be useful when combined with other approaches.[45]

Five Forces Analysis

Harvard Business College Professor Michael E. Porter proposes a model to explain business strategy. This model claims that five forces influence every market and industry. The five forces are Threat of New Entrants, Power of Suppliers, Power of Buyers (Customers), Threat of Substitutes, and Market Competitors. Although designed for "business purposes," its ability to provide insight in other "competitive environments" (e.g., opposing criminal organizations, cartels, rival terror groups) is quite helpful.

Strengths, Weaknesses, Opportunities, and Threats (SWOT) Analysis

SWOT is a useful analytical technique for conducting an environmental scan to determine an organization's internal and external situation. SWOT

---

[45] Z. Hill, eds. K.J. Wheaton, E.E. Mosco, and D.E. Chido, *The Analyst's Cookbook. Volume I*, Mercyhurst College Institute of Intelligence Studies Press, *2006*.

analysis (also known as the SWOT matrix) helps strategists focus on the key issues that they must address in order to enhance a mission's, project's, or organization's success.

Geospatial Analysis

Geospatial analysis is the gathering, display, and manipulation of imagery, GPS, satellite photography, and historical data described explicitly in terms of geographic coordinates or implicitly in other terms (e.g., street address, postal code) as they are applied to geographic models.

Timeline Analysis

Timeline analysis is an excellent technique for revealing patterns and relationships among data. This technique supports trend analyses and situational assessments.[46] Timeline analysis uses a graphic representation showing the passage of time as a line to assist the analyst in visualizing events, associating them time(s) (or time periods), and placing them in a chronological order.

Cost–Benefit Analysis (CBA)

CBA is a framework for assessing and comparing the costs and benefits of an activity, project, or policy over a particular period of time. It uses a systematic approach to estimating the strengths and weaknesses of alternatives that satisfy transactions, activities, or functional requirements.

Sorting

Sorting is a basic structuring technique for grouping information to develop insight to facilitate analysis. It is any process of arranging items systematically. The main purpose of sorting information is to optimize its usefulness for specific tasks. In general, there are two ways of grouping information: by category, for example, a catalogue where items are compiled together under headings such as "terror group," "military," "criminal organization"; by name, by location, by time, and so on; and by the intensity of some property, such as size, for example, from the smallest to largest. Sorting can be used to describe just about every type of ordered information.

---

[46] E.L. Williams-Taliaferro, eds. K.J. Wheaton, E.E. Mosco, and D.E. Chido, *The Analyst's Cookbook*, Volume I, Mercyhurst College Institute of Intelligence Studies Press, 2006.

Event Trees and Fault Trees

Graphical depiction of a potential temporal sequence of events, including potential junctures within the event sequence. Event trees and fault trees are often confused. Event trees can handle better notions of continuity (logical, temporal, and physical), whereas fault trees are most powerful in identifying and simplifying failure scenarios. Fault trees lay out relationships among event whereas event trees lay out sequences of events linked by conditional probabilities.

Diagnostic Techniques

Diagnostic techniques are primarily aimed at making analytic arguments, assumptions, or intelligence gaps more transparent. They challenge the analyst to rethink the basis upon which he or she has made judgments. The following are four diagnostic techniques used to change or validate the analyst's mindset:

- Key Assumptions Check
- Quality of Information Check
- Indicators or Signposts of Change
- Analysis of Competing Hypotheses (ACH)

Key Assumptions Check

The key assumptions check technique lists and reviews the key working assumptions on which fundamental judgments rest.

Quality of Information Check

The quality of information check technique evaluates completeness and soundness of available information sources.

Indicators or Signposts of Change

The indicators or signposts of change technique periodically reviews a list of observable events or trends to track events, monitor targets, spot emerging trends, and warn of unanticipated change.

Analysis of Competing Hypotheses (ACH)

The ACH technique identifies of alternative explanations (hypotheses) and evaluation of all evidence that will disconfirm rather than confirm hypotheses.

Contrarian Techniques

Contrarian techniques explicitly challenge current thinking by adding a diversity of knowledge and beliefs to the analysis process. Four common contrarian techniques used to challenge the analyst's perceptions are as follows:

- Devil's Advocacy
- Team A/Team B
- High-Impact/Low-Probability Analysis
- "What If" Analysis

Devil's Advocacy

The devil's advocacy technique challenges a single, strongly held view or consensus by building the best possible case for an alternative explanation.

Team A/Team B

Use of separate analytic teams that contrast two (or more) strongly held views or competing hypotheses.

High-Impact/Low-Probability Analysis

High-impact/low-probability analysis highlights a seemingly unlikely event that would have major policy consequences if it happened.

"What If" Analysis

"What if" analysis assumes that an event has occurred with potential (negative or positive) impact and explains how it might come about.

Imaginative Thinking Techniques

Imaginative thinking techniques aim at developing new insights, developing different perspectives, developing alternative outcomes, or predicting future events. The following are four imaginative thinking techniques used by the intelligence community:

- Brainstorming
- Outside-In Thinking
- Red Team Analysis
- Alternative Futures Analysis

Brainstorming

Brainstorming is an unconstrained group process designed to generate new ideas and concepts.

Outside-In Thinking

Outside-in thinking is used to identify the full range of basic forces, factors, and trends that would indirectly shape an issue.

Red Team Analysis

Red Team analysis models the behavior of an individual or group by trying to replicate how an adversary would think about an issue. Red Team analysis is not easy to conduct. It requires significant time to develop a team of qualified experts who can think like the adversary.

Alternative Futures Analysis

Alternative futures analysis systematically explores multiple ways a situation can develop when there is high complexity and uncertainty.

Choosing a Suitable SAT

When considering the application of a particular SAT, the analyst should first develop an understanding of the characteristics of the intelligence issue. Some intelligence issues relate to a future state of affairs, but is the future defined as tomorrow, next month, next year, or next decade? Also, other intelligence issues deal with the actions and decisions of individuals, groups, nations, or international entities, and these characteristics may affect your choice of SATs. While understanding the nature of the issue is necessary, it is not enough to make an appropriate choice about the SATs to use. To select appropriate SATs, you should also consider whether the SAT helps you assign meaning to individual pieces of information, the aggregation of information, or both.

In addition, it is essential to consider the nature of the cognition that analysts are trying to aid by using the SAT. This requires an understanding of the cognition associated with analysis, as well as what aspects of cognition are aided by specific SATs.

As mentioned earlier in this chapter, a great deal of emphasis has been placed on the use of SATs. Many classifications of SATs have been done.

The text uses only a sampling of SATs from the intelligence literature (i.e., DIA, CIA courses, and some others) are grouped into four general categories: Pattern recognition, diagnostic, contrarian, and imaginative.

The text does not provide a direct one-for-one mapping of the cognitive factors and the SATs. In addition, many SATs address multiple aspects of thinking and some are designed for individual use, some for group use. However, the book contains multiple matrix tables which identify the more appropriate techniques for given analytical issues/problems.

11

Cognitive Traps for Intelligence Analysis

INTRODUCTION

Intelligence analysis is subject to cognitive bias, or traps, many of which are encountered in other occupations and scientific professions. Besides influencing people's stock picks, car purchases, and new shoe choices, cognitive bias also effects scientific research and philosophy. Psychologists have identified more than 100 individual varieties of cognitive bias. Chapter 11 outlines a few of the more common mental traps also encountered by intelligence analysts. This chapter refers to the first systematic study of the specific pitfalls lying between an intelligence analyst and clear thinking carried out by Richards Heuer, a thought leader in the field of intelligence analysis. According to Heuer, these traps may be rooted either in the analyst's organizational culture or his or her own personality.[1]

BIAS CATEGORIES

Analyst bias fall primarily into specific types or categories: personality bias, confirmation bias, target fixation, improper use of analogy (or model), and organizational culture. There are more, but these are the more

---

[1] Richards J. Heuer Jr., *Psychology of Intelligence Analysis*, Pherson Associates LLC, 2007.

common ones encountered by analysts. Each of these analytical biases, or traps, misdirect the analyst from objectivity and towards subjectivity.[2]

Personality of the Observer

Analysts often start an intelligence project by asking themselves, "How would I do something?" As a result, they discover as they work through the analysis they begin to unconsciously find themselves focusing on data that supports how they would go about performing a task and neglecting data that does not fit their perceptions. This introduction of the observer's personality is called *mirror imaging*. Mirror imaging is one of the more common personality traps where analysts' assumptions presume that the subjects being studied think like the analysts themselves.

Experienced analysts are more likely to notice that they have been snared by

> **TIPS FOR AVOIDING COGNITIVE TRAPS**
>
> - Cognitive traps such as personality bias, confirmation bias, target fixation, improper use of analogy (or model), and organizational culture feed analytical bias and create bad analysis.
> - Most of these traps can be recognized, mitigated, or avoided entirely by use of one or more of the following:
>   - Structured analytical techniques (SATs)
>   - Recognizing the pattern of the trap through critical questioning
>   - Properly framing of the problem
>   - Leveraging other perspectives and using peer reviews

mirror imaging by using structured analytical methods to identify their personal biases. Less perceptive analysts may regard legitimate objections as a personal attack, rather than looking beyond ego to the available evidence. Peer reviews, especially by people from a different backgrounds, can be a prudent precaution.

---

[2] Richards J. Heuer Jr., *Psychology of Intelligence Analysis*, Pherson Associates LLC, 2007.

Confirmation Bias

Multiple scientific studies from the 1960s proved that humans unconsciously seek out, more likely remember, and pay attention to things that agree with and conform to the way they already think.[3] If you do not agree, ask yourself which television or radio station you tune into for news and why? Likewise, we tend to ignore or forget those things that contradict our viewpoints.

Confirmation biases impact how intelligence analysts gather information, but they also influence how analysts interpret and recall information. So why is this detrimental to the analysis process? By not seeking out objective facts and interpreting information in a way that only supports existing beliefs, and only remembering details that uphold these beliefs, analysts often miss important information that might have otherwise influenced their decisions and thereby negatively influences the results of their analysis.

In order to control for confirmation bias, analysts need to proactively take the devil's advocate position in that they need to take the opposite perspective of their stated assessment and spend as much time looking for evidence that proves they are wrong as they spent searching for reasons that they were correct. It is not easy trying to explain that you are not the brilliant analyst you thought you were, but many analysts would prefer their theory disproved that way than to have an outside organization disprove it.

A Mitre Corporation study has shown that using a particular SAT, Analysis of Competing Hypotheses (ACH), to mitigate the effects of confirmation bias is particularly effective.[4] See Chapter 10 for more information on ACH. More information on methods of avoiding cognitive traps is covered later in the chapter.

Target Fixation

Another cognitive trap, *idea* or *target fixation*, is where the brain is focused so intently on an observed object or idea that awareness of other obstacles or hazards are diminished. Some examples of target fixation are when a photographer, fixated on their subject, starts backing up to get a better shot and falls

---

[3] Peter O. Gray, *Psychology*, Worth Publishers, 2011.
[4] Mitre Corporation, Confirmation Bias in Complex Analyses, Mitre Technical Report, MTR 04B0000017, 2004.

into a hole or trips over an obstacle; or when pilots concentrate on delivering their bombs on the mark and they lose sight of the big picture, crashing into the target.

Examples of target fixation might include "terrorists only hijack planes, they don't fly them into buildings" or "all snipers are lone white male gunman, like in the Kennedy assassination." Neither of these statements are true and even if these assumptions are statistically supportable as "more likely" than not, they should be tested against available evidence and validated before analysts inadvertently discount viable leads and reports. To prevent target fixation, intelligence analysts or criminal investigators should develop tests to continuously validate their hypotheses. Criminal investigators do this by checking to see if a potential suspect has a reasonable and verifiable alibi for a crime, like the suspect was incarcerated at the time of the crime.

AUTHOR'S NOTES:
Showing that a suspect cannot be placed at the scene of the crime does not necessarily exonerate them from any involvement in the crime:

- Organized crime or drug cartel murders are most often perpetrated by assailants who are paid killers, as opposed to the individual who ordered the homicide.
- It has been shown that arsonists sometimes have no personal connection with fires they start. Instead they are paid by third parties in order to collect fraudulent insurance claims or for other nefarious reasons. An example of such a case occurred in Russellville, Indiana, whereby Christina Snyder allegedly approached her neighbor and propositioned her with a $5,000 payoff if she would help burn down her house. The neighbor declined and reported Snyder to the police. The claim would have paid out $80,000.

Wrong Analogy

Unsuitable analogies are yet another cognitive trap. Analogies are essentially proposed behavioral models which are used to explain actions, fill in informational gaps, and possibly predict activities. Analogies can be very useful and at the same time very hazardous when misapplied. The danger is when analogies are forced upon the facts (or lack thereof) or untested social assumptions.

Analysts may find sidestepping the path to using inappropriate analogies enormously difficult if they are unaware of the hazard; critical intelligence gaps exist; or when organizational, time, or peer pressure overcomes the will to use a more difficult and structured approach to find answers.

An intelligence organization may be ignorant to the fact that important information which would invalidate the analogy is missing. Additionally, even if the analytical group or analyst does recognize their error, they may be reluctant to admit the lack of knowledge exists, thereby creating another obstacle. Lack of information and negative organizational culture can combine to force the selection of the wrong analogy and push the analysis process down the wrong track toward incorrect answers or at minimum divert critical analytical and collection assets toward useless research and wasted time.

An example of where wrong analogy was avoided is the Oklahoma federal building bombing. On the morning of April 19, 1995, Timothy McVeigh parked a rented Ryder truck in front of the Alfred P. Murrah Federal Building in downtown Oklahoma City. Moments later, a third of the building had been reduced to rubble. Dozens of cars were incinerated and more than 300 nearby buildings were damaged or destroyed.

Coming on the heels of the World Trade Center bombing in New York two years earlier, the media and many Americans immediately assumed that the attack was the handiwork of Middle Eastern terrorists.

On April 20, FBI analysts identified the rear axle of the Ryder truck from the vehicle identification number and traced it to a body shop in Junction City, Kansas. Employees at the shop helped the FBI put together a composite drawing of the man who had rented the van. See Figure 11.1. Agents showed the drawing around town, and local hotel employees supplied a name: Tim McVeigh.[5]

---

[5] U.S. Federal Bureau of Investigation, Famous Cases and Criminals website, Terror Hits Home: The Oklahoma City Bombing, www.fbi.gov/about-us/history/famous-cases /oklahoma-city-bombing.

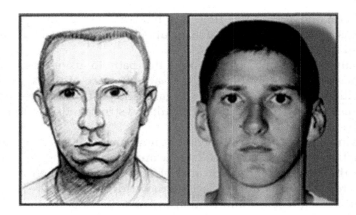

Figure 11.1   FBI composite and actual photo of Timothy McVeigh.

Organizational Culture

Some of the most noted and productive scientific theorists and researchers were nonconvergent thinkers. Albert Einstein fits perfectly under the label "nonconvergent." Einstein's approach to problem solving often diverged from the "groupthink" of his contemporaries. These nonconvergent (or divergent) thinkers often make better intelligence analysts. They can more readily visualize a greater number of possibilities or alternatives. So, what is *groupthink* and how does it relate to organizational culture? Groupthink, a psychology term first seen in the 1970s, occurs when the pressure to conform within a group restricts the whole group's analysis of a problem and causes poor decision-making.

Organizational culture can foster collaborative and extremely productive analysis; it can just as well foster groupthink. Groupthink occurs more often when analytical teams are more concerned with appearances. Supervisors may suppress constructive engagement born of analytical originality because it may "rock the boat" and conflict with analysis performed by other organizations.

To better illustrate the point, let's look at a hypothetical situation. Let us assume that a lone analyst in a county sheriff's office along the U.S./Canada international border has collected significant evidence from multiple sources that terror networks are smuggling arms across the border, specifically through their county. Following standard procedure, they forward their analysis to higher offices and a copy reaches the FBI. The FBI reviews the analysis and does not concur with the assessment. What might be the response? Understandably, the report might better fit conventional paradigms and be more eagerly accepted if the assessment cited "local criminal groups" versus "terror networks" or if the location was along the U.S./Mexico border where previous reporting reflects an ongoing international terror presence. Unfortunately, neither is the case and the potential for ridicule and professional embarrassment exists for the analyst and the local county sheriff's department. In this particular case there are multiple alternatives. Retract the report and apologize—perhaps the analyst could somehow modify the assessment to make it more palatable to the outside organizations; or maybe the analyst should look for supporting data to better prove their point. The most appropriate response would be to continue to collect evidence without bias which either objectively or definitively proves or denies the assessment.

AVOIDING COGNITIVE TRAPS

How can an intelligence analyst avoid cognitive traps? This presents a tremendous question which may not be readily answered. As a goal it is definitely achievable, but not feasibly possible for each and every conceivable situation. Sometimes there simply exists too little data to properly develop an adequate solution and as analysts go through and often repeat the intelligence process, the likelihood of falling into one or more cognitive traps increases.

Recognizing the Patterns

Use critical questions to help recognize the trap. At a minimum, the analyst must ask themselves, "What are the patterns of the cognitive traps I have previously fallen prey to?" "Are these patterns present now?"

This may seem so obvious to be considered trivial. However, to neglect to consider where one has previously fallen prey would satisfy Einstein's definition of insanity:

> The definition of insanity is doing the same thing over and over again and expecting different results.
>
> Albert Einstein

As analysts, pattern recognition is your stock and trade; however, in this case you are looking for patterns in your own analysis. To help you recognize these patterns, ask yourself a question. For example, there is a terror attack and the news media has already labeled it as an "Islamist extremist" attack. You must immediately ask yourself: "Do all (or most) terrorist acts look like Islamic terror acts?" It may very well be an Islamic terror act, but what evidence supports this assertion? Is there a particular signal or prompt that makes marks it as "Islamic terrorism"?

To better illustrate the point, in the Old West there existed a notorious gang of thieves called the James-Younger Gang. When they were active, the gang was accredited with committing many dozens of robberies. Historians generally agree, however, that there were only a total of twenty robberies: Ten banks, seven trains, and three stagecoaches. However, of the twenty not all historians agree, so the total may only be as low as seventeen. Why the discrepancies? There may be several reasons. Criminals may have falsely claimed they were the James-Younger Gang to throw off law enforcement. Newspapers may have just printed the story they knew would sell. Honest mistakes may have also played a part. However, this type of mistake seems to only happen to "notorious" gangs. Perhaps it is some combination of all them. Analysts must be their most meticulous critic to recognize the patterns in their own analysis.

America's adversaries also look for patterns. Criminals, terrorists, and other enemies can also recognize patterns. They observe law enforcement and intelligence organizations to determine our analytical and collection sources and methods and how best to avoid, deceive, and frustrate them. For example, Osama bin Laden used couriers to communicate with his terror network because he understood the signal collection capabilities of the National Security Agency (NSA). Human traffickers (aka coyotes) wait until the U.S. Border Patrol has a shift change to cross the border at remote crossing locations because they know they are less likely to be observed. If certain cues or prompts automatically generate labels like "drug crime" or "gang-related violence," is there a chance criminals and terrorists may be using some of the signals and cues analysts and investigators use to analyze crime and acts of terror?

Authorities now believe Tamerlan Tsarnaev (the Boston Marathon Bomber) may have been responsible for a triple homicide in 2011, which at the time was labeled a "drug-related" killing because thousands of dollars' worth of marijuana and money were left covering the mutilated bodies, and the case was never closed. However, forensic evidence connected Tsarnaev to the scene of the killings, and cell phone records placed him in the area.[6]

Properly Framing Problems

Notice the section is titled "Properly Framing Problems." In this case, the emphasis is placed on the word "properly." Framing problems is essentially just creating mental models to better understand the specifics of a situation or problem set by placing them in some type of context. However, issues arise when framing is done improperly or in a hurried or careless fashion. Unconsciously, humans use frames as mental shortcuts to label things their senses perceive based upon their collected experiences, attitudes, values, and emotions. For example, when you walk into an unfamiliar room and see a lion's head protruding from a plaque on the wall, do you think it is a safari trophy or an actual lion's head sticking through the wall? Most would likely say "it is a safari trophy." See Figure 11.2. But would that perception change if suddenly the lion's head became animated and ferociously growled? Based upon the newly perceived data, you might say it is a real lion … or that, depending on how realistic the animation or roar was, or how startled you were, you might say it was a hoax robot or puppet lion's head. It cannot be all four options (real, robot, puppet, and trophy), but I have shown that it plausibly could be framed as any of the choices presented.

Intelligence analysts routinely use framing to identify potential informational or cognitive traps. By properly framing the problem, the analyst is more fully informed and is in a better position to recognize and avoid the pitfall of choosing the wrong analogy, as discussed earlier. While framing the problem represents the initial step toward a positive resolution, it is also the first place the analysis process can go wrong. Regrettably, frames tend to persist regardless of events and

---

[6] Michele McPhee, Boston Bomb Suspect Eyed in Connection to 2011 Triple Murder, *ABC News*, April 22, 2013.

Figure 11.2   Example of framing.

information that follows. Consequently, if the situation is initially incorrectly framed, the incorrect frame will tend to influence analysts even after conflicting information is revealed. Psychologists commonly refer to this phenomenon as the Law of Primacy (or Serial Position Effect); primacy, the state of being first, often creates a strong, almost unshakable, impression.

Because most problems can be framed, or looked at from more than one perspective, the analysts' personal biases have significant influence on how a particular situation is perceived. Often two or more analysts involved in the same analytical project will see the problem and define it in different ways. To avoid mischaracterizations from the outset, analysts must be objective when initially framing the situation and should try to collaborate with others in the process to gain broader and more diverse perspectives or at a minimum have critical peer reviews of the original representations of the problem.

For example, an analyst who has spent years supporting a fast-paced terrorism operations desk such as National Countertype Terrorism Center (NCTC), which has a high volume of quick response intelligence requests, might have a tendency to look at all intelligence issues as emergent and quickly evolving and therefore needing quick and hurriedly prepared assessments. If one relocates that same analyst from the high operations tempo situation to a slower-paced, more deliberate intelligence atmosphere, a culture shock ensues and it may continue to exist for some period of time until the analyst fully acclimates to the more thorough, methodical, and disciplined analytical environment.

Leveraging Other Perspectives

Take a can of soda and place it on a desk in full view and try to describe it in extreme detail (e.g., Figure 11.3). Take all of your visual descriptions and record them on sheet of paper. Have someone else perform the same task at the same time, but from the opposite side of the desk. Then repeat the process looking at the can from above or involve another sense and listen to the can—perhaps you will hear the carbonation bubbles. Now touch the can and see what its temperature is. Compare all the various descriptions from different perspectives and you will see differences. However, if one combines them, a much more complete and accurate description is generated. The same holds true for analysis, because no two analysts look at any given set of data exactly the same way. See Figure 11.3.

Leveraging other perspectives works best as a collaborative process performed in the same (or as close as possible to the same) time period. Performing a critical peer review later is also a form of leveraging another perspective, but the beneficial early collaborative aspects

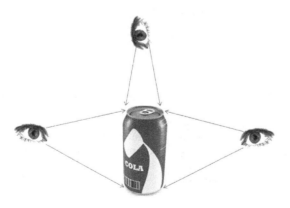

Figure 11.3   Different perspectives provide a more complete picture.

are lost. Ideally, to reduce personal biases, analysts should perform a diverse perspective collaboration followed by one or more independent critical peer reviews.

Structured Analytic Techniques (SATs)

Mentioned earlier in the chapter, SATs are valuable tools in recognizing and mitigating the effects of cognitive traps. Since Chapter 10 goes into detail on the application and benefits of using SATs in the analysis process, SATs will not be discussed again here.

AUTHOR'S NOTES

- Collaborative efforts should be formed from analysts with diverse perspectives (e.g., HUMINT, geospatial, and a SIGINT analyst)
- Independent Critical Peer Reviews also benefit from diversity of perspective (e.g., if a junior team made up of HUMINT, geospatial, and SIGINT analysts produced an intel product, the critical peer review might best be performed by a senior MASINT analyst)

Example of Cognitive Bias

First consider George, a 29-year-old man, married and outgoing. Years ago, during George's college days, he was very involved in animal rights causes, and also participated in People for the Ethical Treatment of Animals (PETA) protests.

Which is more probable about George's occupation today?

a. George is a stock broker
b. George is a veterinarian
c. George is a large animal veterinarian full-time, but remains very active in the animal rights movement (Figure 11.4)

What is your answer? (a) or (b) or (c)? And, in what precise order? Example Solution: The best answer is (a) first (most likely); (b) next; and then (c), in that order.
Supporting Information:

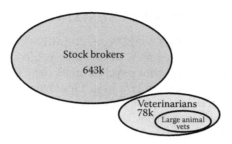

Figure 11.4   Vin Diagram of Professions.

- According to the Financial Industry Regulatory Authority (FINRA), there are 643,298 active brokers in the United States as of October 2015. It is a high-paying career that in most states only requires one of two specific qualification tests and no college or other academic requirement to be eligible.
- According to U.S. Bureau of Labor Statistics Employment Projections program, there are 78,300 veterinarians total in the United States as of October 2014. Veterinarian medicine is a highly competitive and generally well-compensated profession that requires a doctorate-level graduate degree which is only available at roughly 30 universities in the United States.

Note: Large animal veterinarians would be a lesser population than the total number of veterinarians, because it is a subset of the total.

Alternate Solution: (a) or (b), then (c), in that order. Just in case you did not intuitively understand that there are a surplus of stock brokers in America.

The key: If you ranked (c) as more probable than (a) or (b), you are very wrong … and very likely to have answered the question the same as the majority of humanity.

Most people tend to rank (c) before (a) or (b) the first time they face this particular question, and it reflects a very pervasive cognitive bias, technically called a *conjunction fallacy*. (Definition: A fallacy occurs when it is assumed that specific conditions are more probable than a single general one.)

Observing from a strictly statistical perspective, it is more probable that George is a stock broker or veterinarian of any kind than he is likely to be both a large animal veterinarian full-time and also active in the animal rights movement, which is a subset of the category of all veterinarians.

CHAPTER SUMMARY

This chapter expounded the several types cognitive bias (or traps) encountered by intelligence analysts as well as other professional and scientific vocations. It was mentioned that psychologists have identified more than 100 individual varieties of cognitive bias. However, little effort was made to identify or explain them all. It is more important that the analyst realize that cognitive traps exist and they should always be watchful of the effects that these biases have on analysis. That said, Chapter 11 did outline a few of the more common mental traps encountered by intelligence analysts.

Bias Categories

Analyst bias falls mainly into several types or categories: Personality bias, confirmation bias, target fixation, improper use of analogy (or model), and organizational culture. There are more, but these are the more common ones encountered by analysts.

Personality of the Observer

Analysts often start an intelligence project by asking themselves, "How would I do something?" As a result, they discover as they work through the analysis that they begin to unconsciously find themselves focusing on data that supports how they would go about performing a task and neglecting data that does not fit their perceptions. This introduction of the observer's personality is called *mirror-imaging*. Mirror-imaging is one of the more common personality traps where analysts' assumptions presume that the subjects being studied think like the analysts themselves.

Confirmation Bias

Multiple scientific studies from the 1960s proved that humans unconsciously seek out, and more likely remember and pay attention to, things that agree with and conform to the way they already think.[7] If you do not agree, ask yourself which television or radio station do you tune into for news and why? Likewise, we tend to ignore or forget those things that disagree with the way we think.

Target Fixation

Another cognitive trap, *idea* or *target fixation*, is where the brain is focused so intently on an observed object or idea that awareness of other obstacles

---

[7] Peter O. Gray, *Psychology*, Worth Publishers, 2011.

or hazards are diminished. Some examples of target fixation are when a photographer, fixated on their subject, starts backing up to get a better shot and falls into a hole or trips over an obstacle; or when pilots concentrate on delivering their bombs on the mark and they lose sight of the big picture, crashing into the target.

Wrong Analogy
Unsuitable analogies are yet another cognitive trap. Analogies are essentially proposed behavioral models that are used to explain actions, fill in informational gaps, and possibly predict activities. Analogies can be very useful and at the same time very hazardous when misapplied. The danger lies in analogies are forced upon the facts (or lack thereof) or untested social assumptions.

Organizational Culture
Organizational culture can foster collaborative and extremely productive analysis; it can just as well foster groupthink. Groupthink occurs more often when analytical teams are more concerned with appearances. Supervisors may suppress constructive engagement born of analytical originality because it may "rock the boat" and conflict with analysis performed by other organizations.

Avoiding Cognitive Traps

How can an intelligence analyst avoid cognitive traps? This presents a tremendous question which may not be readily answered. As a goal it is definitely achievable, but not feasibly possible for each and every conceivable situation. Sometimes there simply exists too little data to properly develop an adequate solution and as analysts go through and often repeat the intelligence process, the likelihood of falling into one or more cognitive traps increases.

Recognizing the Patterns
Use critical questions to help recognize the trap. At a minimum, the analyst must ask themselves, "What are the patterns of the cognitive traps I have previously fallen prey to?" and "Are these patterns present now?"

As analysts, pattern recognition is your stock and trade. However, in this case you are looking for patterns in your own analysis. To help you recognize these patterns, ask yourself a question. For example, there is a terror attack and the news media has already labeled it as an "Islamist extremist" attack. You must immediately ask yourself: "Do all (or most) terrorist acts look like Islamic terror acts?" It may very well be an Islamic terror act, but what evidence supports this assertion? Is there a particular signal or prompt that makes marks it as "Islamic terrorism"?

Properly Framing Problems

Because most problems can be framed or looked at from more than one perspective, the analysts' personal biases have significant influence on how a particular situation is perceived. Often two or more analysts involved in the same analytical project will see the problem and define it in different ways. To avoid mischaracterizations from the outset, analysts must be objective when initially framing the situation and should try to collaborate with others in the process to gain broader and more diverse perspectives or at a minimum have critical peer reviews of the original representations of the problem.

Leveraging Other Perspectives

Take a can of soda and place it on a desk in full view and try to describe it in extreme detail. Take all of your visual descriptions and record them on sheet of paper. Have someone else perform the same task at the same time, but from the opposite side of the desk. Then repeat the process looking at the can from above or involve another sense and listen to the can—perhaps you will hear the carbonation bubbles. Now touch the can and see what its temperature is. Compare all the various descriptions from different perspectives and you will see differences. However, if one combines them, a much more complete and accurate description is generated. The same holds true for analysis, because no two analysts look at any given set of data exactly the same way.

Leveraging other perspectives works best as a collaborative process performed in the same (or close as possible to the same) time period. Performing a critical peer review later is also a form of leveraging another perspective, but the beneficial early collaborative aspects are lost. Ideally, to reduce personal bias, analysts should perform a diverse perspective collaboration followed by one or more independent critical peer reviews.

Structured Analytic Techniques (SATs)

Mentioned earlier in the chapter, SATs are valuable tools in recognizing and mitigating the effects of cognitive traps. Since the Chapter 10 goes into detail on the application and benefits of using SATs in the analysis process, SATs will not be discussed again here.

12

Probability Estimation

INTRODUCTION

Analysts often ask, "Why bother with probability estimation? Why not just use my gut instincts?" Even today there are intelligence analysts and criminal investigators that subscribe to the philosophy of just following their "gut." Sometimes they are correct, often they are not. Whether they are correct or not, the position of "using your gut" instincts quickly become indefensible when briefing an intelligence assessment to superiors or prosecuting criminals. *Probability estimation* takes some of the guesswork out of assessment and inserts a level of objectivity, reliability, and reproducibility into the intelligence practice that can later be analyzed, explained, repeated, and if required, adjusted to potentially improve the process.

Probability estimation is routinely used in the production of analytic products, criminal profiles, reports, and assessments to convey the likelihood of a future event occurring (or not occurring). Probability has also helped to drive governmental policy decisions (e.g., should we build more or fewer prisons; increase or decrease military spending).

When analysts use probability estimates in assessments or reports, they are expressing the extent of their confidence in the finding. Presently, probability estimation is not a precise science and until recently, its usage was not standard across the U.S. Intelligence Community. This chapter introduces the subject, explains its use, and provides examples of how some of these probability estimates are derived by intelligence and criminal analysts.

This chapter is not a higher math course that teaches in extreme detail how to calculate statistical probability while taking into account various other factors. It only attempts to introduce some of the math concepts involved, how and why probability is used in analysis, show examples of its more recent impact on criminal and intelligence, and provide a few tools to help make analytical probability estimates. Probability estimation tools reported to be in use at the Department of Homeland Security (DHS) are specifically highlighted.

ANALYTICAL APPLICATIONS TO PROBABILITY

Analysts use probabilities estimates to guide intelligence analysis end users in understanding the validity and confidence they have in their intelligence products and analytical judgments to include the data and sources used to make those judgments. Using empirical and research datasets, criminologists use probabilities to create criminal profiles.

Assessment Probability

To avoid unprofessional and hyperbolic assessments like "slam dunk" or "no brainer," analysts need a mechanism that allows them to provide answers to intelligence users in situations where there is not enough raw data to reach proper conclusions. In Chapter 3, we discussed IC efforts to normalize the reporting of assessment analytical uncertainty using the standard as set forth by the Office of the Director of National Intelligence (ODNI). See Table 12.1.

Table 12.1 aids in the standardization of assessment results. Granted, it is not perfect or precise; in point of fact, its variability fluctuates in bell-curve fashion from 5 to 25 percent from one extreme to the other.

In probability theory, the normal distribution is a very common probability distribution (see Figure 12.1). Normal distributions are important in statistics and are often used in the

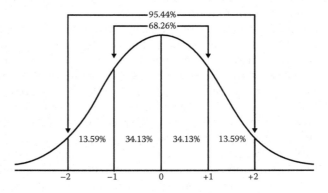

Figure 12.1 Normal distribution, "bell curve."

Table 12.1 ODNI Directive 203, Analytic Standard, Likelihood, or Probability Terminology

Almost No Chance	Very Unlikely	Unlikely	Roughly Even Chance	Likely	Very Likely	Almost Certain
Remote	Highly Improbable	Improbable	Roughly Even Odds	Probable	Highly Probable	Nearly Certain
1–5%	5–20%	20–45%	45–55%	55–80%	80–95%	95–99%

Source: Office of the Director of National Intelligence (ODNI), Intelligence Community Directive #203, Analytic Standards, 2015, http://www.dni.gov/files/documents/ICD/ICD%20203%20Analytic%20Standards.pdf.

natural and social sciences to represent real-valued random variables whose distributions are not known. More on normal distribution calculations and how to use the results will be covered later in the chapter.

Reliability and Credibility of Sources

Analysts do not just use probability to estimate the uncertainty of an assessment. They use probability to estimate the reliability and credibility of collected information that produced the assessment as well. The mechanism used by NATO, most Western Military Intelligence Organizations, and the IC is a 6 × 6 matrix that balances source reliability against the credibility of the information. Known as the NATO system, it has six levels of reliability, each designated by the letters "A" through "F":

- A: Completely reliable
- B: Usually reliable
- C: Fairly reliable
- D: Not usually reliable
- E: Unreliable, and
- F: Reliability cannot be judged

The credibility of the information has six levels as well:

- 1: Confirmed by other sources
- 2: Probably true
- 3: Possibly true
- 4: Doubtful
- 5: Improbable
- 6: Truth cannot be judged

Therefore, if you were to receive a report from a field informant that had a rating of "A-2" it would be reasonable to assess the information to have a high probability (80–95 percent) of being true.

To provide some historical context of how probability is assessed and some insight into the associated problems with the calculation process, let us look at the attack on Pearl Harbor on December 7, 1941. According to diplomatic documents belonging to Joseph Grew, the American ambassador to Japan, discovered sometime after World War II: Grew had received intelligence that Japan was planning to attack Pearl Harbor. Grew received this intelligence from the Peruvian ambassador, who reportedly received it from his chef. The information was dated January 27, 1941, nearly a year before the attack. Ambassador Grew passed this information back to Washington DC, and supposedly Grew's comments referring to the information indicated that he thought the information was unlikely at best.

We use this case as an example where an analyst receiving this information could easily assign a rating of "F-6" to this report based upon the lack of corroborating information and no previous reporting from the source (the Peruvian ambassador's chef) to assess the source's reliability.

SIMPLE INFERENCE

This is the simplest manner of inference using one known, event "A," and one dependent variable, event "B." You can put it in terms of an "if/then" statement, such as, if "A" occurs, then "B" occurs with some estimation of likelihood. Simple inference, or probability, is the likelihood that a specific event will occur, represented by a number between 0 and 1. There are two categories of simple probabilities; Theoretical and experimental. Analysts use both.

Theoretical Probability

Theoretical probability is calculated probability. If every event is equally likely, it is the ratio of the number of ways the event can occur to the total number of possible outcomes. It can be expressed mathematically as

Theoretical probability
$$= \frac{\text{Number of ways to get what you want (or favorable outcomes)}}{\text{Total number of possible outcomes}}$$

Example

There are eight prisoners of war (POWs) with actionable information. Therefore, the number of favorable outcomes equals eight. There is a total of 20 prisoners that were captured in the group. Therefore, the number of total outcomes equals 20.

8/20 = 2/5 In other words, if chosen at random, you have 2/5ths (or 40 percent) chance of interrogating any of the POWs in the group and that POW will have the desired "actionable information" you seek.

The probability of whether a POW has the pertinent (or desired) information is built in the military's interrogation screening process.[1] See Tables 12.2 and Figure 12.2.

Table 12.2   Source Screening Codes

Code	Cooperation level
1	Responds to direct questions.
2	Responds hesitantly to questions.
3	Does not respond to questions.

	Knowledgeability level
A	Very likely to possess PIR information.
B	Might have IR information.
C	Does not appear to have pertinent information.

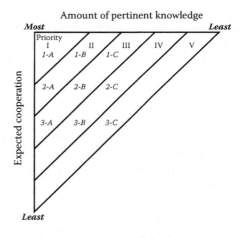

Figure 12.2 Interrogation Priorities by Screening Category.

---

[1] Government Printing Office, U.S. Army, *Field Manual 2-22.3*, Human Collection Operations, Chapter 6, Screening, 2006.

AUTHOR'S NOTES

In Human Collection Operations there is a basic concept involved: Look for information where it is most likely to be found.

An interrogator or a covert operative who spends all of their time interviewing people who have little or no chance of possessing the information pertinent to their mission is wasting their time. Therefore, screening operations are essential to increasing their chances of success.

The example provided is the U.S. Army's process for POW screening operations. By concentrating their efforts on priority "1-A" candidates and utilizing the "1-B" and "2-A" candidates to validate what they learn from the "1-As," they make the most efficient use of their time.

Experimental Probability

Experimental probability is the probability based on data collected from experimentation. It can be expressed mathematically as

$$\text{Experimental probability} = \frac{\text{Number of times the event occurred}}{\text{Total number of outcomes}}$$

Conditional Probability

The concept of conditional probability is one of the most basic, fundamental, and at the same time one of the most important concepts in probability theory. That said, conditional probabilities can also be perfidious and require careful analysis and interpretation.

To explain the concept of conditional probability, let us look at two events: Event "A" and Event "B." If the event of interest is "A" and the event "B" is recognized or expected to have already occurred, "the conditional probability of A given B," or "the probability of A under the circumstance B," is usually written as $P(A|B)$ (in other terms: "Probability" of "A" given that "B" has taken place).

207

CALCULATING RISK OF TERRORIST ATTACK

One would think a straightforward application of the probability concept in terrorism analysis would be to calculate the risk of a potential terrorist attack. The layperson might consider a terror attack as having some level of potential, target susceptibility, and resulting consequences; each of which could be estimated based upon a set of evaluation factors. Experts on risk analysis have put forth the equation of Risk = Consequence × Vulnerability × Threat.[2] Extending this train of thought and laying it out mathematically, Risk of Attack $[P(A)]$ = Consequences $[P(C)]$ × Vulnerability $[P(V)]$ × Threat $[P(T)]$.

The following sections discuss probability calculations of "risk of attack" from both historical and more contemporary perspectives.

Historical Application

Using these risk variables (consequence, vulnerability, and threat), let us look back at the earlier Pearl Harbor example and see how the risk might have been perceived. The potential consequences of losing the U.S. Navy's Pacific fleet were significant. Since Pearl Harbor had a relatively small access channel to the open sea, the Pacific Fleet could easily be bottled up in the harbor. Therefore, the fleet's vulnerability factor was also severe. *So why didn't anyone assess the risk of attack as high?* The logical conclusion is that the "threat" was perceived to be very low.

Naval operational planners at the time correctly pointed out that there were no Japanese-held land-based airfields that could feasibly range Pearl Harbor. Therefore, the only reasonable attack vector remaining was from the sea. Naval analysts would realistically conclude that a significantly large sea-based air strike capability (several carriers and their support auxiliaries) would need to cross thousands of miles of open sea without detection to achieve a successful attack. See Figure 12.3. To assemble and move such a naval force (six carriers, two battleships, three cruisers, nine destroyers, and assorted support vessels and submarines) without detection was considered highly unlikely by most. Unfortunately for the U.S. Navy, that was exactly what Japan planned to do.

---

[2] T. Sandler and H.E. Lapan, The calculus of dissent: An analysis of terrorist's choice of targets. *Synthese*, 76, 245–261, 1988.

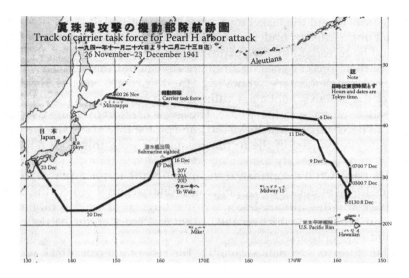

Figure 12.3 Japanese naval taskforce route to and from Pearl Harbor.

A More Contemporary Application

Now to use this type of calculation to estimate terrorist attack risks. Similarly let us start with the first factor, *consequences*. The terrorist likely perceives attacking potential targets (e.g., mass killings, psychological effects, commercial/capital impacts) in terms of their corresponding influence on and beneficial side effects that align with or enhance their strategic and tactical objectives (e.g., increased recruiting, sustained or increased funding). Examples might include attacking and videoing successful attacks on Western military forces to encourage recruitment of terrorist fighters or attacking a high-profile public event or prominent Western landmark to generate funding and mass killings to instill fear. When examining aspects of target selection in relation to a potential benefit to terrorist aims and goals, one can more easily understand why the probability of placing a bomb in an abandoned soccer stadium would not be as likely as the probability for an attack on the stadium hosting the World Cup, especially if the United States or Britain just so happened to be competing. The World Cup is a high-profile event where one could reasonably expect massive press coverage, and the United States and Britain are both well known for their counter-terror efforts.

Vulnerability of the target must then be quantified. It is readily apparent that unguarded or under protected "soft targets" are more desirable to a would-be terrorist. If their purpose is to cause mass killings, the likelihood of their success goes up dramatically should they choose a movie theater or an elementary school (e.g., the Moscow theater terror attack, 2002, or the Beslan school mass killings, 2004) rather than a frontal assault on a police station or military base. The levels of effort for these two types (soft and hard) targets to achieve the same probability of success are vastly disparate on the part of the terror group. However, this does not mean there is zero probability associated with an attack on a police station or military base. On the contrary, if the intent of the terror group is to demonstrate to the masses that the police or military cannot protect the public, the police and the military become prime targets. To see this rationale in action, just look at events over the last several years on the battlefields of Iraq and Afghanistan.

Therefore, to adequately quantify the risk of a terror attack requires cultural knowledge and understanding the motivations, intent, and capabilities of terrorists, in addition to empirical knowledge of historical attack tactics, techniques, and procedures (TTPs), and their relevance to current risks.

Last, we consider the *threat factor* effect on the terror risk equation. Where the vulnerability factor focused on the target/defender, the threat factor focuses on the attacker's capabilities. The premillennial terror threat directed at the U.S. homeland was largely discounted for many of the same reasons the threat on Pearl Harbor was discounted in 1941. The logistics involved to launch a large-scale attack on the continental United States was so significant that most analysts could not conceive of a threat mechanism (barring WMD, e.g., nuclear, chemical, and biological weapons) which could sustain thousands of casualties, and weapons of mass destruction (WMD), in the minds of policy makers and intelligence analysts, required the capabilities of a state sponsor. Similar to events in the wake of the December 7, 1941, attack, the analytical mindset shifted. On 9/11, terrorists, like the Japanese Navy, used creative thinking and "outside the box" meticulous planning and utilized jet airliners as field-expedient WMD to kill thousands. By terrorists co-opting non-weapon items from society and converting them into weapons of mass destruction, calculation of the "threat factor" increased to a markedly higher value.

CRIME PROBABILITIES

Just as intelligence analysis has advanced, likewise, criminal analysis has progressed. Crime scene forensics, recorded media (e.g., audio tape and video), biometrics, DNA analysis, ballistics, and other analytical techniques have revolutionized the court room. Statistical analysis may sway a jury, but solid and irrefutable evidence is the proven way to convict a criminal.

As is the case in the purer forms of intelligence analysis, criminal analysis falls short of perfection and the results must be expressed as a probability. However, that does not imply that probability calculations are without value when it comes to analysis of aggregate crime data or individual crimes. We will look at areas where probability plays significant roles in the solving of crimes and driving law enforcement and criminal justice policy.

Probability in Solving Crime

Can probability solve crimes? The answer is yes. However, usually it is not the only tool used, nor should it be. It is best used to focus the investigation and, when wedded to other pieces of hard evidence, can likely provide a conviction. *So how can probability solve a crime?*

Consider the case of Robert Lee Yates. In Spokane, Washington, in the late 1990s, there existed a serial killer who had eluded police for years and preyed upon prostitutes who worked the skid row area of Spokane. To counter the threat and at a cost of more than $2 million, a taskforce was formed to find the killer. Three years of investigation yielded several similar DNA samples left at the crime scenes, a description of a white male in his 30s or 40s, and reports of a 1977 white Corvette that had been seen in the area after some of the murders. Yates was among hundreds of suspects investigated by a 3 police task force formed recently to investigate the serial killings of 18 prostitutes in the Spokane and Tacoma areas.

Traffic records of a 1977 white Corvette getting a citation in the area produced a name. The name, a DNA test, and some additional questioning ended in the arrest and conviction of Yates for 13 murders dating back to 1990.

At the time of Yates's arrest, he no longer owned the Corvette. The vehicle needed to be located and a search warrant executed to link the vehicle to Jennifer Joseph, a 16-year-old prostitute whose body was found

211

on a farm northeast of Spokane in 1997. The traffic ticket tied Yates to the car and to the area at the time of the murders, but that was circumstantial at best and could easily be discredited in a court of law. The DNA evidence of Jennifer Joseph's blood pushed the probability into "the millions" that this was the vehicle involved in the murder and tipped the scales.

Just as an afterthought, initially police suspected Jennifer Joseph was Yates's first victim. However, according to Yates, Susan Savage, 22, and Patrick Oliver, 21, were his original victims. The couple were picnicking near Walla Walla, Oregon, when Yates chanced upon them in 1975. All of Yates's victims discovered thus far were found within the borders of Oregon and Washington State. He may have been one of those predators who only stalked in familiar hunting grounds. Nevertheless, Yates served in the military for 18 years and was stationed in various military posts in the United States and overseas in Germany, and later, Somalia. According to court documents, Yates hired prostitutes during his two tours in Germany. Based upon his preference for killing prostitutes, there is an argument to be made that there are murder victims in other locations. In light of this information, what is the probability that Yates hunted elsewhere?

Whether there are other victims or not, German police are investigating whether Yates might be involved in the murders of as many as 26 women in that country. Perhaps the "high probability" of association applied to DNA evidence will close some cold cases in other countries and locales.

Probability and Law Enforcement Policy

Probability and statistics not only can be used to identify suspects, support investigations, and obtain convictions, they can also be used to deter criminal behavior.

Data from the National Highway Traffic Safety Administration (NHTSA) repeatedly shows that an estimated 2 million drunk drivers with three or more convictions will be on the America's highways and roads through the holiday season (Thanksgiving to New Year's Day). During this period, approximately 1,500 people nationwide will be killed in crashes that involved a drunk driver.

Based upon a university study of drivers at high risk of driving while impaired or intoxicated, the most important deterrence factors were their perceptions of the likelihood of being stopped or arrested and their support for deterrence laws.[3]

All states have laws on the books to deter impaired driving, but there is little evidence that these laws work to deter high-risk drivers from driving and drinking. However, the study results provide support for the value of high-visibility enforcement campaigns, public safety education, and media efforts. To that end,

December 2014–January 2015
Drive sober or get pulled over alcohol campaign timeline

Figure 12.4 From the NHSTA 2011 pre-holiday campaign.

the NHTSA and law enforcement have pooled efforts and developed annual marketing and enforcement campaigns to deter drinking and driving, particularly during the holiday season. See Figure 12.4.

Probability in Criminal Justice Policy

Next let us look at using probability to shape criminal justice policies and decisions. In the 1990s, in an effort to remove repeat offenders (career criminals) from society, most states adopted what has become known as *three-strike laws*. These laws require three felony convictions and usually one or more of three to be for violent crimes in order to pull the mandatory sentencing trigger.

Crimes that fall under the category of "violent" include: murder, kidnapping, sexual assault, aggravated robbery, and so on. How the three-strike laws are applied varies considerably from state to state, but the laws

---

[3] Emily Smith, MU Professor Recommends Changing Drivers' Perceptions of Law Enforcement to Deter Drinking and Driving, University of Missouri, munews.missouri .edu/news-releases/2008/12-24-Richardson-drinkinganddriving.php.

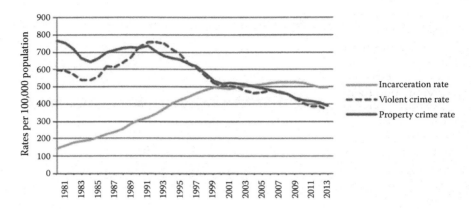

Figure 12.5 Incarceration rates from 1981 to 2013.

generally call for life sentences without possibility of parole for at least 25 years on the third strike.

Some argue that the three-strike rule and other mandatory sentencing laws have led to a steady increase in U.S. incarceration rates. See Figure 12.5.

Coinciding with the rise in incarceration rates, there has been a reduction in violent and property crimes.

Several recent studies argue that increased incarceration rates have some impact on reducing crime rates, but the scope of that impact is limited.[4] See Figure 12.6.

Looking at the precipitous drop in crime between 1992 and 1997, imprisonment was responsible for just 25 percent of that reduction and the remainder was attributable to factors other than incarceration.[5] As a result, pundits contend that incarceration may not be the most effective way to increase public safety.

This presents a developing societal issue in a period of limited funding for new prisons and the ever-rising cost of incarceration. *What are the*

---

[4] William Spelman, What recent studies do (and don't) tell us about imprisonment and crime, *Crime and Justice*, 27 419, 2000.
[5] William Spelman, Jobs or jails? The crime drop in Texas, *Journal of Policy Analysis and Management*, 2000.

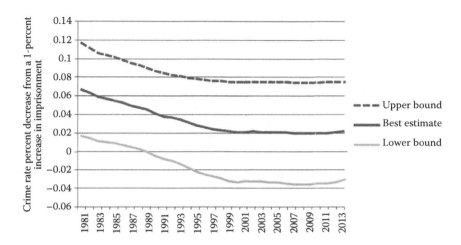

Figure 12.6 Crime percentage decrease from a 1-percent increase in imprisonment.

cost–benefits associated with continued growth in incarceration? Does it prevent considerably fewer, if any, crimes? If so, at what cost to taxpayers?

TOOLS FOR CALCULATING PROBABILITY

Complex events, such as the attack on Pearl Harbor or a hypothetical major terror attack on the homeland, are difficult to assess directly. Breaking the events/attacks down into subparts as demonstrated in the earlier section, Calculating Risk of Terrorist Attack, is useful in estimating overall event probability.[6]

There are several tools available to break events into their component parts. In this chapter we will only discuss two: Event trees (Figure 12.7) and decision trees. Event trees and decision trees are cited by a recent RAND study to be in use at DHS's Office of Intelligence and Analysis to identify and assess current and future threats to the United States. According to the RAND study, the DHS is moving to greater use of risk analysis and risk-based resource allocation, a process that is designed to

---

[6] Barry Charles Ezell, Steven P. Bennett, Detlof von Winterfeldt, John Sokolowski, and Andrew J. Collins, Probabilistic risk analysis and terrorism risk, *Society for Risk Analysis*, Vol. 30, No. 4, 2010.

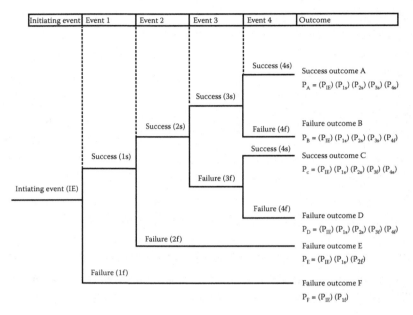

Figure 12.7 Event tree.

manage the greatest risks instead of attempting to protect everything.[7,8] Event and probability (decision) trees can be used to model a sequence of uncertain events in order to estimate event likelihoods.

Event Trees

Event trees use a Boolean logical diagram in which an event is analyzed along a time-driven path of subsequent events or consequences. This methodical segmented analysis provides a visual flow path of events and subsequent potential effects and provides a basis for assessing a terrorism risk. See Figure 12.7.

---

[7] Henry H. Willis, Tom LaTourrette, Terrence K. Kelly, Scot Hickey, and Samuel Neill, *Terrorism Risk Modeling for Intelligence Analysis and Infrastructure Protection*, RAND Corp, 2007.

[8] Barry Charles Ezell, Steven P. Bennett, Detlof von Winterfeldt, John Sokolowski, and Andrew J. Collins, Probabilistic risk analysis and terrorism risk, *Society for Risk Analysis*, Vol. 30, No. 4, 2010.

Probability Trees

The probability tree is also a branched diagram representing multiple sequential events and their associated probability variables. The branches stemming from each node signify the different variables associated with the decision node. Event trees are an extension of probability trees by adding the initiating event, mitigating events, and consequences (or outcomes). Consequences are added for each probability path.[9] Each branch leads to what are called *endpoints*. Each endpoint represents the final result of a path from the root node of the decision tree to that endpoint.

When using a probability tree to perform decision analysis, trees provide a support tool to find and weigh alternatives. In terrorism attack calculations, they allow analysts to better structure arguments graphically by laying out an attacker's actions in the form of a series of perceived decisions with associated probability percentage values for choices and chances of success. See Figure 12.8.

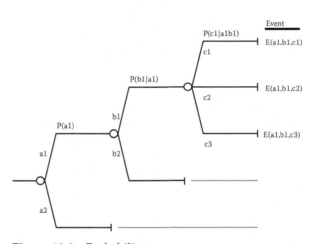

Figure 12.8 Probability tree.

Calculating Probability Distribution/Density Using Excel

As mentioned in the introduction, this chapter is not a higher math course that teaches statistics in extreme detail, but some basic concepts and calculations are necessary to understand collected datasets.

---

[9] Barry Charles Ezell, Steven P. Bennett, Detlof von Winterfeldt, John Sokolowski, and Andrew J. Collins, Probabilistic risk analysis and terrorism risk, *Society for Risk Analysis*, Vol. 30, No. 4, 2010.

POTENTIAL PITFALLS OF PROBABILITY AND STATISTICS AND HOW TO AVOID THEM

Potential Misuses

- Manipulating scale to change the appearance of the distribution of data
- Eliminating high/low data points for more coherent presentation
- Inappropriately focusing on certain variables to the exclusion of other variables
- Presenting correlation as causation

Measures to Avoid the Pitfalls

- Testing results for reliability and validity
- Testing for statistical significance
- Critically reading statistical results

One conceptual method is called *probability distribution*. Probability distribution describes the proportion of a population having a specific range of values (or density) for a specific attribute. Analysts and researchers use the calculation to better visualize and understand datasets. In this section, you will use MS Excel software as an expedient calculation tool to assist in visualizing a global terror dataset.

Statistical Terminology and Concepts

Rarely will one find data spread across populations or geographical areas in a homogenous format. Most datasets will possess values that are near the average (or mean), some have

AUTHOR'S NOTE

There are many spreadsheet and statistical software tools available today and this should not be considered an endorsement of the Microsoft Excel product. However, most college students are at least familiar with Excel, and therefore Excel is considered the best choice to present the information in this section.

amounts that are farther away from the average, and some have amounts exceptionally distant from the average.

The *standard deviation* of a dataset is a measure of the spread (or deviation) of the data from its mean. For the purposes of this discussion we are referring to large datasets (in the hundreds or thousands), not single or double digits. *Normal distributions* usually contain roughly 68 percent of a sample within one standard deviation of the mean and 95 percent within two standard deviations.

The *z value* is the distance between a particular data point and the mean in terms of standard deviations.

Three other terms we need to cover before we start the exercise are mean, mode, and median.

- The mean is the average of the dataset.
- The mode is the number that occurs most often (highest frequency) in the dataset.
- The median is the number in the middle of the dataset.

Normal Distribution

There are several cases where the data tends to collect around a central value with no bias left or right, and it gets close to a normal distribution, as shown in Figure 12.9.

Many things found in nature and made by man closely follow a normal distribution. Examples include the following:

- Zebra stripes
- People's height
- Measurement errors
- Blood pressure
- Test scores
- Financial and sales data

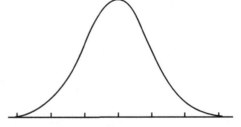

Figure 12.9 The "normal" distribution curve.

Simply stated, data is considered to be "normally distributed" when the data symmetrically clusters around a central data point, 50 percent of values are less than the mean and 50 percent are greater than the mean, and the mean, mode and median are equal.

Normal distributions are important in statistics and probability calculations. It is important to understand whether data is (or is not) normally distributed, because if data is treated as normal when it is not, significant errors can be introduced into your analysis.

Visualizing the Data

Often it is helpful to plot datasets on a chart to better understand the data and the underlying problem, or problems, the dataset represents.

Example

Federal law requires the U.S. Department of State to include in its annual report on terrorism "to the extent practicable, complete statistical information on the number of individuals, including United States citizens and dual nationals, killed, injured, or kidnapped by each terrorist group during the preceding calendar year." As an exercise we will visualize the dataset by calculating the "distribution" using this dataset. See Table 12.3.

As an intelligence analyst you may be tasked to plot the data. As a class exercise, we will plot the underlying dataset which supports the U.S. State Department's report on terrorism worldwide, 2014.

Table 12.3 Terrorism Worldwide 2014

Country	Total Attacks	Total Killed	Total Wounded	Avg. Killed per Attack	Avg. Wounded per Attack
Iraq	3370	9929	15137	3.07	4.79
Pakistan	1821	1757	2837	0.99	1.61
Afghanistan	1591	4505	4699	3.16	3.25
India	763	426	643	0.59	0.9
Nigeria	662	7512	2246	12.8	6.31
Syria	232	1698	1473	8.24	9.32
All Other	5024	6900	7756	1.37	1.12
Totals	13463	32727	34791	2.43	1.06
Averages	68.69	166.97	177.51	0.01	0.01

Source: U.S. Government, State Department, Annex of Information, Country Reports on Terrorism 2014, http://www.state.gov/documents/organization/239628.pdf.

PRACTICAL EXERCISE

The practical exercise is a learning activity designed to assist you in under-standing methods of visualizing data and determining whether a dataset is considered normal. To begin you will need some additional data besides what is in Table 12.3. This data will be provided by the instructor as part of a Practical Exercise—Handout.

AUTHOR'S NOTES

Before you can do most statistical data cal-culations using Excel, you must activate the Excel "Analysis ToolPak" add-in. To do so, perform the following steps:

1. Click on the File tab and choose "Options."
2. When the "Excel Options" dialog box appears, choose "Add-Ins" from the list. Check to ensure "Excel Add-Ins" is displayed in the "Manage" win-dow and click the "Go" button.
3. When an "Add-Ins" dialog box appears, click the check box for "Analysis ToolPak" and then click the "OK" button.

TIPS FOR CALCULATING PROBABILITY USING MS EXCEL

- In most cases, Excel probability functions can replace statis-tical tables. Excel produces values for the probability den-sity function, cumulative probabilities, as well as inverse probability for most common theoretical distributions.
- Be aware that
  - Excel offers minimal help for probability calculations, so if you do not understand the results given by Excel, Excel can lead you astray.
  - Before starting, ensure you comprehend the function being evaluated and its associated limits.

221

CHAPTER SUMMARY

This chapter described what probability is, pointed out its importance to intelligence and crime analysis, and identified some of the more common applications. *Probability estimation* takes some of the guesswork out of assessment and inserts a level of objectivity, reliability, and reproducibility into the intelligence practice that can later be analyzed, explained, repeated, and, if required, adjusted to potentially improve the process.

Some of the math concepts involved in probability and statistical analysis were introduced, as well as the "how" and "why" probability is used in intelligence analysis. Those "how" and "whys" were demonstrated using historical and more recent examples of analytical probability. Lastly, some probability estimation tools reported to be in use at the Department of Homeland Security (DHS) were specifically highlighted.

Analytical Applications to Probability

Analysts use probability estimates to guide intelligence end users in understanding validity and improve confidence in their intelligence products and analytical judgments to include the data and sources used to make those judgments. Using empirical and research datasets, criminologists use probabilities to create criminal profiles.

Assessment Probability

To avoid unprofessional and hyperbolic assessments, analysts need a mechanism that allows them to provide answers to intelligence users in situations where there is not enough raw data to reach proper conclusions. The IC has "normalized" the reporting of assessment analytical uncertainty using the standard as set forth by the Office of the Director of National Intelligence (ODNI). See Table 12.1.

Table 12.1 aids in the standardization of assessment results. Granted, it is not perfect or precise, in point of fact, its variability fluctuates in a bell-curve fashion from 5 to 25 percent from one extreme to the other.

In probability theory, the normal distribution is very common (see Figure 12.1). Normal distributions are important in statistics and are often used in the natural and social sciences to represent real-valued random variables whose distributions are not known.

Reliability and Credibility of Sources

Analysts do not just use probability to estimate the uncertainty of an assessment. They use probability to estimate the reliability and credibility of collected information that produced the assessment as well. The mechanism used by NATO, most Western Military Intelligence Organizations, and the IC is a 6 × 6 matrix that balances source "reliability" against the "credibility" of the information.

Simple Inference

This is the simplest manner of inference using one known, event "A," and one dependent variable, event "B." You can put it in terms of an "if/then" statement, such as, if "A" occurs, then "B" occurs with some estimation of likelihood. Simple inference, or probability, is the likelihood that a specific event will occur, represented by a number between 0 and 1. There are two categories of simple probabilities: Theoretical and experimental. Analysts use both.

Theoretical Probability

Theoretical probability is calculated probability. If every event is equally likely, it is the ratio of the number of ways the event can occur to the total number of possible outcomes. It can be expressed mathematically as

$$\text{Theoretical probability} = \frac{\text{Number of ways to get want you want (or favorable outcomes)}}{\text{Total number of possible outcomes}}$$

Experimental Probability

Experimental probability is the probability based on data collected from experimentation. It can be expressed mathematically as

$$\text{Experimental probability} = \frac{\text{Number of times the event occured}}{\text{Total number outcomes}}$$

Conditional Probability

The concept of conditional probability is one of the most basic and fundamental and at the same time one of the most important concepts in probability theory. That said, conditional probabilities can also be perfidious and require careful analysis and interpretation.

Calculating Risk of Terrorist Attack

Experts on risk analysis have put forth the equation of Risk = Consequence × Vulnerability × Threat.[10] Extending this train of thought and laying it out mathematically, Risk of Attack [P(A)] = Consequences [P(C)] × Vulnerability [P(V)] × Threat [P(T)].

Historical Application
Using these variables (consequence, vulnerability, and threat), let us look back at the earlier Pearl Harbor example and see how the "risk" might have been perceived. The consequences of possibly losing the U.S. Navy's Pacific fleet were significant, and the vulnerability factor was also severe. However, the "threat" was perceived to be very low, because naval analysts could not recognize that a significantly large sea-based air strike capability (several carriers and their support auxiliaries) would be able to cross thousands of miles of open sea without detection to achieve a successful attack.

A More Contemporary Application
Estimating risk of terrorist attack starts similarly with the first factor, consequences. The terrorist likely perceives attacking potential targets (e.g., mass killings, psychological effects, commercial/capital impacts) in terms of their corresponding influence on and beneficial side effects which align with or enhance their strategic and tactical objectives (e.g., increased recruiting, sustained or increased funding).

The next factor, vulnerability of the target, must then be quantified. It is readily apparent that unguarded or under-protected "soft targets" are more desirable to a would-be terrorist. If their purpose is to cause mass killings, the likelihood of their success goes up dramatically should they choose a movie theater or an elementary school rather than a frontal assault on a police station or military base. The levels of effort for these two types (soft and hard) targets to achieve the same probability of success are vastly disparate on the part of the terror group. However, this does not mean there is zero probability associated

---

[10] T. Sandler and H.E. Lapan, The calculus of dissent: An analysis of terrorist's choice of targets. *Synthese*, 76, 245–261, 1988.

with an attack on a police station or military base. On the contrary, if the intent of the terror group is to demonstrate to the masses that the police or military cannot protect the public, the police and the military become prime targets.

Therefore, to adequately quantify the risk of a terror attack requires cultural knowledge and understanding the motivations, intent, and capabilities of terrorists, in addition to empirical knowledge of historical attack tactics, techniques, and procedures (TTPs), and their relevance to current risks.

Lastly, we look at the threat factor's effect on the terror risk equation. Terrorists co-opting non-weapon items from society and converting them into weapons of mass destruction, calculation of the "threat factor" has increased to a markedly higher value.

Crime Probabilities

Crime scene forensics, recorded media (e.g., audio tape and video), biometrics, DNA analysis, ballistics, and other analytical techniques have revolutionized the court room. Probability plays significant roles in the solving of crimes and driving law enforcement and criminal justice policy.

Probability in Solving Crime

Probability can be used to solve crimes. However, usually it is not the only tool used. It is best used to focus the investigation and, wedded to other pieces of hard evidence, can likely provide a conviction.

The DNA evidence of Jennifer Joseph's blood pushed the probability into "the millions" that the white Corvette was indeed the vehicle involved in the murder and tipped the scales.

Probability and Law Enforcement Policy

Probability and statistics not only can be used to identify suspects, support investigations, and obtain convictions, they can also be used to deter criminal behavior.

Data from the National Highway Traffic Safety Administration (NHTSA) repeatedly shows that an estimated 2 million drunk drivers with three or more convictions will be on the America's highways and roads through the holiday season (Thanksgiving to New Year's Day).

Based upon a university study of drivers at high risk of driving while impaired or intoxicated, the most important deterrence factors were their perceptions of the likelihood of being stopped or arrested and their support for deterrence laws.[11]

The study results provide support for the value of high-visibility enforcement campaigns, public safety education, and media efforts. To that end, the NHTSA and law enforcement have pooled efforts and developed annual marketing and enforcement campaigns to deter drinking and driving, particularly during the holiday season.

Probability in Criminal Justice Policy

Probability is also used to shape criminal justice policies and decisions. This section looked at statistical studies of repeat offender laws adopted by most states known as *three-strike laws*. These laws require three felony convictions and usually one or more of three to be for violent crimes in order to pull the mandatory sentencing trigger.

Several recent studies argue that increased incarceration rates have some impact on reducing crime rates, but the scope of that impact is limited.[12] Students are asked to ponder the cost–benefits associated with continued growth in incarceration. *Does it prevent considerably fewer, if any, crimes? If so, at what cost to taxpayers?*

Tools for Calculating Probability

Complex events are difficult to assess directly. Breaking the events/attacks down into subparts, as demonstrated in an earlier section, is useful in estimating overall event probability.

There are several tools available to break events into their component parts. In this chapter we only discussed two—event trees and decision trees. Event trees and decision trees are cited by a recent RAND study to be in use at DHS's Office of Intelligence and Analysis to identify and assess current and future threats to the United States. According to the RAND study, the DHS is moving to greater use of risk analysis and risk-based resource allocation, a process that is designed to manage the

---

[11] Emily Smith, *MU Professor Recommends Changing Drivers' Perceptions of Law Enforcement to Deter Drinking and Driving*, University of Missouri, munews.missouri.edu/news -releases/2008/12-24-Richardson-drinkinganddriving.php.

[12] William Spelman, What recent studies do (and don't) tell us about imprisonment and crime, *Crime and Justice*, 27, 419, 2000.

greatest risks instead of attempting to protect everything.[13,14] Event and probability trees can be used to model a sequence of uncertain events in order to estimate event likelihoods.

Event Trees
Event trees use a Boolean logical diagram in which an event is analyzed along a time-driven path of subsequent events or consequences. This methodical segmented analysis provides a visual flow path of events and subsequent potential effects, and provides a basis for assessing terrorism risk.

Probability Trees
The probability tree is a branched diagram representing multiple sequential events and their associated probability variables. When using a probability tree to perform decision analysis, trees provide a support tool to find and weigh alternatives.

Calculating Probability Distribution/Density Using Excel
One conceptual method is called *probability distribution*. Probability distribution describes the proportion of a population having a specific range of values (or density) for a specific attribute. Analysts and researchers use the calculation to better visualize and understand datasets. The book covers use of MS Excel software as an expedient calculation tool to assist in visualizing a global terror dataset.

Statistical terminology and concepts were introduced. Normal distribution curve, standard deviation, Z values, mean, mode, and median were among the terminology discussed.

The normal distribution curve was explained, and how it is used to calculate probabilities of things found in nature and made by man, the normal distribution's significance to statistics and probability calculations, as well as understanding whether data is (or is not) normally distributed.

---

[13] Henry H. Willis, Tom LaTourrette, Terrence K. Kelly, Scot Hickey, and Samuel Neill, *Terrorism Risk Modeling for Intelligence Analysis and Infrastructure Protection*, RAND Corp, 2007.

[14] Barry Charles Ezell, Steven P. Bennett, Detlof von Winterfeldt, John Sokolowski, and Andrew J. Collins, Probabilistic risk analysis and terrorism risk, *Society for Risk Analysis*, Vol. 30, No. 4, 2010.

13

Creating an Analytical Plan

INTRODUCTION

Effective intelligence on an adversary's operations, movements, or plans rarely just happens. Unless the adversary is extremely careless, inept, or has a nefarious reason for wanting his or her enemies to have the information, effective intelligence must be developed. Developing and executing an analytical plan to provide needed intelligence is far superior to hoping for a situation where you are fortunate enough to have a careless or inept opponent.

This chapter begins with a discussion of the various areas of analysis and then identifies the starting point, milestones/steps in the analysis process, and the desired outcomes associated with creating an analytical plan. Each step of creating an analytical plan is broken into supporting activities, resources required, the schedule development process, and the actual production of a written analytical production plan.

From an intelligence perspective, analysis is a process by which an item (e.g., weapon, communications equipment, vehicle), entity (key political/military leader, terrorist), or organization (criminal cartel, army, terror network, supply system) is separated or broken into parts for individual study. The sum of the constituent parts or the relationship between parts can also be studied. Intelligence analysis delves into the operation, interrelationships, and linkage between parts, which are carefully examined to better understand their functions, strengths, and weaknesses. What aspects are analyzed and to what extent; the resources and processes to be used; and the order, schedule, and priorities involved all should be addressed in the analytical plan. It all begins with an initial appraisal.

During the discussion of this topic, we will use a common (perhaps oversimplified) analogy to explain how to create an analytical plan. The analogy is "making a shopping list." As we go through the steps, you'll notice the striking similarities, or perhaps you may think, "I did not think that making a shopping list was this complicated." In either case, the analogy will aid in your understanding of the subject matter.

The process begins with a tasking. The task may be to find a terrorist, bring down a criminal cartel, crush an insurgency, or some combination thereof. For our "shopping list" we will choose two tasks. One is immediate in nature—getting a few items for a dinner party—and one is more long-term—stocking the family's isolated mountain cabin with winter supplies and provisions for an extended winter vacation.

INITIAL APPRAISAL

There are many analytical disciplines (e.g., HUMINT, SIGINT, IMINT) and a given analytical product may contain one or any combination of these disciplines. Although the collection, processing, exploitation, and analysis subtasks of each discipline may differ, the major steps of the overall analytical planning process do not.

So, to start the process, a basic review is performed to conduct an inventory of sorts to identify and validate what is known. This review also determines the "unknowns" or intelligence gaps.

For our purposes, the task requirement(s) has already been defined and comes down through organizational channels.

This initial appraisal may seem to be a simple process, but appearances are deceiving. If the initial appraisal is not performed, or if it is completed improperly, or not revisited periodically, the results can be catastrophic.

To illustrate the point, we look to before December 7th, 1941. At this time, Japanese

Figure 13.1 U.S. fleet dispositions at Pearl Harbor.

230

Intelligence possessed a large body of fairly accurate information regarding U.S. military strength and disposition in the Pacific theater. See Figure 13.1.[1] Despite a fundamental understanding that the American industrial base was conservatively 10 times larger than Japan's, Japanese intelligence assessed that once the Pacific fleet stationed in Pearl Harbor was removed from the picture, America would be unable to respond militarily in the Pacific and, faced with this fact, would immediately sue for peace. Various factors contributed to this inaccurate perception of the American public's likely response and the U.S. military's strategic ability to expeditiously recover from the significant setback of essentially losing the entire U.S. Pacific fleet.

First, we review Japanese naval history. The Japanese navy's battle history demonstrated the possibility for success of the Pearl Harbor attack plan. In 1905, the Japanese destroyed two-thirds of the Russian Imperial fleet. The decisive destruction of the Russian navy caused an immediate hostile reaction from the Russian people, which prompted a peace treaty shortly after without any further conflict. This pivotal victory over a seemingly much larger and stronger nation had no doubt been engrained in the minds of every officer on the Japanese military general staff.

Next, let us examine the "limited" nature of the information the Japanese had in reference to U.S. military capabilities prior to World War II. At the conclusion of the war, Japan General Staff Office Operations Bureau member, former Captain Shinobu Takayama recollected the following:

> As one responsible for operations, I should have more thoroughly investigated the situation regarding the U.S. and Great Britain, and of the U.S. in particular. I should have respected the opinions of the individuals in charge of U.S. and British intelligence within the General Staff office, as well as Japanese officers resident in other places such as those, and other, neutral countries.[2]

Japanese intelligence utilized the American news media to collect open source information about the U.S. military and assess the mood and morale of the American public. Several contemporary pieces of open source information may have contributed to Japanese intelligence's

---

[1] U.S. National Archives, U.S. Naval Fleet Chart Found in a Downed Japanese Aircraft, December 7th, 1941.
[2] Shinobu Takayama, Sanbo Honbu Sakusenka, General Staff Office Operations Bureau, Fuyo Shobo, 1985.

inaccurate assessment of American military status and recuperative abilities.[3]

In the 1930s, the United States Navy and Army were seriously under-funded, which left them equipment-deprived to a great extent. This predica-ment would result in the United States entering the Pacific War with a large number of obsolete war-ships, only six front-line aircraft carriers to deploy in the Pacific and Atlantic, and a large number of obsoles-cent military aircraft.

Figure 13.2 Excerpts from pre–World War II news reels.

U.S. news reels of military training exercises depicted a poorly prepared U.S. Army. See Figure 13.2.

There was no U.S. military draft, and in 1940, the combined total strength of all U.S. military forces was 458,365 personnel.[4] Whereas, dur-ing the same timeframe, the Imperial Japanese Army alone numbered more than three times that number. During the 1930s, America had entered a period of isolationism that exhibited a marked unwillingness to be involved in foreign issues that did not directly affect American national interests.

History demonstrates that these data points were readily accessible to the general public via multiple newspapers and other open media sources and therefore, likely influenced the Japanese assessment. Had the Japanese exer-cised due diligence and vetted and discounted some of these misperceptions, they perhaps would have chosen another course of action.

Using the "shopping list" analogy, suppose you went off to the store without first looking in the cupboard to see what you are out of or what

---

[3] Kotani Ken, Japanese Military Intelligence: "Why Is Intelligence Not Used?", Tokyo: Kodansha, 2007.

[4] US World War II Museum, New Orleans, US Forces by the Numbers, (http://www .nationalww2museum.org/learn/education/for-students/ww2-history/ww2-by-the -numbers/us-military.html), 2016.

items you already have. You may end up buying unneeded items or not getting essential supplies. The results could be a failed dinner party, or your family gets snowed in and starves, or both.

PRACTICAL EXERCISE

This learning activity illustrates to the student the need for vetting the so-called "knowns."

Exercise Scenario

For this exercise, let us assume that you are an intelligence analyst working for the Department of Homeland Security (DHS). As a DHS intelligence analyst, you have been given the task of identifying and locating terror threats to the United States and its citizens. More specifically, you have been tasked to locate a known terrorist reported to be traveling to America in order to carry out an attack on a high-profile target. Your initial database pull found the following pieces of related information.

(**Note:** All items in this exercise scenario are fictitious. Any resemblance to real people, living or dead, is unintended.)

Subject Name: Abdul Rajid Raffman

- AKA: "A J" Raffman
- Age: 34
- Height: 5'10"/178 cm
- Weight: Approximately 200 lbs/ 91 kgs
- Eye Color: Brown
- Complexion: Dark skin with severe acne scarring
- Hair Color: Dark brown
- Build: Average
- Scars: Missing two fingers from right hand, index and thumb.
- DNA and fingerprints on file.
- Nationality: French
- Photo(s): No photo available

Background Information: Raffman, Abdul Rajid, is a known international terrorist and bomb maker. Wanted in France, Germany, Jordan, Israel, Iraq, and Saudi Arabia. Born in France to naturalized Iraqi parents. Speaks Arabic and French fluently, understands and speaks marginal English and German. Has some technical training in residential electrical wiring. Worked as an electrician's apprentice for two years in Paris, France. Reportedly travelled to Iraq and radicalized in 2004. Originally linked to Al Qaida in 2004–06 and associated with several IED attacks in Iraq against Iraqi Army and Coalition Forces. Since September 2007, Raffman is known to be offering his services to the highest bidder without regard to ideological or religious affiliation. Reportedly lost two fingers from right hand due to bomb-making accident in or around June 2007. Raffman usually travels alone and prefers not to fly, has difficulty driving (reason unknown), and there is no known record of him ever having a driver's license.

Using the information provided, run data mining routines on multiple intelligence and law enforcement databases. Most information matches what you have on file; however, there are discrepancies.

Your database search results are as follows:

- Height: 6'/183 cm
- Eye Color: Blue
- Eye Color: Sandy brown
- Inconsistent reporting of missing fingers on right hand.

New Information:

- Other aliases include: "Raffles"; "Raj"
- Last known location/ date: Tripoli, Libya,

AUTHOR'S NOTES:

Some analysts would argue that there is little need for SIRs, because everybody already knows what to look for. However, this is rarely the case.

The police patrolman and the common foot soldier often do not have the same understanding of the PIR that the analyst possesses.

Look at the PIR example provided: "Report all evidence of improvised explosive devices (IEDs) in the operational area." Now ask yourself, if you were the "guy on the ground" wouldn't you prefer the SIR: "Report all evidence of IEDs in and around OBJ Mike, especially any areas of upturned earth, suspicious packages, suspicious debris in roadway, or loose wires sticking out of ground" rather than the PIR used in the example? Doesn't the SIR more clearly define exactly what you are looking for?

234

one week ago (Source: Confidential Informant, known to have periodic contact with subject and to have reported reliably in the past)

Make an "initial appraisal" of the information provided and take some time to discuss what may have caused these database discrepancies.

IDENTIFYING AND PRIORITIZING THE INTELLIGENCE GAPS

Once the "knowns" are vetted to an acceptable level, the intelligence gaps are listed and prioritized. This is necessary because all information is not equal and rarely are there adequate analysis and collection resources available to thoroughly investigate all the gaps identified. Analysts refer to these as priority intelligence requirements (PIRs). The United States Department of Defense (DoD) defines a PIR as an intelligence requirement, stated as a priority for intelligence support, that the commander and staff need to understand the adversary or the environment.[5]

There are no one hard-and-fast rules for generating PIRs. PIRs and the supporting specific information requirements (SIRs) are based upon the needs of the intelligence consumer. Each PIR generates multiple SIRs. SIRs contain the information required to answer all or part of an intelligence requirement. For example, the PIR: "Report all evidence of improvised explosive devices (IEDs) in the operational area" would generate the SIR: "Report all evidence of IEDs in and around OBJ Mike, especially any areas of upturned earth, suspicious packages, suspicious debris in roadway, or loose wires sticking out of ground."

In the military (division and below), PIRS are generally tied to the tactical mission/objective and analysts work with commanders to determine what the PIRs should be. Above division (corps/theater-level), PIRs become more strategic in nature.

Commanders/leaders (e.g., military, law enforcement, government):

- Focus on capabilities and intentions of adversaries (e.g., enemy combatants, criminal, rogue states)
- Analyze the operational environment (e.g., battlefield, areas of jurisdiction, sovereign borders)

---

[5] U.S. DoD Joint Publication 3-0, Joint Operations, 2006.

- Identify adversary centers of gravity and critical vulnerabilities (e.g., lines of communication, threat finance, populace motivators)
- Monitor events in the joint force commander's area of interest (e.g., enemy activities, criminal activities, rogue state activities)
- Support the planning and conduct of campaigns (e.g., invasion of enemy homeland, disruption/destruction of a criminal cartel, destabilize/overthrow of rogue state)

Determining and prioritizing the type and level of intelligence resources helps collectors to better schedule and allocate limited resources. Intelligence staffs use intelligence requirements as a basis for formulating statements of intelligence interest to the IC, justifying tasking of national collection resources, and justifying requests for intelligence capabilities.

Intelligence analysts review existing databases for potential answers to intelligence and information requirements. If the intelligence does not already exist, the requestor issues a request for information (RFI). An RFI is a specific time-sensitive informal requirement for information or intelligence products, distinct from other more standardized requirements or scheduled intelligence production. An RFI can lead to a production requirement. If possible, the request should be answered with information on hand. If the requested information is unavailable, outdated, in doubt, or somehow considered unreliable, it can generate a collection requirement. Projected production requirements are normally expressed in the form of analytic tasks and subtasks.

> **TIPS FOR "PRIORITIZING INTELLIGENCE GAPS"**
>
> - **Do an initial assessment of "knowns" first**
> - **List all of your intelligence gaps and place them in a matrix (as shown in the example)**
> - **Identify if there are both tactical and strategic considerations to account for**
> - **Justify each intelligence gap and place the justification adjacent to the intelligence gap it is justifying**
> - **Adjust priorities accordingly (most important first)**

Revisiting our "shopping list" analogy, try looking at the "dinner party" as a tactical requirement and "stocking up the mountain cabin" as a more strategic requirement. In this analogy, you have the benefit of being the analyst as well as one of the intelligence consumers. However, there are other consumers whose needs you want to consider. For the dinner party, your spouse and other guests might provide input to shape your collection plan. Perhaps your guests previously showered you with compliments for the ribeye steaks you prepared. For the mountain cabin analogy, your spouse, other family members, or anyone else who may share the cabin with you may provide input. When considering intelligence priorities for the mountain cabin, be aware that one of your children suffers from diabetes and there is no hard line telephone or cell phone coverage at the cabin. Based upon the scenario information provided, review and consider the analysis plan entries listed in Table 13.1.

Items to note in regards to Table 13.1:

- All items are based upon needs of the consumer(s)
- More critical items have higher priority
- Answers to higher-priority intelligence gaps often effect lower-priority items, sometimes reducing or negating their importance
- Strategic items tend to have greater importance/significance and have to be considered over time periods farther into the future

DEVELOPING THE COLLECTION PLAN

Any collection requirements generated should have supporting SIRs created to allow the allocation of the appropriate collection capabilities to satisfy them. If the requestor (usually the analyst) does not provide SIRs, the collection manager should consult with the requestor to determine the indicators of activity against which to focus collection capabilities so that appropriate SIRs can be developed.[6]

For more information, the various aspects of collection planning were covered in far greater detail in Chapter 9.

---

[6] U.S. DoD Joint Publication 2-0, Joint Intelligence, 2013.

Table 13.1 Prioritizing Intelligence Gaps

		Shopping List Analysis Plan		
Intel Gap Priority	Dinner Party (Tactical)	Justification	Stocking the Mountain Cabin (Strategic)	Justification
1.	Ask butcher where you intend to purchase steaks, determine cost/availability	• Potentially most expensive item (limited funds) • Critical item for success of dinner party, based upon guest's past compliments • Steaks may not be in stock	Request 90-day prescription for child's medical condition	• If drugs unattainable, trip may too risky • <90 day supply may affect length of trip
2.	Ask guests/spouse about menu items	• Individual tastes may have changed • Guests may have started diet • Information from item #1 may affect menu	Research renting, purchasing, or borrowing a satellite phone	• If snowed in, satellite phone would provide way to call for help
3.	Ask guests/spouse about dinner entertainment	• Is simple dinner conversation more desirable? • Would spouse/guests be more interested in table games or other party games?	Calculate cost of purchasing large quantities of non-perishable food stuffs	• Food will not go bad if you lose power • Enough to get through winter, if snowed in

Allocating Resources and Schedule Development

Often, significant effort is put into the collection planning aspects of the intelligence cycle, however, planners generally provide little consideration to the allocation and scheduling of analytical resources as the information is collected. Generally, resources are assigned ad hoc as the information trickles in from information sources and collection platforms.

The processing/exploitation, analysis, and production aspects of the intelligence cycle also require careful planning. Recognize that collection assets can fail or are routinely delayed, priorities are changed, and assets miss their collection windows/opportunities and have to be rescheduled; therefore, flexibility in the planning process is imperative.

Processing and Exploitation

A significant percentage of U.S. intelligence resources is devoted to processing and exploitation of raw data into usable form for intelligence analysis. Processing and exploitation can take the form of decoding messages, translating foreign media, interpreting imagery, manipulating data from one computer language to another for processing, storage and retrieval—the list goes on and on. Each process takes time and resources which must be accounted for in the planning process.

Collected, processed, and exploited information is fed via secure, and to varying degrees, classified computer networks, to intelligence analysts from all sources related to their assigned areas. To aid the planning process, if not already available, a step-by-step work breakdown should be performed and time intervals required for the processing and exploitation steps need to collected (and updated periodically) for each type of intelligence (e.g., SIGINT, IMINT, ELINT). Additionally, these collection and processing times need to be adjusted for data volume and who is doing the processing/exploitation. This information should then be tabulated and put into a project management format or a work breakdown structure (WBS) either by hand or using software. By going through these steps, one can better predict when the processed/exploited information will arrive for analysis.

239

Analysis Phase

In the IC and law enforcement, intelligence analysts are generally assigned to a particular geographic or functional specialty (e.g., Southwest Asia, Counter-Terrorism, Counter-Narcotics). Most intelligence organizations do not allow analysts to work alone. The more established and better funded organizations utilize an analytical grouping practice of peer review and oversight by more senior analysts.

Intelligence planners should use their familiarity with these analytical groups or teams and their understanding of the expected availability of information submitted for collection to make appropriate tasking decisions based upon analytical skill sets and combined experience of the group.

Allocating Resources and Schedule Development Example

(**Note:** All items in this exercise scenario are fictitious. Any resemblance to real people, living or dead, is unintended.)

> You have a tasking to determine if a particular criminal cartel (the Durango Drug Cartel) is acquiring/purchasing the bomb-making skills of a terror group (the Kraznovian Liberation Army or KLA) in order to wage war on a rival criminal organization. In your organization there is an SIGINT analytical team with generic regional expertise for the subject area, an all-source team with significant improvised explosive device (IED) experience, a (HUMINT-based) team with subject matter expertise on the terror group, and another (open source) team with expertise with criminal cartels in the region.
>
> Collection requests were submitted to fill the following intelligence gaps:
>
> - Who are the bomb makers associated with the KLA? (HUMINT) What are their skill sets? (HUMINT and SIGINT) Have any of them come into the country? (HUMINT, SIGINT, and database search) Of the bomb makers identified, do any have known contacts in the region? (Police/government database search and HUMINT) What are their names/locations? (Open source and police/government database search)

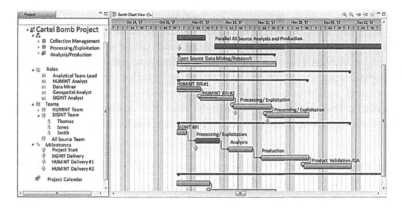

Figure 13.3 Cartel bomb project.

- Which criminal cartels is the Durango Drug Cartel feuding with? (open source and HUMINT) What is the status of the feud(s)? (open source and HUMINT)
- Have bombs/IEDs been used by the Durango Drug Cartel in the past? (open source and police/government database search) When? Where? What type(s)? (open source and police/government database search)

The application of project management principles has been advocated for in the open press for more than ten years.[7] However, the practice is not widespread in the IC. Referring to the project management chart depicted in Figure 13.3, notice how basic project management mechanisms can be used to streamline the analysis production cycle.

Breaking the intelligence production process steps down into component parts and knowing (or at least estimating) the performance periods for each step creates a work breakdown structure (WBS). Using the WBS and inputting the project data into an off-the-shelf project management application allows for a much more efficient use of analysis and production resources.

The Gantt chart for the Cartel Bomb Project example demonstrates how the allocation and scheduling of intelligence resources might appear. Be aware, like any other non-intelligence project, no project plan is perfect and schedules must be regularly monitored and adjusted to reflect unforeseen changes.

---

[7] Jerry H. Ratcliffe, *Strategic Thinking in Criminal Intelligence,* Federation Press, 2009.

241

Referring to our "shopping list" analogy for analysis planning, consider that the shopping list was our list of RFIs and the various trips to the supermarket, sporting goods store, and other specialty shops to get food and supplies was the intelligence collection process. As the groceries and supplies are brought in they must be handled, put away, stored, and refrigerated until needed (intelligence processing/exploitation).

Finally, the dinner party is held and the mountain cabin vacation takes place (analytic production and dissemination).

AUTHOR'S NOTES

The adoption of project management tools in analysis production in the IC is spotty at best and the Cartel Bomb Chart displayed in the text is completely notional.

I am not advocating the creation of a project management file for all intelligence production. I concede that answering simple RFIs would amount to gross overplanning. However, I have used project management processes and software in several of my more-complex intelligence production efforts and I have encountered resistance from peers and other intelligence professionals for using project management tools. To date, no one has voiced a valid reason not to adopt the practice for the more resource intensive efforts other than "it is not the way I was taught." That said, an objective observer can easily see how judicial usage of project management techniques can facilitate the allocation and usage of resources more efficiently.

Besides the more obvious efficiency benefits of using project management tools, the collection of cost–project data would aid in better intelligence budget forecasting for the IC.

PRODUCTION AND DISSEMINATION

Once the analysis is completed, it must be reviewed and vetted. In simple terms, it is reviewed for completeness and accuracy by answering the questions: "Did it answer the original question asked (RFI) and is the answer correct?"

Besides completeness and accuracy, the results of analysis should be compared to previous results and the analysis of other outside groups. This vetting is not done to mimic others in the IC or participate in some form of groupthink; rather it is to ensure nothing major was overlooked or misinterpreted. If major discrepancies exist, new questions should be asked and satisfactorily resolved to ensure the conflicting intelligence results are erroneous and not your own.

Time and resources for this analytical product review and vetting step must also be allotted and planned for. Once your team is satisfied with the product review and vetting step. The final product is disseminated to the intelligence consumer in a format that best communicates the requested information.

TIPS ON ANALYTICAL PLANNING

- Use the "shopping list" approach to visualize the planning process until the intelligence planning steps become more routine
- Use the "intelligence production cycle" to provide your overall major process planning steps
- Break down each major step into discrete subtasks for planning purposes and allocate time and resources to each subtask
- Use project management techniques for more complex intelligence production efforts

CHAPTER SUMMARY

Chapter 13 began with a discussion of the various analytical disciplines and then identified the starting point, milestones/steps in the analysis process, and the desired outcomes associated with creating an analytical plan. Each step of creating an analytical plan was broken into supporting activities, resources required, the schedule development process, and the actual production of a written analytical production plan.

What aspects are analyzed, to what extent, what resources and processes are to be used, the order, and the schedule and priorities involved should be addressed in the analytical plan—and it all begins with an initial appraisal.

A "shopping list" analogy was introduced to assist you in visualizing the steps involved in analytical planning. For the "shopping list" you were given two tasks: One is immediate in nature—getting a few items for a dinner party—and one more long-term—stocking the family's isolated mountain cabin with winter supplies and provisions for an extended winter vacation.

Initial Appraisal

To start the process of analytical planning, a basic review is performed to conduct an inventory of sorts to identify and validate what is known. This review also determines the "unknowns" or intelligence gaps.

This initial appraisal may seem to be a simple process, but appearances are deceiving. If the initial appraisal is not performed, completed improperly, or not revisited periodically, the results can be catastrophic.

Identifying and Prioritizing the Intelligence Gaps

Once the "knowns" are vetted to an acceptable level, the intelligence gaps are listed and prioritized. This is necessary because all information is not equal and rarely are there adequate analysis and collection resources available to thoroughly investigate all the gaps identified. Analysts refer to these as *priority intelligence requirements*. The United States Department of Defense (DoD) defines a priority intelligence requirement (PIR) as an intelligence requirement, stated as a priority for intelligence support, that the commander and staff need to understand the adversary or the environment.[8]

There is no one hard-and-fast thumb-rule for the creation of PIRs. PIRs and the supporting specific information requirements (SIRs) are based upon the needs of the intelligence consumer. Each PIR generates multiple SIRs. SIRs contain the information required to answer all or part of an intelligence requirement. For example, the PIR: "Report all evidence of improvised explosive devices (IEDs) in the operational area" would generate the SIR: "Report all evidence of IEDs in and around OBJ Mike, especially any areas of upturned earth, suspicious packages, suspicious debris in roadway, or loose wires sticking out of ground."

Use the Tips for Prioritizing Intelligence Gaps to assist in the prioritization process.

Determining and prioritizing the type and level of intelligence resources helps collectors to better schedule and allocate limited resources. Intelligence staffs use intelligence requirements as a basis for formulating statements of intelligence interest to the IC, justifying tasking of national collection resources, and justifying requests for intelligence capabilities.

---

[8] US DoD Joint Publication 3-0, Joint Operations, 2006.

Developing the Collection Plan

Any collection requirements generated should have supporting SIRs created for to allow the allocation of the appropriate collection capabilities to satisfy them. If the requestor (usually the analyst) does not provide SIRs, the collection manager should consult with the requestor to determine the indicators of activity against which to focus collection capabilities so that appropriate SIRs can be developed.[9]

For more information, the various aspects of collection planning were covered in far greater detail in Chapter 9.

TIPS FOR "PRIORITIZING INTELLIGENCE GAPS"

- **Do an initial assessment of "knowns" first**
- **List all of your intelligence gaps place them in matrix (as shown in the example)**
- **Identify if there are both tactical and strategic considerations to account for**
- **Justify each intelligence gap and place the justification adjacent to the intelligence gap it is justifying**
- **Adjust priorities accordingly (most important first)**

Allocating Resources and Schedule Development

Often significant effort is put into the collection planning aspects of the intelligence cycle. However, planners generally provide little consideration to the allocation and scheduling of analytical resources as the information is collected. Generally resources are assigned ad hoc as the information trickles in from information sources and collection platforms.

Processing and Exploitation

A significant percentage of U.S. intelligence resources is devoted to processing and exploitation of raw data into usable form for intelligence analysis. Processing and exploitation can take the form of decoding messages; translating foreign media; interpreting imagery; manipulating data from one computer language to another for processing, storage, and

---

[9] U.S. DoD Joint Publication 2-0, Joint Intelligence, 2013.

retrieval—the list goes on and on. Each process takes time and resources which must be accounted for in the planning process.

Analysis Phase

In the IC and law enforcement, intelligence analysts are generally assigned to a particular geographic or functional specialty (e.g., Southwest Asia, Counter-Terrorism, Counter-Narcotics). Most intelligence organizations do not allow analysts to work alone. The more established and better funded organizations utilize an analytical grouping practice of peer review and oversight by more senior analysts.

Intelligence planners would use their familiarity with these analytical groups or teams and their understanding of the expected availability of information submitted for collection to make appropriate tasking decisions based upon analytical skill set and combined experience of the group.

Production and Dissemination

Once the analysis is completed, it must be reviewed and vetted. In simplistic terms it is reviewed for completeness and accuracy by answering these two questions: "Did it answer the original question asked (RFI) and is the answer correct?"

Besides completeness and accuracy, the results of analysis should be compared to previous results and the analysis of other outside groups. This vetting is not done to mimic others in the IC or participate in some form of groupthink; rather, it is to ensure nothing major was overlooked or misinterpreted. If major discrepancies exist, new questions should be asked and satisfactorily resolved to ensure the conflicting intelligence results are erroneous and not your own.

Time and resources for this analytical product review and vetting step must also be allotted and planned for. Once your team is satisfied with the product review and vetting step, the final product is disseminated to the intelligence consumer in a format that best communicates the requested information.

14

Preparing and Conducting Intelligence Briefings

INTRODUCTION

This chapter will cover one of the most important duties of intelligence analysts, namely, the preparation and conduct of briefings. Though the material presented here will emphasize military intelligence briefings, the instruction coupled with the practical exercises, if adhered to and mastered, are applicable in any vocation, particularly the law enforcement community, since it is a paramilitary environment. The ability to stand before a group of individuals and deliver material in a professional, informative manner (Figure 14.1), such as is taught in the military intelligence briefing protocol, prepares one to accomplish this task in law enforcement or business environments in the most effective manner possible. Preparing and delivering an effective briefing, especially in a challenging environment to a challenging audience, allows individuals to demonstrate their professionality and capability. See Figure 14.1.

Intelligence analysts will provide analyzed data to the appropriate individuals and sections in many forms but the most often-used method is the intelligence briefing. Although briefing material will be provided to the recipient or commander—often referred to as "the customer" in written form—before the actual briefing, the briefing is an opportunity for a verbal exchange and more detailed explanation of the data. Although, as will be reiterated later in this chapter, the principal recipient of the intelligence brief is the commander, or "customer," the briefing also serves as

Figure 14.1 Briefing in a "classroom" and "field" environment.

an opportunity for analysts to update others involved in a mission or a project as to their state of readiness and preparation.

In addition to the written material, during mission planning and operations, the briefing is a standard method of discussing the analyzed intelligence. Written intelligence reports will still be developed and distributed but in light of the critical nature of the mission itself, briefings are mandated by virtually every commander. The briefing is also the venue most often used to explain deductions and predictions based upon the intelligence available. Additionally, though some dread the PowerPoint presentation, PowerPoint is the most effective method of conducting the intelligence brief. This too, will be discussed later in this chapter.

Briefings are conducted at every level in the command structure. The analysts who develop the intelligence analysis data will deliver it verbally in a briefing to their most immediate command initially, then repeat it at every level right up to the mission command level. This is part of the "dissemination" stage in the intelligence cycle (Figure 14.2) but it is also the most traditional method of getting the data to those who should receive it. Additionally, for

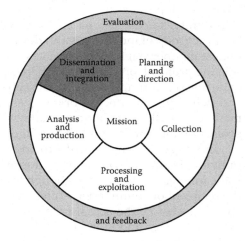

Figure 14.2 U.S. military intelligence cycle. (From *Joint Publication* 2.0.)

mission analysis, an updated briefing will normally be held on a regular schedule leading up to the actual mission launch. This briefing session will be conducted by representatives of all sections involved in mission planning, of which intelligence is only a single (albeit most agree the most important) part.

AUTHOR'S NOTE

This will be stressed at several points throughout this chapter, but the role of the intelligence analyst, although it may not be specifically referred to as such, is performed by specific, trained, and prepared individuals in law enforcement and, to an extent, business environments. Virtually every aspect of the intelligence analysts briefing, discussed in this chapter, is applicable to these arenas.

Research into causes of increased stress levels in humans has always indicated that public speaking is the most stressful thing that we humans are occasionally called upon to do. In the intelligence community, analysts are most responsible for delivering intelligence data in this manner. Those who actually gather intelligence either in the form of HUMINT or SIGINT or any other data-gathering discipline are rarely called upon to stand before their command staff and give account. Intelligence analysts are required to do this on a regular basis and often several times a day, depending on the mission and the stage of mission completion.

Once a mission warning order is issued and the actual planning stage of the mission has commenced, normally all those responsible for assuring success of the mission, including operations, support, logistics, weather, and intelligence, will gather at predetermined times to update the mission commander as to their progress or lack thereof. As the mission launch nears, the briefings will be more frequent. This, or a highly similar, format and process is followed in law enforcement agencies and in many cases, the business environment. Consider, in support of this point, that in the business environment, major decisions and major changes are highly similar to combat or military missions and operations in their significance and process. Few would argue against the point that law enforcement, (especially in the process of planning and launching law enforcement operations) being a paramilitary process, mimics precisely the military planning process. See Figure 14.2.

Additionally, on occasion, special briefings will be held to inform visiting dignitaries or adjacent commands. Appropriate dignitaries or commands will be provided briefings, assuming they have the requisite "need to know" and appropriate clearance levels.

The briefing process, in addition to keeping the command informed of progress or lack thereof, also allows for a lateral exchange of information between sections. For instance, if logistics plans to use a specific piece of equipment or materials in the mission and that equipment will be adversely affected by certain weather conditions, this variable may be identified and discussed between weather and operations at the briefing. During Operation Desert Storm mission planning, for example,  there was little interchange or discussion between weather and logistics as to adverse conditions for air operations. This lack of proper exchange of information in the briefing process contributed to various setbacks that could have been avoided. This should have been realized during the daily commander's update briefings.

Ethical considerations, which will be covered extensively in another area of this text set, have always been an issue in intelligence analysis. The customer, or mission commander, most often has a great deal at stake aside from mission accomplishment, and one of the purposes for the organized formal briefings is to allow for a clear objective analysis to be openly discussed.

In the initial months of Operation Iraqi Freedom, intelligence analysts had to deliver the less-than-optimal news that things weren't going as planned and signs of an imminent insurgency were present. Command briefings gave the analysts an opportunity to be blunt and open in reference to their analysis. The news is not always well accepted, but the fact that the objective data is delivered accurately and publicly (in the sense that several individuals received the same information at the same time and place) assures an opportunity to discuss and defend analysis.

BRIEFINGS IN LAW ENFORCEMENT AND BUSINESS

Virtually every facet of the briefing process is applicable to law enforcement as well as the business environment. Operations in law enforcement are not unlike operations in the military and they require a level of planning that is similar too if not specifically like those in the military. The objectives and goals accomplished by briefings in the military are very similar to those accomplished in law enforcement. In the business community, important business decisions are often followed by a period of planning and decision-making. Meetings in which a process similar to the military briefings process are held often, leading up to the actual business decision being made. In the military environment briefings are used to explain and instruct, thus, the principles addressed are perfectly comparable to the law enforcement and business environments.

RESPONSIBILITIES OF INTELLIGENCE ANALYSTS

One of the most highly debated areas of intelligence analysis, especially among analysts themselves, is the role of the analyst involved in making predictions. Those who argue for a lower profile in this area point out that a commander is better served by being given data and allowed to make his or her own assumptions. They would also argue that analysts are criticized much less when they don't make predictions that may well be proven false.

The other side of this argument is that an analyst's job is to make, well supported, well researched, and analyzed predictions and that these decisions should be voiced to the command during briefings. In either case, the command always has the option of accepting or rejecting these predictions.

In fairness to those who argue the safer route, many commanders can be fairly brutal in their reaction when a recommendation or prediction goes against that which they prefer. During the initial stages of Operation Iraqi Freedom, CIA analysts were often excoriated when they predicted a civil war in Iraq following the overthrow of Saddam Hussein, but history proved they were right.

251

The fact is, an analyst is only effective when he or she makes well-thought-out, well-researched predictions. A commander, or customer, needs to hear bad news or predictions of unfavorable scenarios even if he or she doesn't want to. This, coupled with the fact that in the long run, the most effective intelligence analysts are those who are willing to suffer the consequences, supports the risk of always telling the truth and taking a stand on your intelligence. Commanders will always respect those who take this route.

AUTHOR'S NOTE

Another consideration along these lines, and one that will be discussed at length in other areas of this text, is the mistake analysts often make, in adhering to an assumption they have when the evidence refutes it. Analysts should make predictions, but they should always be willing to make predictions which prove their assumptions wrong. Our ideas are like our children; we are often too protective of them, and unwilling to accept evidence that proves them wrong.

PREPARATION OF BRIEFING SLIDES

Many people have an aversion to PowerPoint presentations but the simple fact is, using PowerPoint to conduct a briefing has been proven to be the most effective method and the preferred method of the majority of customers in the military and in law enforcement. The fact that recipients of such briefings always have paper copies of all slides plus more voluminous supportive narratives to review adds to the effectiveness of this method of conducting a briefing. Of utmost importance, however: If the briefing is classified, the level of classification must appear on each slide, normally top-center. If the presentation is for a law enforcement agency or a business and it is considered confidential, that too should appear on each slide.

The PowerPoint also serves the purpose of keeping the briefer on track to as he or she moves through the material. One of the most important things about conducting a briefing is to keep it brief.

The slides help to do this by minimizing the chance that a briefer will digress from his narrative. The preparation of slides is vitally important. When preparing slides, a briefer must remember that he

Figure 14.3   Examples of briefing slides.

or she is basically telling a story. Slide and information sequencing is very important. Each slide and each sequence of information should follow logically on that which came immediately before it. See Figure 14.3.

If you are telling someone a story, for instance, you would not relate the ending or the climax at the beginning. Such would obviously be confusing. There is one exception to this in brief slide preparation but that will be covered later in this chapter. In telling a story, it is vital to lay some type of foundation first. The easiest way to explain this is by using an information briefing format (see section on types of briefings).

In an information briefing, the briefer is relating data in a well-thought-out format, building on a foundation that is laid first. The most explanatory in terms of sequencing of information is a country brief which is designed to provide data, for instance, about an environment in which an operation is to take place. The first few slides in a country briefing would most likely be maps. In preparing map slides, obviously the purpose would be to detail the location of the area of operation (AO). These slides are always constructed big to small. For instance, in a briefing for an operation that would take place in an AO such as Baghdad, Iraq, the first slide would likely show the country of Iraq, including bordering countries such as Syria to the west, Jordan and Saudi Arabia to the south, and Iran to the east, with a small box or indicator over Baghdad in the central part of Iraq. Borders separating countries or AOs from nonoperational areas should be clear and easily discernable.

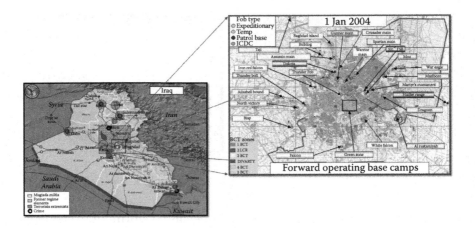

It is important to indicate who the neighbors are when discussing an AO and where they are located in conjunction to the AO. The second slide would zoom in but would probably show the country of Afghanistan (at least the northern part), including the AO, in this case, Balkh Province. Such a slide would indicate the distance from important areas such as the capital, Kabul.

Even though maps include distances, it is convenient, and most customers who aren't extremely familiar with a spe-

cific AO appreciate the inclusion of "referencing" type data. For instance, a slide showing Balkh Province and Kabul might include a short note indicating that the distance between Balkh Province and Kabul is roughly the distance between DC and Baltimore, or that the city of Mazer-i-Sharif, center of Balk Province, is roughly the size of San Antonio, Texas. Other helpful references in terms of demonstrating distance is referring to the shorter distances as comparable to X number of football fields, or some other well-known, easily conceptualized distance. These little references are greatly appreciated and provide a more instantaneous visual.

Once location has been established in information briefing slides, a briefer should limit the remainder of the slides to only vital information, and by that, I mean information vital to the success of the mission. The ethnic breakdown of the Balkh Province would be important. The ethnic breakdown of the country of Afghanistan may not be.

A leadership slide when briefing an AO is very important and would probably follow ethnic breakdowns. A leadership slide demonstrates the power brokers in a specific area. These individuals may not always be the most obvious, such as the political leaders or the tribal leaders. They are often individuals of influence for other reasons. It is important to know who these decision-makers are.

Again, remember, you are providing information that flows from big to small. An AO briefing would most likely conclude with local issues. It is important for a commander or mission leader to know what is most likely on the minds of most of the people in an area at the time his or her forces will be there.

The data on a slide should be as simple as possible while still getting the necessary information to the recipient. Occasionally a briefer will try to cram a lot of information into a slide in order to account for his or her analysis. Remember, the recipient of the briefing is usually pressed for

AUTHOR'S NOTE

The best way to gauge current events that people in a specific area determine to be important is to access the local media and read the letters to the editor, if this is available. If not, look for some other type of sounding board that is open to the local population. Most communities have something comparable to this and it is a great source for local complaints. If a commander is going to be conducting a mission in an area, it is important to know of the things that the "man on the street" deem important.

time and has to absorb a lot of information prior to making command decisions. This is true in law enforcement operations as well as with business decisions that must be made.

The best method of conducting a briefing slide by slide is to pull up the next slide and point out two or three key items on it, preferably without reading it word for word, then allow the recipient to peruse the remaining data until he or she is ready to proceed to the next slide. Information on briefing slides should always be in bullet points. They do not have to be complete sentences, but they do need to convey complete thoughts or points (Figure 14.4). As the customer has to read most of the data, this information should be as concise as possible. Do not use slang or jargon unless you absolutely have to.

4 types of military briefings

- Information briefing
  - to inform
- Decision briefing
  - to obtain a decision
- Mission Briefing
  - the mission is .....
- Staff briefing
  - combined staff action for Cdr

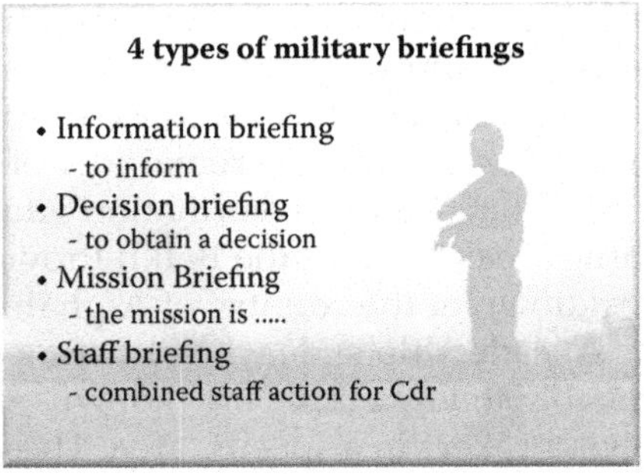

Figure 14.4 Informational briefing slide example.

Keep the information as simple as possible, always assuming the recipient is not as clear and knowledgeable as you are. This is most often true. Use common sense. It may not be necessary to identify Ashraf Ghani as the president of Afghanistan if the AO is in Afghanistan, but it would be wise, for instance, to identify Rashid Dostum as first vice president of Afghanistan. See Figure 14.4.

AUTHOR'S NOTE

Don't apologize for your pronunciation of names. Take your best shot and go with it.

If you are operating in a foreign country, such as Afghanistan, for instance, and the names are difficult to pronounce, practice first then take your best shot at pronunciation.

In PowerPoint presentations, background and color schemes are important as well. The print media should contrast fairly sharply with the background to avoid confusion—no light print on light background or vice versa. A general rule of thumb in bullet points is no more than five per page and no more than seven words per point, and this should of course be adjusted to compensate for visuals. If you have an important, vital visual for a slide, it is more important to get it in and adjust your bullet points to compensate, rather than diminishing the size of the visual to allow for the print media. The background or print color should not change throughout the briefing. Actually, most units or intelligence teams have standard master slide backgrounds and color schemes. If this is the case, you should always stay with this scheme. Font sizes should always remain standard throughout your brief unless it is absolutely necessary to change. Font styles such as Times New Roman should never change. Visuals such as pictures or charts are always helpful as long as they pertain specifically to the information provided. For instance, if you are providing a briefing about a specific border crossing point, an actual photograph of the area or a photograph of a border officer actually working in the area would be appropriate and informative. A photograph of an unrelated border area would not.

You should never use moving visuals or fade in narratives unless they are necessary to get the information across. Media or moving visuals, for entertainment purposes or for humor, is never a good idea.

Earlier in this section it was pointed out that there was an exception to the rule of sequencing of information or staying with a logical format. The exception is the BLUF, or "bottom line up front." You wouldn't ordinarily find a BLUF in a simple information type briefing, but you would definitely find it in a decision briefing. The BLUF states an analyst's conclusion at the beginning of a briefing, "The Taliban will reinforce a specific location" or "The Taliban will abandon a location as soon as they are challenged and fall back to location X."

The BLUF, of course, is followed by detailed analysis and supportive information but it gives the customer a short specific overview of what the briefing will be about at the outset. If the briefing recipient has this vital BLUF at the beginning of the briefing it is easier for him or her to look for and determine if the appropriate analysis has been done and if the BLUF is supported by the follow-on data.

ROLES AND RELATIONSHIPS

An intelligence analyst has a unique role and relationship with his or her command. In light of the fact that the analyst most often has the best "detailed view" of the upcoming mission, or the state of affairs at the ground level in ongoing operations, he or she has an opportunity to determine whether the command is asking the right questions or establishing the right priorities.

Most often the command or the ultimate customer or decision-maker doesn't have time to get down into the weeds or micromanage an operation and, therefore, relies on the analyst to advise if he or she is overlooking something or putting too much or too little emphasis on an issue. The briefing allows this interchange to take place and most command level individuals really appreciate the guidance.

Much of the command in Operation Iraqi Freedom, for instance, had little insight as to public perception of American forces. So much of their intelligence requirements and priorities were focused elsewhere. Intelligence analysts had a perfect opportunity during briefings, mostly to refocus the command on the public perception of coalition efforts and whether that perception was positive or negative.

Analysts often have to assist their command in redirecting priorities and most commanders understand this and appreciate the advice. Analysts must know their commanders and understand the mission needs. They must also be prepared to advise the command when they may be making tactical errors. This, also, is most effectively done during the briefings. The most important thing analysts must do in this sense is know their infor-

mation, and to the extent possible, know their customer or commander. Briefing rehearsals are vital in assuring this confidence in the knowledge and delivery of the data.

Most analysts who had an opportunity to brief General David Petraeus during Iraqi Freedom came to know several things about him and about his preferred method of receiving information. General Petraeus was a voracious reader and was therefore knowledgeable of most of the information he would receive from his analysts during briefings. Hearing what he already knew from someone else, however, often gave him a different perspective. Analysts will find this to be true of most command staff or supervisory operational staff.

Another issue that analysts have to deal with in a briefing is the demeanor of the customer or command. Some recipients of command level briefings are terse and abrupt and will occasionally criticize their briefer, but normally this is done in a constructive manner. Individuals at this level are often pressed for time. While General Petraeus was more patient, his second in command, General Ray Odierno, was often abrupt. This is another reason analysts and briefers need to know their material and know their customer.

PRACTICING YOUR BRIEFING

A briefer should spend at least three times as much time in practicing a brief as he or she intends to spend actually briefing. Briefings should be practiced before other analysts who understand the process but who are not as familiar with the data to be presented. The reason this is recommended is to detect areas of confusion or areas in which information is too sparse and needs to be supplemented. Other analysts understand the process and if they are confused or feel they haven't been provided enough data in a specific area, the customer obviously will feel that way too. Often a briefer will assume the command or the customer knows things they do not know and practicing will bring this out. Additionally, it is not a good idea to have to go back with your slides. If a customer has to ask you to go back a slide or two in your briefing, it means you didn't provide enough information or you didn't provide it clearly enough. Practice will likely identify these areas. Remember, in a briefing you are imparting data. You are not lecturing. You are not carrying on a two-way conversation. You are not shooting the breeze, and you are not looking for direction. You should be providing direction. Practice enough that you do not have to use filler noises such as "uhh" or "umm" and never, ever use the word "like," as in, "similar to." Your diction should be simple and without jargon, and it should be professional.

Body Positioning

Body positioning during a briefing is vitally important, not only in military briefings but in any type of public presentations. The simple rule is "never turn your back on your customer." Risking redundancy, it must be reiterated that knowing your material solves a multitude of briefing issues, this one included.

A briefing always begins with an introduction and ends with a completion statement. The introduction and the entire briefing as well as the completion statement is always directed to one person, not the entire audience. The introduction is always, "Good morning/afternoon/evening sir/ma'am, I am ——- and I will be briefing you on ——." The briefing always ends with, "Pending your questions, this concludes my briefing," followed by a pause of no more than five seconds waiting for any questions. Most often the recipient or customer will nod, indicating no questions.

Analysts conducting briefings may sometimes make the mistake of having to turn to face their projected slides if they aren't familiar enough with their material, and find themselves having to refresh their memory as to what is being displayed. This can be avoided, again, by knowing your material, although it is appropriate to have notes in your hand if you need to refresh your memory. Maintaining facial and body contact with your customer, however, is always best. Again, the best plan is to be familiar with the material and data and practice, practice, practice.

Another trick to assure you do not turn your back on your customer is to back up as close as possible to your actual display or to your slides in the case of a PowerPoint presentation. If you have your back close to the actual screen or display and you find yourself having to glance at the slides, you will often have to do little more than turn your head slightly. Your shoulders will more than likely remain squared off toward your customer.

In preparing for the actual presentation, follow these steps: Position yourself as stated with your back close to the wall or the presentation screen. Focus all your attention on your principal customer or commander. As far as you are concerned, there is one person in the room and that is the customer, or in the case of briefing dignitaries, the principal individual among the recipients. Do not scan your audience as you would in a general lecture of some type. All attention is focused on one person. When you have briefed a slide and provided all the data you need to provide from that slide, look at your customer's eyes. He or she will either be reading something from the slide or scanning something you've presented on the slide. Either way, he or she will nod, or glance back at you indicating he or she is finished. Go to your next slide at that point and continue the process. Upon completion of your slides, you will always conclude with the statement, "Pending your questions, this concludes my briefing." Stand for a second to ascertain if there are questions, then move out.

One last note, not specifically pertaining to body positioning: Never read your slides to your customer or commander. KNOW YOUR MATERIAL. When a new slide is presented, point out one or two important items on the slide or, for instance, if something needs to be pointed out on a map with a laser do so, then watch your customer's eyes until he or she indicates he or she has absorbed everything necessary from the slide and is ready for you to move on.

Types of Briefs

There are many different types of briefings and though a few military examples will be provided here, all have comparable examples in law enforcement and business. Three of the most often utilized types of briefings are simple information briefings, decision briefings, and mission briefings.

Information briefings are general in nature. For instance, if a military operation is going to be conducted in a specific area or part of the world, an information briefing is conducted simply to familiarize the command of the geography, politics, culture, and current events, or important issues in cultural or political issues, all of which may or may not conform to things the command is familiar with concerning the area. The current political environment or issues of current concern are probably most important to the command, but again, the basic information briefing is designed to lay a foundation upon which the remainder of the mission planning will be built.

A corollary in law enforcement would be a similar briefing to provide all foundational information pertaining to a specific area in which a law enforcement type operation will be conducted. A specific example would be the many varied operations to implement new border and immigration policies upon the change of administration when President Trump took office.

Prior to launching these operations, commanders had to be updated on areas with which they may have been familiar but in which many cultural and environmental changes had occurred since previous immigration enforcement operations had taken place.

Similarly, in the business community, such information briefings are valuable in laying foundations upon which larger, more encompassing business ventures may take place.

The decision briefings in the military take place at points in the mission planning cycle at which the command has to burn bridges, so to speak. At times, a command must take a path which precludes going back and rethinking issues or decisions. The military refers to such decisions, euphemistically, as "drop dead" decisions. Though a command has generally been prepared for these decisions and is ready to move in specific directions, the "last-minute" decision serves to either cement his or her choices or decisions or provide him or her with any last-minute data needed. Decision briefings are held throughout the mission planning process but obviously the most important decision briefing will be held shortly before the all-important mission launch decision. As before, these same type of briefings are held in the law enforcement and business communities.

Mission briefings are similar to decision briefings but are more encompassing. A mission briefing is held shortly before mission launch

261

and is designed to clear up any concerns, last minute issues, and to ensure everyone knows their role and has no questions.

SUMMARY AND REVIEW

To summarize, some of the most important aspects of the intelligence briefing are as follows:

- Know your material. The importance of this cannot be stressed enough.
- Practice your actual briefing and be receptive to constructive criticism.
- Have notes available but try to brief from memory and rely on your notes as little as possible.
- Do not read your briefing slides.
- Focus on one individual, normally the commander or customer.
- Stress the major points in a slide but do not read verbatim.
- Focus on your customer or commander and read his or her expression as a guide when to advance in your briefing.
- Be prepared for questions but do not be afraid to indicate that you do not know the answer (don't guess. If you don't have some piece of information your command is asking for, simply advise and assure him or her that you will get the information to him or her as soon as it is available to you).

15

Best Practices

INTRODUCTION

Chapter 15 introduces the concept and identifies methods or techniques accepted by the IC and recognized as standards/benchmarks in the practice of intelligence analysis. The chapter also describes selected analytical practices which are broadly used in the intelligence community and have specific application to Homeland Defense Intelligence Analysis.

Beginning with the generic concept, a "best practice" is a method or technique that dependably demonstrates results far greater than those achieved using other means. Best practices are employed as a standard or benchmark.

Best practices in the field of intelligence are inherently difficult to objectively observe, recognize, and appropriately and empirically measure simply because of the secretive nature of the intelligence profession. Consider for a moment that Russia, France, China, or the United States commissioned a university research group or think tank to crawl through mounds of highly classified data and finished intelligence so they could publish and critique their country's flawed intelligence practices or tell the world how they propose to improve their intelligence collection and analysis practices. The likelihood of such an event occurring is negligible. One could envision the study being performed on a limited basis, perhaps under multiple levels of security, and shared on a limited basis with their countrymen and possibly a few close allies, but not shared with the general public under any circumstances. That said, however, on June 21, 2007, the Director of National Intelligence (DNI) signed and implemented Intelligence Community Directive (ICD) Number 203, Analytic Standards, governing the production and evaluation of intelligence analysis and analytical products.[1]

The DNI, via ICD 203, established programmatic requirements to improve the quality, applicability of, and confidence in the analysis and conclusions of intelligence products produced for policy makers, government leaders, and military commanders.

This chapter outlines, explains, and where practical, demonstrates the IC's best practices as defined by ICD 203.

ICD 203'S LIST OF NINE STANDARDS

A direct result of the miscalculations in the National Intelligence Estimate (NIE) on Iraqi weapons of mass destruction (WMD) stimulated Congress to establish an office of the Director of National Intelligence (DNI). One of the DNI's major tasks was to develop and ensure compliance with analytic quality standards. ICD 203 contains nine analytic quality standards (or best practices) for use by DHS and throughout the IC.

Additionally, ICD 203 enables analysts from across the IC to communicate more directly with each other and thus reduce the negative effects of insular groupthink. The goal of adopting common IC standards (best practices) and other analytic common tools, and encouraging analytic collaboration is the improvement and value enhancement of the final analytic product in the eyes of the intelligence consumer.

ICD 203 presents these analytic standards as product "attributes" or "qualities." All nine are listed in the following:

1. Properly describe quality and credibility of underlying sources, data, and methodologies.
2. Properly express and explain uncertainties or confidence in analytic judgments.
3. Properly distinguish between underlying intelligence and analysts' assumptions and judgments.
4. Incorporate analysis of alternatives.
5. Demonstrate customer relevance and addresses implications.
6. Use clear and logical argumentation.
7. Explain to/or consistency of analytical judgements.

---

[1] Office of the Director of National Intelligence, Analytic Standards, Intelligence Community Directive 203 (ICD 203), 2007.

8. Make accurate judgements and assessments.

9. Incorporate effective visual information where appropriate.[2]

The remainder of this chapter further describes each of these nine analytic best practices and, where appropriate, provides or points to other chapters for supporting examples.

PROPERLY DESCRIBE QUALITY AND RELIABILITY OF UNDERLYING SOURCES

How reliable is your intelligence source? Failure to properly evaluate the quality or reliability of an intelligence source can negatively impact analytical conclusions and completely invalidate the final product. Let us examine the reliability of a few intelligence disciplines, starting with imagery intelligence (IMINT). IMINT provides the user with an actual picture. Many would argue that if one has photographic evidence, there is no room for doubt or argument, but this is not the case. Other disciplines also have their reliability shortfalls. HUMINT sources lie or can be mistaken. SIGINT can be misinterpreted or deliberately falsified. ELINT can be jammed or faked, and the list continues. The more sophisticated the adversary, the higher the possibility of deception.

Analysts generally receive some level of training to help them evaluate sources, spot errors, and recognize deception. These concepts are discussed in more detail in Chapter 4. Consistently assessing sources and validating collected information prevents bad or deceptive information from being included in the assessment and allows analysts to identify intelligence gaps requiring additional collection efforts.

Guidance to Better Describe Quality and Credibility of Underlying Sources

By organizing and tying analytic judgments to the supporting data and intelligence, analysts create a type of pedigree for their assessments and associated findings. The more clearly organized and complete the judgment pedigree is, the easier it is for peers and analysis team supervision to review and detect bad data, analytical bias, analytical errors,

---

[2] Office of the Director of National Intelligence, *Analytic Standards*, Intelligence Community Directive 203 (ICD 203), 2007.

or adversarial deception. Guidance and an example of how to better build this judgment-source pedigree is explained in the next paragraph.

Analysts exercise this best practice by tying analytical judgments to specific supporting information and to their underlying sources. When tying judgments to the source, use as much detail as allowed to describe the source's placement, access, reliability, and performance history. Analyst comments should also address the vulnerability of the source (or technical method) information to deception, denial, or in the case of HUMINT-provided information, the source's motivations or possible biases. Where possible, weighting factors should be associated with information that drives the product's assessment. Where practical, call out specific sources that played a prominent role the final assessment. Use of a sources and methods summary statement is helpful to assist the consumer in understanding the amount and types of sources used to develop the product. This can be one or two sentences that identify the number and types of pertinent sources reviewed, how many supported the assessment findings, and how many conflicted (e.g., *Assessment findings based upon IMINT only; imagery analysis consists of 347 images of the designated collection area from 17 surveillance aircraft sorties on different dates, 9 day and 8 night, 7 sorties [42 percent of the time, 6 night and 1 day] target not spotted in imagery. Analyst comment: During the 7 negative collection sorties, target may have been away from designated area, undercover and obscured, possibly asleep.*)

Practical Exercise

This practical exercise illustrates the point quite well. Go to the practical exercise on Evaluating the Quality or Reliability of Intelligence Sources.

PROPERLY CAVEAT AND EXPRESSES UNCERTAINTIES OR CONFIDENCE IN ANALYTIC JUDGMENTS

Communicating analytical judgments and levels of uncertainty in such a way that commanders and policymakers fully understand has long vexed the intelligence profession. When commanders and policymakers are given advanced and accurate warnings by intelligence gatherers, they are often disregarded for manifold reasons. I cite Stalin's multiple warnings from Soviet intelligence prior to the 1941 Nazi invasion of Russia as an example (Operation Barbarossa) and the accurate and timely assessment to Custer of the size and disposition of enemy Sioux forces in the Little Big Horn valley (Custer's Last Stand) by his command's Dakota scouts as two conspicuous historical examples.

As discussed in Chapter 12, analytic products should express a level of confidence in the judgments and clarify a basis for endorsement and acceptance of analytical results. The intelligence product should highlight intelligence gaps and contrary reporting. In addition, products should identify indicators that would augment or decrease confidence thereby pointing to possible reconsideration of existing analytical judgments.

Spoken and written expressions of uncertainty such as "possible," "probable," and "unlikely," as well as many other adjectives, are subjective statements of probability. When trying to express uncertainty, quantifying and articulating the level of uncertainty as a range is often the most the intelligence professional can reasonably accomplish. Despite the lack of precise definitions promulgated by ICD 203, the IC directive does set "range parameters," or standards for expressing uncertainty to better assist communication among analysts and between analysts and the intelligence consumer.

Guidance to Ensure Explanation and Expression of Uncertainties or Confidence in Analytic Judgments

Use the ICD 203 probability terminology to convey the level of analytic certainty/uncertainty in assessment results. If significant uncertainties exist, to the extent possible, identify, quantify, and explain the rationale for the uncertainty (e.g., uncertainties exist due to generally reliable but conflicting HUMINT source reporting, significant intelligence gaps, and so on). To assist the consumer's understanding of the confidence level, identify confidence levels and their associated percentages in a table or legend for easy reference. If intelligence gaps exist that potentially could significantly sway assessment findings for better or worse, identify them to the consumer for further collection and reassess findings as required (e.g., cloud obscuration of the target area negatively impacts assessment finding confidence levels, findings being released as preliminary, new high-priority imagery collection request submitted, report will be updated and re-released upon receipt of new target imagery.)

PROPERLY DISTINGUISH BETWEEN UNDERLYING INTELLIGENCE AND ANALYSTS' ASSUMPTIONS AND JUDGMENTS

An assumption is a proposition that analysts have accepted as a fact and forms the basis of the assessment. Using SATs to evaluate and re-evaluate an assumption is valuable at any time prior to finalizing a judgment to insure the assessment is not tied to or resting on a defective premise. See Chapter 10 for more information on using SATs to evaluate key analytical assumptions. Unambiguously stating assumptions or judgments made by analysts focuses the cognitive processes of intelligence consumers on what the supported facts and analytical judgments are, allowing them to have confidence in or ignore assessments or judgments as appropriate.

Guidance on How to Properly Distinguish between Underlying Intelligence and Analytical Assumptions and Judgments

Clearly identify any assumptions and judgments used. Segregate assumptions and judgments from underlying reporting and supporting data and intelligence. Use analytical verbiage to state assumptions and judgments in the assessment findings, such as "consider, assess, calculate, judge, estimate, determine," and "assume."

INCORPORATE ALTERNATIVE ANALYSIS WHERE APPROPRIATE

The Intelligence Reform and Terrorism Prevention Act of 2004 (IRTPA) obligated DNI to develop a process to ensure the effective use of alternative analysis to counter an inclination for analysts to focus their efforts down a single path of reasoning.[3] The argument that analytic products should identify and explain strengths and weaknesses of alternative hypothesis, viewpoints, or outcomes in light of both available information and information gaps stemmed indirectly from criticism contained in the flawed assessment of Iraq's weapons of mass destruction (WMD) program. The Commission on the Intelligence Capabilities of the United

---

[3] U.S. Government, Intelligence Reform and Terrorism Prevention Act, 2004.

States Regarding Weapons of Mass Destruction, also known as the WMD Commission, report identified: The IC, in the 2002 National Intelligence Estimate (NIE), assessed with high confidence that Iraq has biological weapons (BW).[4]

Guidance on How to Incorporate Alternative Analysis Where Appropriate

Arguably, where time and resources are available, analysts should incorporate insights from the application of structured analytic techniques. These techniques include, but are not limited to, analysis of competing hypotheses, argument mapping, and comparative analysis to decide if a potential alternative perspective or conclusion is more likely or trending towards higher probability. Using structured analysis to assess indicators and facts using a matrix or table where each column is a differing competing hypothesis aids in excluding an alternative hypothesis, thereby identifying the most likely hypothesis as the one with the least amount of contradicting evidence.

AUTHOR'S NOTES

Performing Alternative Analysis of Competing Hypotheses requires additional time and personnel. For example, if one has five competing hypotheses, you would potentially require five times the resources needed to fully develop one hypothesis. These additional resources are often difficult to obtain, or may be completely unavailable, due to competing mission priorities. Therefore, intelligence planners should be judicious in the application of alternative analysis techniques.

Table 15.1 displays a representative example of one method of comparing and scoring competing hypotheses. See Chapter 10 for more information on using SATs to incorporate alternative analysis.

---

[4] Commission on the Intelligence Capabilities of the United States Regarding Weapons of Mass Destruction, Report to the President of the United States, Washington, DC: Government Printing Office, 2005.

Table 15.1 Sample Alternative Hypotheses Table

Example of Alternative Hypothesis Matrix

Intelligence Requirement: Will Krasnovia retaliate for the United States bombing its intelligence headquarters?

Hypotheses:

H1: Krasnovia will publically protest but will not retaliate.

H2: Krasnovia will publically protest and sponsor a few low-level terrorist actions.

H3: Krasnovia will mount a major attack/terror action on an equivalent U.S. intelligence-related target.

	Reliability	Credibility	H1	H2	H3
E1: Krasnovian FM denounces U.S. attack at the UN	Medium	High	+	+	+
E2: Krasnovian president announces that "he will not retaliate"	Medium	High	+	+	+
E3: Absence of terror retaliation after past U.S. attacks	Medium	Medium	+	+	–
E4: Assumption: Krasnovia would not want to further provoke United States	N/A	N/A	+	+	–
E5: SIGINT chatter has increased between Krasnovian government and field operatives	Medium	High	–	+	+
E6: Krasnovian embassies have higher security postures than before HQ bombing	Medium	Medium	–	+	+
E7: Assumption: No retaliation would be perceived as a sign of weakness to Krasnovian public/president's inner circle	N/A	N/A	–	+	+
E8: Assumption: No retaliation would be perceived as a sign of weakness to Krasnovian neighbors/adversaries	N/A	N/A	–	+	+

DEMONSTRATE CUSTOMER RELEVANCE AND ADDRESSES IMPLICATIONS

For any intelligence analyst, a common goal should be to provide analytic products that address the consumer's questions and information requirements, offer insights on relevant and related concerns, and to update existing products. For analysts working inside the U.S. IC, products should highlight information that has "national security aspects" (e.g., potential damage to U.S. trade or the economy, strengthen/weaken foreign relations, endanger U.S. nationals), particularly if the information is something the consumer (e.g., government leader, policymaker, or military commander) does not know or fully understand. Intelligence products should add value by addressing implications, context, threats, or factors affecting opportunities for planned or potential actions, for the intended audience.

Guidance on How to Ensure Customer Relevance and Address Implications

A successful analyst "answers the question." However, best practice encourages the analyst to go further. For example, when producing an analytic product that answers a question with limited scope (e.g., Will the enemy attack Hill 293?), the analyst should first fully answer the intelligence requirement (e.g., answer: The enemy will almost certainly attack Hill 293). See Figure 15.1 (upper half).

Then the analyst would endeavor to provide added value (e.g., enemy will most likely attack at night from the West using improved roads for armored vehicles and unimproved roads for lighter vehicles/dismounted troops to maximize speed of advance of heavy armored forces). Additionally,

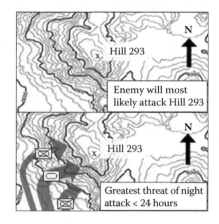

Figure 15.1 Success vs. best practice.

the analyst includes any relevant near and far-term implications (e.g., near-term, <24 hours, rapid assault from the West implies the enemy is prepared to take heavy casualties in order to sustain momentum and possibly take

271

the initiative in this sector; a delayed assault, >24 hours, implies the enemy is consolidating forces, awaiting resupply and replacements, and the main effort is likely in another sector). See Figure 15.1 (lower half).

As one can see, both responses successfully answer the intelligence consumer's question (e.g., Will the enemy attack Hill 293?). However, if the supporting data is available, the analyst should also provide other relevant information to aid the consumer's understanding of the problem and the associated near- and far-term implications and thereby paint a much fuller picture of the situation.

USE LOGICAL ARGUMENTATION

Analytic products should present a clear main analytic message upfront. Products containing multiple judgments should have a main analytic message that is drawn collectively from those judgments. All analytic judgments should be effectively supported by relevant intelligence information and coherent reasoning. Language and syntax should convey meaning unambiguously. Products should be internally consistent and acknowledge significant supporting and contrary information affecting judgments.[5]

Guidance on Using Logical Argumentation

A logical argument should consist of a series of related statements crafted to establish a clear proposition. When making a logical argument, there should be a premise, inference, and conclusion as illustrated in Figure 15.2.

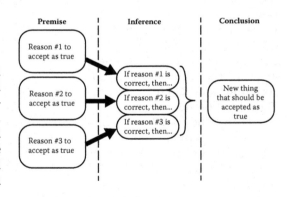

Figure 15.2 Logical argument.

---

[5] Office of the Director of National Intelligence, Analytic Standards, Intelligence Community Directive 203 (ICD 203), 2007.

Stage One: The Premise
Usually more than one premise is needed to adequately support an argument. Premises need to be clear and succinct assertions. Premises should consist of evidence and logical reasoning and should use supporting language to aid in identifying that this is the premise, such as "since," "because," or "if/then" statements. Premises are the evidence (or basis) for accepting the argument and its conclusions.

The premise of the argument is italicized in the following examples:

- *Since the volume of drug cartel–associated violence is significantly increasing,* one can logically expect it to spill outside the areas where it is presently reported.
- *Because the informant has reported with 100-percent reliability for three years,* he will likely report reliably in the near future.
- *If the enemy has advanced radar technology and did not have a supporting R&D program,* they likely got the technology from other sources.

Stage Two: Inference
The premises of the argument are used to obtain further propositions. This process is known as *inference.* In inference, begin with one or more propositions that have been accepted. Following this, derive a new proposition. There are various forms of valid inference.

The inference of the argument is italicized in the following examples:

- Since the volume of drug cartel–associated violence is significantly increasing, *one can logically expect it to spill outside the areas where it is presently reported.*
- Because the informant has reported with 100-percent reliability for three years, *he will likely report reliably in the near future.*
- If the enemy has the advanced radar technology capability and did not have a supporting R&D program, *they likely got the technology from other sources.*

The conclusions arrived at by inference may then be used in further inference. Inference is often denoted by phrases such as "implies that" or "therefore."

Stage Three: Conclusion

Finally we arrive at the conclusion of the argument: Another proposition. The conclusion is often stated as the final stage of inference. It is affirmed on the basis of the original premises and the inferences from them. Conclusions are often indicated by phrases such as "therefore," "it follows that," "we conclude," and so on.

The conclusion of the argument is italicized in the following examples:

- Since the volume of drug cartel–associated violence is significantly increasing, one can logically expect it to spill outside the areas where it is presently reported. *Therefore, we expect a marked rise in the volume of drug cartel associated violence outside the areas where it is presently reported.*
- Because the informant has reported with 100-percent reliability for three years, he will likely report reliably in the near future. Provided he continues to have required access, *we conclude that he will continue to report reliably.*
- If the enemy has the advanced radar technology capability and did not have a supporting R&D program, they likely got the technology from other sources. Without a working R&D effort of their own, *it follows that the enemy will continue to seek outside assistance or covert procurement means to maintain or improve their radar technology capability.*

EXHIBIT CONSISTENCY OF ANALYSIS OVER TIME, OR HIGHLIGHTS CHANGES AND EXPLAINS RATIONALE

Analytic products should state how their judgments on a topic are consistent with or represent a change from those in previously published analysis, or represent initial coverage of a topic. Products need not be lengthy or detailed on explaining change or consistency. They should avoid using boilerplate language, however, and should make clear how new information or different reasoning led to the judgments expressed in them. Recurrent products such as daily crisis reports should take note any changes in judgments. Absent changes, recurrent products need to confirm consistency with previous editions. Significant differences in analytic judgment, such as that which may occur between two IC analytic elements, should be fully considered and brought to the attention of customers.[6]

Guidance on Consistency of or Explaining Changes to Analytical Judgments

There are only three approaches open to the analyst:

- You agree with previous reporting and explain and support why you agree.
- You disagree with previous reporting and explain why and support why you disagree.
- This in new coverage on a topic not previously reported on.

You Agree with Previous Reporting

Consistency of analysis over time directly relates to properly expressing uncertainties and significance. Consistency ultimately builds confidence and credibility with the intelligence consumer. This begins with the analyst evaluating or critiquing their own work and asking the question, "Are my (or the previous analyst's) judgments still valid?" If it is consistent with previous products, does your analysis provide any new insights? Don't waste the intelligence consumer's time by making them read another product that does not add to their understanding.

You Disagree with Previous Reporting

Again, the analyst asks the question, "Are my (or the previous analyst's) judgments still valid?" However, this time the answer is "no." Now the analyst must determine why the previous reporting was erroneous (e.g., they/you missed something or collections sensors were fooled). Perhaps the conclusion was correct but the circumstances upon which the conclusion was made changed or perhaps the right answer just changed (e.g., enemy moved to another location, the previous leader of a crime organization was usurped, and so on). In either case the analyst highlights the change and explains and supports the rationale for change and possible implications associated with the change.

---

[6] Office of the Director of National Intelligence, *Analytic Standards*, Intelligence Community Directive 203 (ICD 203), 2007.

New Coverage on a Topic Not Previously Reported On

When reporting on a topic not previously covered, the process is much the same as with topics that have previous reporting associated with them. It still requires the analyst to critique his or her own work and ensure his or her judgments are valid. However, in this case there is a higher level of due diligence in the sense that everything is done from scratch. There are no previous assessments to review and gain potential insights. The analyst must look at every piece of data and build the assessment from the ground up.

MAKE ACCURATE JUDGMENTS AND ASSESSMENTS

Analytic products should apply expertise and logic to make the most accurate judgments and assessments possible based on the information available and known information gaps. In doing so, analytic products should present all judgments that would be useful to customers and should not avoid difficult judgments in order to minimize the risk of being wrong. Inherent in the concept of accuracy is that the analytic message a customer receives should be the one the analyst intended to send. Therefore, analytic products should express judgments as clearly and precisely as possible, reducing ambiguity by addressing the likelihood, timing, and nature of the outcome or development. Clarity of meaning permits assessment for accuracy when all necessary information is available.[7]

Guidance on Making Accurate Judgments and Assessments

Analysts, like most professionals, pride themselves in doing the job right. In contrast to most other professionals, an analyst's mistake may result in significant loss of life, property, or even the defeat of a nation. The possible magnitude and significance of a wrong judgment or assessment implores the analyst to be clear, expeditious, precise, and get it right the first time and every time. It is impossible to be correct every time; nevertheless, it is the goal.

So how is it done? The application of individual intellectual honesty and the recognition that no one is right all the time, along with critical and independent reviews will greatly enhance the quality of analysis and the accuracy of the products which result from the process. If analysts and

---

[7] Office of the Director of National Intelligence, Analytic Standards, Intelligence Community Directive 203 (ICD 203), 2007.

agencies across the IC wholeheartedly adopt and train to the standards, as laid out in ICD 203, analytic processes and analytic product accuracy should improve significantly.

INCORPORATE EFFECTIVE VISUAL
INFORMATION WHERE APPROPRIATE

Analytic products should incorporate visual information to clarify an analytic message and to complement or enhance the presentation of data and analysis. In particular, visual presentations should be used when information or concepts (e.g., spatial or temporal relationships) can be conveyed better in graphic form (e.g., tables, charts, images) than in written text. Visual information may range from plain presentation of intelligence information to interactive displays for complex information and analytic concepts. All of the content in an analytic product may be presented visually. Visual information should always be clear and pertinent to the product's subject. Analytic content in visual information should also adhere to other analytic tradecraft standards.[8]

Guidance on Incorporating Effective Visual
Information Where Appropriate

If the visual you are planning on incorporating does not improve, or confuses or distracts from, the analytic story you are trying to present, you should not use it. A simple, clear message delivered with confidence and accuracy is the objective. Avoid using too

TIPS FOR INCORPORATING VISUALS INTO INTELLIGENCE PRODUCTS

- If visuals confuse or distract from the message, *don't use them.*
- Use visuals where they can best support the primary findings/judgments of an analytical product.
- Keep visuals simple, uncluttered, clear, and concise.
- Visuals should agree with the written text and reinforce the message.

---

[8] Office of the Director of National Intelligence, Analytic Standards, Intelligence Community Directive 203 (ICD 203), 2007.

many distracting colors, images, or confusing text. The visual should be consistent with the written portion of the product. It should complement, simplify, and strengthen product findings. Visuals are most effective when they are tied to the main judgment of the assessment.

As discussed in Chapter 6, visuals not only communicate on a cognitive level, they also can communicate on an emotional level. Visual clues help us decode text and attract attention to information, increasing the likelihood that the audience will remember.[9] Graphics engage our imagination and heighten our creative thinking, leading to a more profound and accurate understanding of the presented material.[10] See Chapter 6 for more detailed information.

CHAPTER SUMMARY

Chapter 15 introduced the concept of best practices and identified methods or techniques accepted by the IC and recognized as standards/benchmarks in the practice of intelligence analysis. The chapter also described selected analytical practices that are broadly used in the intelligence community and have specific application to Homeland Defense Intelligence Analysis.

Beginning with the generic concept, a *best practice* is a method or technique that dependably demonstrates results far greater than achieved using other means, and is employed as a standard or benchmark. This chapter outlined, explained, and, where practical, demonstrated the IC's Best Practices as defined by ICD 203.

ICD 203's List of Nine Standards

A direct result of the miscalculations in National Intelligence Estimate (NIE) on the Iraqi weapons of mass destruction (WMD) stimulated Congress to establish an office of the Director of National Intelligence (DNI). One of the DNI's major tasks was to develop and ensure compliance with analytic quality standards. ICD 203 contains nine analytic quality standards (or best practices) for use by DHS and throughout the IC.

---

[9] W.H. Levie and R. Lentz, Effects of text illustrations: A review of research, *Educational Communications and Technology Journal*, 1982.

[10] D. Bobrow and D. Norman, Some Principles of Memory Schemata, Representation and Understanding: Studies in Cognitive Science, New York: Academic Press, 1975; D. Rumelhart, Schemata: The Building Blocks of Cognition, Theoretical Issues in Reading Comprehension, Hillsdale, New Jersey: Lawrence Erlbaum Associate, 1980.

Additionally, ICD 203 enables analysts from across the IC to communicate more directly with each other and thus reduce the negative effects of insular groupthink. The goal of adopting common IC standards (best practices) and other analytic common tools, and encouraging analytic collaboration is the improvement and value enhancement of the final analytic product in the eyes of the intelligence consumer.

ICD 203 presents these analytic standards as product "attributes" or "qualities." All nine are listed in the following:

1. Properly describe quality and credibility of underlying sources, data, and methodologies.
2. Properly express and explain uncertainties or confidence in analytic judgments.
3. Properly distinguish between underlying intelligence and analysts' assumptions and judgments.
4. Incorporate analysis of alternatives.
5. Demonstrate customer relevance and addresses implications.
6. Use clear and logical argumentation.
7. Explain to/or consistency of analytical judgements.
8. Make accurate judgements and assessments.
9. Incorporate effective visual information where appropriate.[11]

Describing Quality and Reliability of Underlying Sources

"How reliable is your intelligence source?" Failure to properly evaluate the quality or reliability of an intelligence source can negatively impact analytical conclusions and completely invalidate the final product.

Proper Caveats and Expressing Uncertainties or Confidence in Analytic Judgments

Communicating analytical judgments and levels of uncertainty in such a way that commanders and policymakers fully understand has long vexed the intelligence profession. Even when commanders and policymakers are given advanced and accurate warning by intelligence gatherers, it is often disregarded for manifold reasons.

---

[11] Office of the Director of National Intelligence, *Analytic Standards*, Intelligence Community Directive 203 (ICD 203), 2007.

As discussed in Chapter 12, analytic products should express a level of confidence in the judgment and clarify a basis for endorsement and acceptance of analytical results. The intelligence product should highlight intelligence gaps and contrary reporting. In addition, products should identify indicators that would augment or decrease confidence, thereby pointing to possible reconsideration of existing analytical judgments.

Distinguishing between Underlying Intelligence and Analysts' Assumptions and Judgments

An assumption is a proposition that analysts have accepted as a fact and forms the basis of the assessment. Using SATs to evaluate and re-evaluate an assumption is valuable at any time prior to finalizing a judgment to insure the assessment tied to or resting on a defective premise. See Chapter 10 for more information on using SATs to evaluate key analytical assumptions. Unambiguously stating assumptions or judgments made by analysts focuses the cognitive processes of intelligence consumers on what the supported facts and analytical judgments are, allowing them to have confidence in or ignore assessments or judgments as appropriate.

Incorporating Alternative Analysis Where Appropriate

Intelligence Reform and Terrorism Prevention Act of 2004 (IRTPA) obligated DNI to develop a process to ensure the effective use of alternative analysis to counter an inclination for analysts to focus their efforts down a single path of reasoning.[12]

Demonstrating Customer Relevance and Addresses Implications

For any intelligence analyst, a common goal should be to provide analytic products that address the consumer's questions and information requirements, offer insights on relevant and related concerns, and update existing products. For analysts working inside the U.S. IC, products should highlight information which has "national security aspects," particularly if the information is something the consumer does not know or fully

---

[12] U.S. Government, Intelligence Reform and Terrorism Prevention Act, 2004.

understand. Intelligence products should add value by addressing implications, context, threats, or factors affecting opportunities for planned or potential actions for the intended audience.

Using Logical Argumentation

Analytic products should present a clear main analytic message upfront. Products containing multiple judgments should have a main analytic message that is drawn collectively from those judgments. All analytic judgments should be effectively supported by relevant intelligence information and coherent reasoning. Language and syntax should convey meaning unambiguously. Products should be internally consistent and acknowledge significant supporting and contrary information affecting judgments.[13]

Exhibiting Consistency of Analysis over Time, or Highlights Changes and Explains Rationale

Analytic products should state how their judgments on a topic are consistent with or represent a change from those in previously published analysis, or represent initial coverage of a topic. Products need not be lengthy or detailed on explaining change or consistency. They should avoid using boilerplate language, however, and should make clear how new information or different reasoning led to the judgments expressed in them. Recurrent products such as daily crisis reports should take note any changes in judgments; absent changes, recurrent products need to confirm consistency with previous editions. Significant differences in analytic judgment, such as between two IC analytic elements, should be fully considered and brought to the attention of customers.[14]

Making Accurate Judgments and Assessments

Analytic products should apply expertise and logic to make the most accurate judgments and assessments possible based on the information available and known information gaps. In doing so, analytic products should

---

[13] Office of the Director of National Intelligence, Analytic Standards, Intelligence Community Directive 203 (ICD 203), 2007.

[14] Office of the Director of National Intelligence, Analytic Standards, Intelligence Community Directive 203 (ICD 203), 2007.

present all judgments that would be useful to customers, and should not avoid difficult judgments in order to minimize the risk of being wrong. Inherent in the concept of accuracy is that the analytic message a customer receives should be the one the analyst intended to send. Therefore, analytic products should express judgments as clearly and precisely as possible, reducing ambiguity by addressing the likelihood, timing, and nature of the outcome or development. Clarity of meaning permits assessment for accuracy when all necessary information is available.[15]

Incorporating Effective Visual Information Where Appropriate

Analytic products should incorporate visual information to clarify an analytic message and to complement or enhance the presentation of data and analysis. In particular, visual presentations should be used when information or concepts can be conveyed better in graphic than in written text. Visual information may range from plain presentation of intelligence information to interactive displays for complex information and analytic concepts. All of the content in an analytic product may be presented visually. Visual information should always be clear and pertinent to the product's subject. Analytic content in visual information should also adhere to other analytic tradecraft standards.[16]

---

[15] Office of the Director of National Intelligence, Analytic Standards, Intelligence Community Directive 203 (ICD 203), 2007.

[16] Office of the Director of National Intelligence, Analytic Standards, Intelligence Community Directive 203 (ICD 203), 2007.

16

Operations Security (OPSEC)

INTRODUCTION

The military has a process, common also, to business and law enforcement and much of the business environment aptly named *After Action Review* (AAR). The process, simply put, involves critiquing another's decisions with the benefit of hindsight. Though seemingly unfair criticism, the process is invaluable in understanding how and why mistakes were made in order to avoid them in the future. In this light, this book was written and edited by the authors as America was experiencing the 2016 presidential campaign and election and the first year of President Donald Trump's administration. A dominating issue throughout the campaign and throughout much of President Trump's administration has been and continues to be related to intelligence, security classifications, and classified material in general. As this chapter is devoted to the all-important intelligence analysis issue of operations security (OPSEC), these events and occurrences must be considered and discussed for instructional purposes, or in effect, subject to a type of AAR. These issues will be discussed purely for instructional and educational purposes, as they are extremely important tools in the study of intelligence analysis and its processes and procedures.

THE FOUNDATION OF OPSEC

Operations security at its core is directed toward information protection and as such, asset protection. Assets, in terms of intelligence, are those individuals who seek out (most often under the most dangerous of conditions) information and provide that information to us. For myriad reasons, those individuals and their identities must be protected at all costs. Compounding this is the fact that the slightest hint of leaked information or the slightest scrap of information can, in the hands of professionals, lead to the identity of assets. Our adversaries know when a piece of information relating to them or their operations has been released. Often, they know how many people had access to that particular bit of information, and even who the individual people were. In many cases all they need is a single bit of data, released inadvertently by someone who didn't practice appropriate OPSEC, and they can then identify that individual.

OPSEC practices are also in place to protect information associated with upcoming operations, available weaponry and technology, and a number of other situations and conditions, but to understand the importance and reasoning behind the confusing rules and regulations related to OPSEC, recognizing the vital importance of asset protection provides clarity and understanding.

OPSEC Process

The OPSEC process denies adversarial governments access to information about the capabilities and intentions of the United States government. The concept of OPSEC is interwoven into the process of force protection (FP). *Force protection* is the term used to describe efforts by the United States government to protect service members and their families, facilities, and equipment. OPSEC and the process of force protection is, of course, everyone's responsibility, but both of these areas fall under the control and authority of the government's counterintelligence operations.

OPSEC itself involves primarily identifying, analyzing, and controlling critical information in order to prevent this information from falling into the hands of our adversaries, or, in some cases, our allies. Of course, it must be understood that at all times, our enemies and adversaries are attempting to obtain this information as we are attempting to a great extent to do the same thing to them. A major part of maintaining military superiority over those who would do us harm and maintaining the highest level of safety and security in our country is knowing to some extent the capabilities and intentions of those who would do us harm. Those who would do us harm in turn seek the same advantage over us. The process of our gaining this information relative to our adversaries is called *intelligence* and *intelligence gathering*. The process of preventing our adversaries from gaining such advantage over us is called *counterintelligence*. In order to "counter" our enemy's efforts in this area, we must have in place appropriate restrictions and practice the highest levels of OPSEC. Again, this is everyone's responsibility, but assuring this is the ultimate responsibility of our counterintelligence operations.

In this process our counterintelligence operatives are constantly identifying actions that can be observed by our adversaries and determining what actions can be taken by us to assure to the greatest extent that our enemies are unsuccessful in their efforts.

In order to fully understand the concept of OPSEC, one must have a basic knowledge of security classifications, security clearance processes, document markings, and "need to know." These will be covered in more detail later in this chapter. The simple objective of OPSEC, however, can be stated in one word with, "awareness."

AUTHOR'S NOTE

Throughout this chapter, keep in mind that our adversaries, especially our more sophisticated adversaries, are mirroring basically everything we do to gain intelligence advantages as well as to deny our gaining the same advantages on them. Encapsulated, they do the same things we do.

As long as men have waged war or sought to protect themselves from others who would wage war against them, there has been a need for secrecy. OPSEC itself is the process of maintaining a level of secrecy. Conversely, as long as men have waged war or sought to protect themselves from those who would wage war against them, there has been a need to uncover the secrets of adversaries. From these simply stated albeit extremely complicated processes come the need for and the intricacies of OPSEC. OPSEC is practiced by us and our allies but it must be understood that to a degree, it is also practiced by our enemies.

Intelligence vs. Counterintelligence

In OPSEC there are two related concepts, intelligence and counterintelligence. At its core, intelligence is the process of uncovering or deciphering the secrets of our enemy. Counterintelligence, at its core, is the process of preventing the enemy from uncovering or decipher- ing our secrets. OPSEC is a frame of mind that is vital to the process of counterintelli- gence. It is further the job and responsibility of everyone.

During World War II, civilians were subtly trained or indoctrinated in the con- cept of OPSEC. Posters warn- ing "Loose Lips Sink Ships" along with depictions of the disastrous results of those loose lips could be seen on every corner, mostly in Great Britain, but also in the United States. Though the need for OPSEC wasn't born or conceived, during WWII, these posters and urgings to avoid discus- sions of confidential matters of which one may be knowl- edgeable most often comes to mind when one considers the history of OPSEC.

The Ambassador of the United States of America
Donald Teitelbaum and Ms. Julianna Lindsey
request the pleasure of your company to commemorate the
234th Anniversary of the United States of America

on Wednesday, June 30, 2010
3:00 p.m. - 6:00 p.m.

Guests Arrive: 3:00 - 3:35 p.m.
Presentation of Colors: 3:45 prompt
National Anthems and Remarks: 4:00 p.m.

Regrets Only   *46 Independence Avenue*
Tel: 030-2741-505, 030-2741-672   *Accra*
Dress: Open Collar/National Dress

Please bring this card with you
Please see enclosed leaflet for directions to parking lots

Figure 16.1 Invitation to a state dinner party.

The direct connection between OPSEC and aware- ness is obvious. One must always be aware of who they are interacting with and the level of that interaction (Figure 16.1) when anything remotely connected to our nation's security is discussed or contemplated. And though OPSEC training and emphasis is most prevalent with our armed forces and government agencies such as the State Department and Department of Defense, it is an issue about which we all need to be aware and conscious.

Family members, close friends, and associates of individuals involved in national security are constantly coming into possession of subtle pieces of information from which an adept adversarial counterintelligence operator can derive more complicated and detailed data.

Figure 16.2 OPSEC in personal communications.

AUTHOR'S NOTE

There exists a fairly large community of Civil War relic hunters, in the south, particularly. When preparing to search out places to dig, these hunters first read and review the millions of letters available that were written by soldiers fighting in particular battles. Even these soldiers, so many years ago, followed that simple human need to let their loved ones know exactly where they were at the writing of the letter. Soldiers would always start a letter home with a sentence such as "We are camped 200 yards south of a creek that runs east and west through a corn field just north of the town of Clarksdale," or something to that effect.

For example, a service member or member of one of the aforementioned agencies who may be separated from family or friends and communicating by letter or digitally almost always adheres to a simple principle of human interaction, we always want our friends and loved ones to know where we are. (See Figure 16.2.)

That slight innocuous category of data has historically provided a link to untold intelligence of value to our adversaries. In the right hands, an individual's location can lead to much more detail, which can be used against us.

287

Complicating this pursuit of appropriate levels of OPSEC is the enormous amount of information that is available to us and to our adversaries. A category of intelligence referred to as *open source* (OSINT) actually refers to that information that is available to anyone who has access to a newspaper, television, radio, or computer. OSINT provides a vast amount of information to our own intelligence analysts, but the problem is, that same information is available to the entire world.

The ease of obtaining information today makes OPSEC more important and more difficult to maintain. Today "loose lips" still "sink ships."

Enforcing OPSEC

A simple albeit foundational statement is that "OPSEC is the responsibility of everyone." It is most definitely the responsibility of everyone in the military because individuals in the military or individuals associated with military operations, however indirectly, have access to information that could be advantageous to our adversaries if it were divulged.

Those in the military holding the least sensitive level of classifications are occasionally in possession of vital information, such as troop movements, troop strength, troop morale, leadership changes, and myriad seemingly innocuous bits and pieces of operational data, even though they are not involved directly with operational planning or execution. OPSEC is as much their responsibility as it is that of the intelligence analyst who works in the high-end Secret Compartmented Information Facility (SCIF).

The function of assuring that everyone maintains OPSEC at all times, however, falls within the preview of counterintelligence (CI) operations. As stated earlier in this chapter, intelligence is the process of gathering and analyzing information on our adversaries and counterintelligence is the process of preventing our adversaries from gathering that same type information on us. Assuring OPSEC compliance, therefore, quite easily becomes the responsibility of counterintelligence.

While CI cannot control open source (OSINT), all other venues for release of data can be monitored and controlled to a certain extent. Additionally, in the event that classified information is released on open source, if that information was obtained illegally or in violation of our security related laws, CI operations can intervene, resulting in criminal charges.

Counterintelligence personnel are responsible for detecting, identifying, assessing, and neutralizing adversarial threats and insider threats to our national security. This involves not only identifying attempts launched by our enemies to exploit us, but additionally to identify and neutralize actions either conscious or inadvertent by our own people. Counterintelligence operations identified and brought down Aldrich Hazen Ames (Figure 16.3), a former CIA analyst who was convicted of spying for the Russian KGB in 1994. At the other end of the spectrum, counterintelligence operations developed and continue to modify all the training material used in the military and civilian government agencies to train individuals to avoid the unintended divulging of information.

The well-known euphemistically titled "dumpster dive" is also the responsibility of counterintelligence operations. Dumpster diving (Figure 16.4) involves going through the trash and discarded items of a functioning SCIF or other department charged with dealing with classified items to see what is being discarded and determine whether these items could be used to gain information. (See Figure 16.4.)

Figure 16.3   Aldrich Hazen Ames.

The well-known "red teams," though often manned and conducted by special operations personnel, are normally organized and supervised by counterintelligence operations. Red Teams are teams of undercover individuals who attempt, test, and exploit the operations security of agencies and departments for constructive, instructional purposes.

Figure 16.4   CI officer searching through trash.

Open Source Information (OSINT) and Its Effect on OPSEC

OSINT obtained by us or our enemies is generally not classified information.

289

It is most often information that supplements or substantiates classified information. For instance, if our intelligence analysts come into possession of classified information relating to a potential meeting of high-level officials from adversarial governments but the meeting has not been confirmed, a news report detailing a planned trip of an official from one of these governments to the supposed meeting location at that time may help to confirm.

OSINT is CI-monitored, but as stated, not easily controlled. Freedom of information in America and in most other countries prevents our counterintelligence operators from controlling the release of information that has been obtained by news sources. Fortunately for us, however, our adversaries often have the same problem making OSINT from our enemy nations a valuable source of intelligence for us.

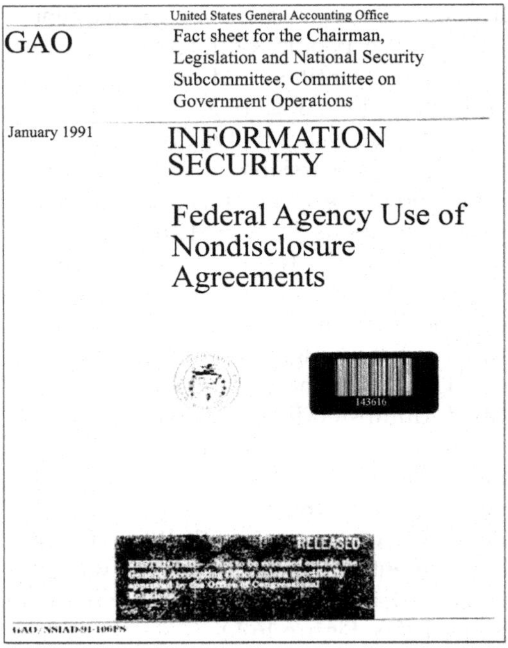

GAO

United States General Accounting Office

Fact sheet for the Chairman, Legislation and National Security Subcommittee, Committee on Government Operations

January 1991

INFORMATION SECURITY

Federal Agency Use of Nondisclosure Agreements

143616

RELEASED

RESTRICTED—Not to be released outside the General Accounting Office unless specifically approved by the Office of Congressional Relations.

GAO/NSIAD-91-106FS

Figure 16.5 NDA regulations.

All other areas of potential OPSEC violations, however, are more easily controlled and monitored, especially when those areas involve service members or DoD employees. The most effective method of control, assuring appropriate and effective levels of OPSEC, however, is through simple training. All service members are given regular OPSEC briefings and, depending on their assignment, are required to sign a non-disclosure agreement (NDA; see Figure 16.5) verifying their knowledge of OPSEC and the penalties associated with divulging information. Additional NDAs are also required of service members and civilian employees on specific missions.

OPSEC briefings and trainings cover myriad information but the focus is on knowing who our adversaries are, knowing what they want to obtain in the way of information, knowing how they might attempt to obtain it, and knowing what we can do to assure they do not obtain it. As stated earlier in this chapter, OPSEC in today's environment is much more difficult because our entire world operates on through the process of providing and receiving information, and in this day when virtually everyone shares intimate details about their lives on OSINT social media, it is that much more difficult.

In a Perfect World

The concept of OPSEC is fairly innocuous. As such, it is something most people do not concern themselves with. After all, keeping your mouth shut should not take concentration or a conscious effort. The fact is, however, that trained counterintelligence operatives functioning for our adversaries depend on our lack of conscious effort. The vast majority of intelligence gathered by our enemies has been obtained from people and in circumstances in which the fact was never known. In most cases the individual providing the information may never know they did it. A very minute percentage of intelligence is gathered through overt espionage. Talking about your level of job satisfaction or your coworkers with an acquaintance you've known casually for a long time, as example, may provide volumes of data over a period of time. Trained opposition or adversarial CI operators are adept at listening to and piecing together minute bits of information over a long period of time, until they have a clear picture of a secure environment or process.

In order to understand the significance of any concept, it is best to visualize it as functioning perfectly, in a perfect world. In a perfect world, OPSEC is accomplished on different levels. Vital intelligence information is shared among those who need it, based upon their clearances. The United States clears individuals to receive and transmit levels of classified material following extensive investigations into their background and, of course, commensurate with the level of classified material they need, in order to do their jobs. The lowest level of clearance granted is "confidential." The vast majority of military personnel are given this very basic level of clearance and, under normal circumstances, the extent of an investigation conducted for one enlisting in the service is sufficient to warrant issuance of a "confidential" clearance. Confidential classifications are applied to information that reasonably could be expected to cause damage to national security if disclosed to unauthorized sources.

The next step in clearance levels is "secret." Secret classifications are applied to information that could reasonably be expected to cause serious damage to the national security if disclosed to unauthorized sources. The secret clearance, like subsequent clearances, is granted following an investigation into one's past, which includes criminal records, illegal drug involvement, financial delinquencies, mental health counseling, alcohol-related incidents and counseling, military service, prior clearances and investigations, civil court actions, misuse of computer systems, and of course subversive activities. The number of years of information required on the form (the clearance request form is SF86. Most of it is available online and can be completed online by those seeking a clearance) varies from question to question. Many require seven years; some require ten years.

A step up from secret is the "top secret" clearance. It is granted following the same basic process only the investigation is much more thorough and goes back much further. Additionally, most interviews conducted by clearance investigators are conducted face to face, whereas secret-level investigations may be done more informally.

Finally, for the vast majority of servicemen, the addition of Secret Compartmented Information (SCI) may be added if and when necessary for an individual to do his job. The SCI clearance is "mission-specific" in that it is generally granted for specific missions. The SCI addition accompanies the top secret clearance when an individual needs access to compartmented information. This is also required for an individual who needs access to a Secret Compartmented Information Facility (SCIF), which is a secured area in which such information can be used or stored. SCI access eligibility is divided into three sensitivity levels, each with a different investigative requirement. They are Single Scope Background Investigation (SSBI) without polygraph, Counterintelligence with polygraph, and full-scope polygraph.

Each of these clearance levels can be granted on an interim basis when needed. An interim clearance is based on the completion of minimum investigative requirements and granted on a temporary basis. It is most often granted pending the completion of the full investigative requirements for the final clearance. Interim clearances can be granted in a few days once the clearance granting authority receives a properly completed SF86, or application for access. Interim Top Secret clearances take one or two months longer.

The interim clearance is granted in cases where an individual needs priority access to information in order to do his or her job. The granting of interim clearances is tightly controlled but the option remains when necessary.

In addition to the appropriate clearance, access to information is restricted to "need-to-know." Simply having the top secret clearance, for example, doesn't automatically grant one access to all top secret data. Need-to-know can be either a formal or an informal determination. An individual may have need-to-know for one portion of a mission, for instance, but not for the entire mission.

Finally, when an individual is granted access at the SCI level, he or she goes through a process referred to as being "read on" and must sign a non-disclosure agreement (NDA). Once he or she leaves the SCIF facility permanently or the mission, he or she is "read off." The read on and read off process is required, but normally simply reinforces the need for secrecy while on the operation or having access to the information and the need for non-disclosure once the mission is competed or an individual leaves the mission or facility. An individual with the appropriate clearance will go through a similar read on and read off process each time they begin work on a new operation or mission. There are higher levels of classification and access but these are limited to a very few individuals.

> **AUTHOR'S NOTE**
>
> A security clearance or a clearance review and update can only be requested by a governmental agency or a civilian organization authorized to conduct affairs or business related to the government and in the interest of the government. An individual may not request a security clearance background investigation on their own.

Nuts and Bolts

The remainder of this chapter will focus less on pure OPSEC and more on the functions of counterintelligence operators in assuring OPSEC maintenance. Basic OPSEC can be summed up in four words: *Keep your mouth shut*. The difficulty in OPSEC and, therefore, the more vital information for this section is how we maintain OPSEC.

Another simplistic OPSEC concept is the fact that OPSEC is everyone's responsibility. The role of assuring and validating appropriate levels of OPSEC, however, falls to counterintelligence operations. Counterintelligence operatives among their other functions, routinely take measures and steps to assure that individuals and facilities are maintaining OPSEC.

A key component of developing and maintaining an effective OPSEC program for individual operations and individual installation is much the same as that for the entire nation. At the foundation is a process of identification of critical information. In other words: What specific information and processes should be the subject of the most intensity of security?

While it is obvious that everything that happens within a military installation and surrounding an operation of some type is and should be classified, maintaining such a level of secrecy is not practical. Much of what happens on installations and even in the run up to certain operations is information the public should be aware of.

Take the operations Enduring Freedom and Iraqi Freedom as examples. In the planning stages and near the commencement of both these operations, it was important that the general public knew what the United States was planning in general and why. Support of the people could not have been obtained otherwise.

Operation Enduring Freedom, America's invasion of Afghanistan in the wake of the attacks of 9/11, was a necessary and appropriate response to our being attacked. The optimum OPSEC in relation to this mission would have been better maintained had we not said anything to the American people until the mission had been launched and the operation commenced. Though we maintained a level of secrecy until around the time of mission launch, many people within the government knew what we were going to do and much of the purpose and objectives were announced to the public.

As a nation, America operates along a fine line between the necessity of maintaining operation security and the public's right to know. Honest mistakes are made along the way on both sides of this line, but as long as we maintain objective OPSEC and consistently return to the principles of appropriate OPSEC, we will be accomplishing the objective.

STARS AND BARS

OPERATION ENDURING FREEDOM

Deadly jihadi ambush on US forces shows new danger in African region

Determining what that line should be is stage one. Determining what information should under no circumstances be compromised and what information is appropriate to release is stage one. Indeed, in the recent campaign for the office of president, the idea or issue of what information should be classified and what should be available to those without clearances came up often. Stage one is therefore determining and identifying CI. CI is determined for two reasons. The need to know what to emphasize as being subject to classification and the need to know what information our adversaries are seeking. Both of these types information are considered CI.

The next stage in OPSEC is searching for indicators. Intelligence and counterintelligence operators and analysts spend their careers focusing on indicators. Indicators, very simply, are signals that certain actions are highly likely to follow friendly detectable actions or open source information that can be interpreted or pieced together by an adversary to derive critical information.

Troop movements, for instance, are large-scale indicators. Significant individuals from certain nations traveling to a specific location at the same time are indicators. Indicators that are most valuable, however, are the subtlest ones. Counterintelligence operators charged with OPSEC maintenance constantly look for these subtle indicators. They also look for indicators that might be detected by our adversaries and determine how they would be used. During the 2016 presidential campaign season, many indicators referencing attempts to access polling and election information were available, leading to an emphasis on OPSEC, relating to America's information technology structure. The FBI used such indicators to urge the DNC to be vigilant with their email and Internet communications.

As stated, CI searches for indicators that we provide inadvertently or out of necessity and determine how the enemy would use them. If damaging, CI will recommend or mandate different methods of operation in order to mask the indicator and confuse the enemy. A pattern of deception may be recommended. Searching for indicators is a second step in the OPSEC cycle, but it is a continuous step.

Identifying indicators often leads to the next steps, developing threat assessments, and vulnerability analysis. The aforementioned red teams are used quite frequently in these efforts. Again, red teams, often comprised of special operations personnel, are tasked with penetrating security

AUTHOR'S NOTE

This cannot be stressed enough, not only in this section but in the entire study of intelligence. Remember, everything we do in intelligence and counterintelligence is mirrored by our adversaries and our enemies. The character George Smiley, in John le Carré's *Tinker Tailor Soldier Spy*, famously told his nemesis, Russian master spy Karla, "We spend our lives searching for the weaknesses in one another's systems." His comment sums this up perfectly.

measures set up to comply with appropriate OPSEC efforts. These individuals are trained and conditioned to carry out such missions targeting enemy OPSEC, so it is natural that they be called upon to test our OPSEC standards and efforts. If they can't break through, it is unlikely our adversaries can.

A threat assessment generally includes the identification and detection of adversaries and their associated capabilities, limitations, and intentions. Vulnerabilities are very simply weaknesses.

An example in the business world of attempting to manage vulnerabilities can be seen in automobile design. In many European countries where auto manufacturers such as Volvo, Mercedes, Porsche, and Volkswagen are located in close proximity and of course wish to protect their design while still testing their vehicles on open roads, the use of odd painting schemes such as polka dots or zebra stripes are employed to prevent clear photographs of

a vehicle's design lines. Threat assessments and analyses are developed as tools to give us an idea where we are and what steps need to be taken to improve our OPSEC. They are completed on a national level, focusing on broad pictures, such as determining whether training programs meet the current threat, and they are done for missions and operations that are much smaller scaled and have a defined beginning and end.

These assessments most often offer suggestions though sometimes mandate actions be taken. Of course, the suggestions cannot always be followed. Military missions, by their very nature, are dangerous, and though it would be advantageous to eliminate all threats, this is often impossible.

In applying the appropriate OPSEC measures, the immediate objective of "mission success" must take precedence. In austere environments we just have to do the best we can.

DOCUMENT MARKINGS AND CLASSIFICATIONS

This chapter will cover very basic classification markings and the reasoning behind the markings. This issue also came up often in the 2016 presidential campaign. The regulations and laws dealing with who has the authority to classify documents and when these decisions are made are not complicated and must be understood by anyone dealing with this material. A very common-sense general rule, however, is, "Any time there is confusion as to the level of classification of a document or a piece of information, err on the side of caution."

The classified markings found on a classified document are as follows, from lowest to highest: Unclassified (U), Confidential (C), Secret (C), Top Secret (TS). These markings appear at top center and bottom center and indicate the highest level of classification of information on that page. Further, most classified documents classify each paragraph.

All printed material, whether PowerPoint presentations, documents, or photographs dealing at any level with classified material must be clearly marked indicating the level of classification of the material in the documents. This marking appears in several locations on the documents.

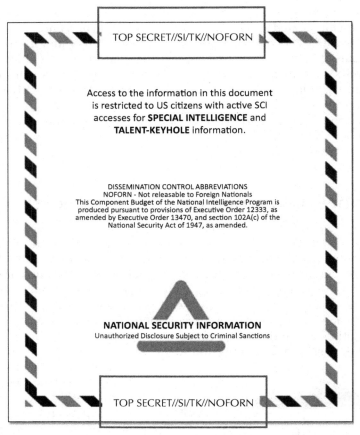

Assuming a document has a cover, the highest classification of a document is marked at the top and bottom of the outside cover and the title page. This is also true of the first page, and the outside of the back cover or back side of the last page.

Each page in the document is marked top and bottom with the highest classification of information on the page. If, for instance, a document page primarily has classified material no higher than secret, but happens to have one sentence or phrase that is actually top secret, the entire page must be marked (TS) top and bottom.

Since it is possible that attachments and annexes to a document may become separated from the document itself, they should be marked as if they were separate documents.

Classified documents must also indicate the agency and office that wrote and produced the document, and the date it was produced. The data must be sufficient enough to allow someone to contact the agency or office that created the document for questions.

Once these documents are written and produced, they are circulated to all with a "need-to-know" (refer to the intelligence cycle). Normally, if a receiving office reviews a document and determines that someone else outside of the receiving group needs the information, they will obtain permission from the originating department or office.

The originating office has the authority to determine the original classification of a document. This makes perfect sense since they, and they alone, know how the information was obtained; who, in some cases, obtained it; and what damage might conceivably be done if the information is compromised.

Declassifying a document is somewhat more complicated. Some documents have a specific declassification date at which time, due to their age and the fact that anyone involved in the collection of the information will likely no longer be alive, coupled with the fact that the document may have historic value, they will automatically become open records, available to the general public. The originating agency of a document, may request an exemption from this automatic declassifying date if they have sufficient cause.

AUTHOR'S NOTE

The President of the United States retains the ultimate authority to declassify any document.

In order for a classified document to be made available, all those who are to be given access, must have a clearance level equal to or greater than the highest classification of the document, and they must have a need-to-know. The need-to-know obviously means they must be assigned to a mission or an activity to which the document is pertinent.

Practical Exercise

This project is based on one of the responsibilities of a counterintelligence operative: The responsibility of enforcing OPSEC, or overseeing a unit's OPSEC practices for the purpose of recommending changes or alterations to practices. This is often done by virtue of an activity known as "dumpster diving." Though the practice actually involves going through vast amounts of discarded material, such as that which would be found in a dumpster, for purposes of the exercise, a trash container from an often-used office will suffice. Have the students, in teams of four or five, obtain permission from an office supervisor, or a fellow professor, to go through his trash as collected at the end of a day. Have the students lay out all the items in a trash can and categorize them for the purposes of indicating which items are connected in some way, if any. Once these items are categorized, have the students compile a list of information, however small, that can be obtained from the discarded items. Applying this to a classified facility, comparisons can be made to what might be inadvertently discarded, thus providing valuable classified information to anyone taking the time to sift through the discarded items.

CHAPTER SUMMARY
Foundations and History of OPSEC

Operations security at its core is directed toward information protection and as such, asset protection. Assets, in terms of intelligence, are those individuals who seek out (most often under the most dangerous of conditions) information, and provide that information to us. For myriad reasons, those individuals and their identities must be protected.

Intelligence vs. Counterintelligence

This section delineated the concepts and practices of intelligence and counterintelligence. In OPSEC there are two related concepts: intelligence and counterintelligence. At its core, intelligence is the process of uncovering or deciphering the secrets of our enemy. Counterintelligence, at its core, is the process of preventing the enemy from uncovering or deciphering our secrets.

Enforcing OPSEC

The process of enforcing and assuring appropriate OPSEC practices is never-ending. This chapter reinforced some of these practices. A simple albeit foundational statement is that "OPSEC is the responsibility of everyone." It is most definitely the responsibility of everyone in the military because individuals in the military, or individuals associated with military operations, however indirectly, have access to information that could be advantageous to our adversaries if it were divulged.

Nuts and Bolts

The Nuts and Bolts section is the "how to" guidance. This chapter, for obvious reasons, was practical and hands-on in nature. Basic OPSEC can be summed up in four words: Keep your mouth shut. The difficulty in OPSEC, and therefore the more vital information for this section, was how we maintain OPSEC.

Another simplistic OPSEC concept is the fact that OPSEC is everyone's responsibility. The role of assuring and validating appropriate levels of OPSEC, however, falls to counterintelligence operations. Counterintelligence operatives, among other functions, routinely take measures and steps to assure that individuals and facilities are maintaining OPSEC.

Document Markings and Classifications

This chapter covered very basic classification markings and the reasoning behind the markings. This issue came up often in the 2016 presidential campaign and is still timely. The regulations and laws dealing with who has the authority to classify documents and when these decisions are made are not complicated or ambiguous. They are consistently reinforced and must be understood by anyone dealing with this material. A very good common-sense general rule, however, is, "Any time there is confusion as to the level of classification of a document or a piece of information, err on the side of caution and consider it classified at the highest level."

INDEX

Page numbers followed by 'f' and 't' refer to figure and tables, respectively.

Printed in the United States
by Baker & Taylor Publisher Services